Electrical and Electronic Principles 3

S.A. Knight B.Sc (Hons) Lond.

Second Edition

Newnes
An imprint of Butterworth-Heinemann Ltd
Linacre House, Jordan Hill, Oxford OX2 8DP

A member of the Reed Elsevier group

OXFORD   LONDON   BOSTON
MUNICH   NEW DELHI   SINGAPORE   SYDNEY
TOKYO   TORONTO   WELLINGTON

First published 1980
Reprinted 1982, 1986
Second edition 1988
Reprinted 1989, 1990, 1991, 1992, 1993

© S. A. Knight 1980, 1988

British Library Cataloguing in Publication Data
Knight, Stephen Alfred
  Electrical and electronic principles.
  3
  1. Electric engineering
  I. Title
  621.3   TK145

ISBN 0 7506 0117 5

Printed by Hartnolls Ltd, Bodmin, Cornwall

Contents

Preface

Since this book was first published, a number of changes have been made in the BTEC syllabus for Electrical and Electronic Principles 3 for which it was originally written. With a new edition, an opportunity has been taken to bring the text into line with the most recent bank of objectives recommended by the BTEC Council under Unit U86/329. This edition, therefore, covers as fully as possible the contents of the revised Electrical and Electronics Principles 3 unit.

The major changes have been, as much as anything, additions to and extensions of the earlier Unit U75/360. Most of the original material is therefore retained, with additions to Sections 1, 2, 4, 7 and 9 covering the new material of attenuation and decibel measurements, active differentiating and integrating circuits, selectivity and bandwidth of tuned circuits, stepping motors and digital instrumentation, and completely new sections covering the fresh material of modulation and detection, and second-order control systems. It is hoped that the book, used in conjunction with associated laboratory work (as it should be) and the lecturer's notes, will now satisfy all pertinent aspects of the revised guidelines. Students and lecturers may therefore choose the relevant parts of the text to suit their course structure.

The layout of the book remains unchanged and is identical with the format of *Electrical and Electronic Principles 2* and *4/5*. There are two groups of example problems included in the text. One group comprises worked examples which illustrate method and procedure; these are prefaced by the heading Example ( ). The second group are self-assessment problems which are for students to work out for themselves before proceeding to the next part of the text. They should not be skipped, even if there are some which might prove difficult at that particular point. These problems (which also appear in an overall testing capacity at the end of each section) are simply given a number in parentheses: ( ), and are intended to illustrate those parts of the text immediately preceding them, though they might refer to earlier work as well. All examples in both groups are on a tinted background and are numbered throughout each section in order; this makes the checking of solutions a simple matter. Some solutions contain comments which can be considered as an extension of the text.

Of course, no book ever kept everybody completely satisfied, but I hope that the present text will be of use to the majority of its readers. I would very much appreciate receiving any comments, suggestions or useful criticisms that may be forthcoming.

S.A. Knight
Market Harborough 1987

1 Circuit elements and theorems

Aims: At the end of this Unit section you should be able to:
Differentiate between passive and active circuit elements. Explain the concepts of constant-voltage and constant-current equivalent generators.
State Thevenin's and Norton's theorems.
Solve simple problems using these theorems.
State the maximum power transfer theorem.
Solve problems involving maximum power conditions in resistive circuits.
Calculate gains and losses in decibels.

CHARACTERISTICS OF CIRCUIT ELEMENTS

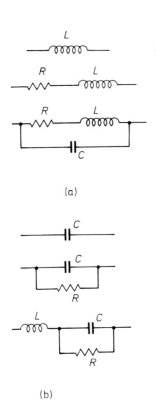

(a)

(b)

Figure 1.1

Circuit theory is founded on Ohm's Law and the two laws which are attributed to Kirchhoff. We are already acquainted with these laws and their applications, together with the superposition theorem, most of the work in Electrical Principles for the previous year having been based on them.

However, circuit problems are not solved simply from a knowledge of circuit laws; it has also been necessary to know the characteristic properties of each circuit element so that its behaviour can be predicted when subjected to any specific variation of current or voltage. There is, for example, a class of circuit elements in which the current is proportional to the applied voltage.

The most obvious of these elements is that of a resistor, the ratio V/I being the resistance of the element, R ohms. This is the fundamental example of Ohm's law. For another element in this class the current is proportional to the applied voltage, but the ratio V/I is not unvarying as it is in the case of resistance, but depends upon the frequency of the supply. Such elements are in the group of reactors, the ratio V/I being the reactance of the element, X ohms. Inductors and capacitors come into this category; for a given frequency the reactance has a certain value and for this condition the ratio V/I is constant.

No elements conform exactly to the ideal concepts of resistance, inductance or capacitance. All practical elements are a combination of these in varying degrees of magnitude. In *Figure 1.1(a)* an inductor to a first approximation can be represented as a coil of wire. But a coil of wire has resistance, and so a second approximation shows the ideal elements of inductance and resistance in series. Finally, there is capacitance between the turns of wire on the coil and between the terminals, and a third approximation brings in the parallel ideal element of capacitance. *Figure 1.1(b)* shows the same progressive approximations applied to a capacitor.

It is not possible, of course, to separate out any practical component into discrete ideal elements in the way these diagrams suggest. Resistance, inductance and capacitance are intimately combined and any such points as the junction shown for L and R in *Figure 1.1(a)* have no physical reality.

Circuit elements which may be represented in this way, as an equivalent network made up of resistance, inductance and capacitance are known as *passive* elements and the circuits in which they act are known as *linear* circuits.

Terminal p.d V is always less than
the generated e.m.f E when a load
is connected

Figure 1.2

There is a second class of circuit elements which are known as *active* elements. These elements are primarily sources of e.m.f. and may consist of d.c. or a.c. generators. The voltage appearing at the terminals of an active element is not the same in general as the e.m.f. generated. We have already encountered an elementary example of this in the case of a battery with internal resistance; when the battery is connected to an external load resistor R_L, as in *Figure 1.2*, the terminal voltage is less than the generated e.m.f. by the drop in voltage across the internal resistance r when the circuit current flows through it. For a full circuit analysis therefore, it is necessary to know the terminal voltage of a particular generator under all conditions of loading.

Again, just as we did with passive elements above, we can represent a practical active element as an equivalent circuit made up of a combination of ideal elements in which the fundamental action of the generation of e.m.f. is conveyed by an ideal active element, completely free of loss, in association with a passive element (or elements) representing the internal resistance or impedance. There are two basic equivalent circuits we use for this purpose:

(i) The constant-voltage generator shown in *Figure 1.3* which is represented as an ideal generator, generating an e.m.f. of E volts and having *zero* internal resistance, in series with a passive element, in

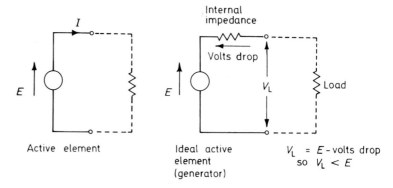

Figure 1.3

this case a resistor, across which the internal voltage drop occurs. The load voltage at the terminals is then always less than the generated e.m.f. The term constant-voltage generator is applied to this circuit because it produces the stated e.m.f. E under *all* conditions of load.

(ii) The constant-current generator shown in *Figure 1.4* which is represented as an ideal generator, generating a current I as stated under *all* conditions of load and having an *infinite* internal resistance; in parallel with a passive element, in this example a resistor, through which a part of the generated current is lost. The load current is then always less than the generated current.

This last form of generator may be a new concept to you and you may find it curious in the sense that current is the *effect* which follows from the *cause* of e.m.f. But you should keep in mind that in analysing a circuit it is not e.m.f. or current alone which interests us but the relationships between them. So it is not necessary to treat either current or voltage as being the more fundamental quantity and the

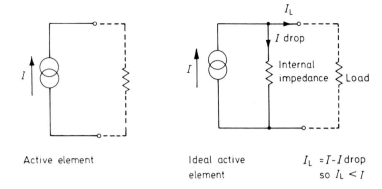

Figure 1.4

concepts of constant-voltage and constant-current generators are equally feasible. The actual generators may consist simply of batteries or other sources of direct current, or they may consist of a.c. sources such as alternators, oscillating systems or the outputs of electronic amplifiers.

You should make a note at this stage of the symbols used for these equivalent generators.

Although, as always, there are no ideal constant-voltage or constant-current active elements, very close approximations can be obtained to them. Part of your electronics course will cover power supplies which perform as almost ideal constant-voltage generators.

Figure 1.5

Example (1). The circuit of *Figure 1.5* feeds a load resistor R_L which can be varied from 0 to 100 kΩ. What will be the variation of current in the load throughout this range of load resistance?

Notice that the battery has a very high effective internal resistance. When the load is zero, the current

$$I_L = \frac{E}{R} = \frac{10}{10^6} \text{ A} = 0.01 \text{ mA}.$$

When the load is set at 100 kΩ (= 0.1 MΩ)

$$I_L = \frac{10}{(1 + 0.1) \times 10^6} \text{ A} = 0.009 \text{ mA}$$

Hence I_L changes by only 0.001 mA even though the load changes from 0 to 100 kΩ. The circuit obviously behaves as a constant-current generator. This will always be so providing the resistance of the source is very *high* compared with the load.

(2) By assuming now that the battery has an internal resistance of only 0.1 Ω show that the output voltage is practically constant for a load which varies from 10 Ω to 100 Ω.

We shall now apply two important network theorems to the solution of problems associated with combinations of passive and active elements.

THEVENIN'S THEOREM   A network in which all the passive elements remain constant can be solved by the application of Kirchhoff's laws and the superposition theorem. Look at *Figure 1.6* and suppose the load impedances Z_1, Z_2 and Z_3 are to be connected in turn to the output terminals of the active network drawn within the broken lines. It is obvious that the evaluation of the load currents and voltages in each of the three cases is likely to prove heavy going if we apply Kirchhoff to the problem. However, by the use of Thevenin's theorem we can replace the active network with a single equivalent circuit and most of the tedious work is eliminated.

Figure 1.6

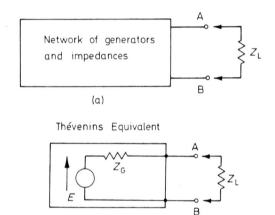

(a)

Thévenins Equivalent

(b)

The current flowing in the load Z_L will be the same in both cases

Figure 1.7

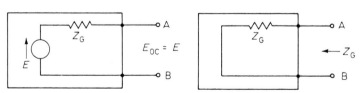

$E_{OC} = E$

With no load connected the voltage at terminals A and B is the same as the generator e.m.f. E

The impedance seen at terminals A and B with the generator removed is equal to Z_G

Figure 1.8

Thevenin's theorem tells us that in any linear active network having output terminals A and B as shown in *Figure 1.7(a)*, the circuit behaves *as far as measurements at the output terminals* are concerned as though it consisted of a single constant-voltage generator of e.m.f. E volts in series with a single passive impedance Z_G as shown in *Figure 1.7(b)*. So if a load impedance Z_L is connected to the terminals A-B of the network of generators and impedances as shown at (*a*), the current that will flow in the load will be *exactly* the same as if it was connected to the simple network shown at (*b*). What we require to find then are the component parts of the equivalent circuit.

Figure 1.8 shows the equivalent circuit again. If there is no load connected to terminals A-B, the voltage measured there will be equal to E since there will be no voltage drop across impedance Z_G. This is then the open-circuit voltage E_{oc}, and E_{oc} (= E) is the voltage measured across terminals A-B of the network with the load impedance Z_L removed. The internal impedance Z_G is the impedance measured between A-B with the generator replaced by its own internal impedance. Let us illustrate this in a little more detail.

Suppose points A and B in *Figure 1.9(a)* to be the output terminals of a network of resistance R_1 and R_2 and a source of e.m.f. E having an internal resistance r. A load resistor R_L is connected across A and B; what will be the current through this load resistor?

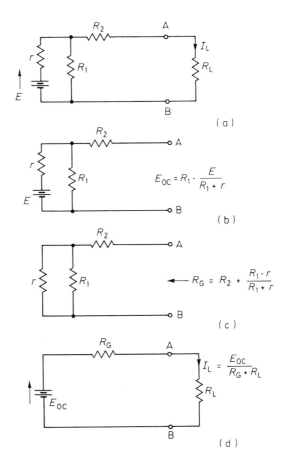

Figure 1.9

With R_L disconnected as in *Figure 1.9(b)* the current through R_1 will be $E/(R_1 + r)$ and so the voltage drop across R_1 will be

$$R_1 \frac{E}{(R_1 + r)}$$

This will also be the open-circuit voltage E_{oc} across terminals A and B since there will be no voltage drop across R_2. This gives us one of the equivalent circuit elements, E_{oc}.

We now remove the source of e.m.f. and replace it by its internal resistance r as shown in diagram (*c*). Looking back into the network from terminals A and B we see a resistance R_G where

$$R_G = R_2 + \frac{rR_1}{R_1 + r}$$

This gives us the other component of the equivalent circuit, R_G. Hence the Thevenin equivalent of the circuit of *Figure 1.9(a)* is as shown at (*d*) which consists simply of a source of e.m.f. (= E_{oc}) in series with a resistance R_G of the value determined above. Hence the current through *any* load resistor R_L will be

$$I_L = \frac{E_{oc}}{R_G + R_L}$$

We shall normally work with circuits in which only resistances are present for this stage of the course. Bear in mind that the circuits and theorems we are discussing are of course valid for impedances in general which are indicated in the appropriate places by the symbol Z.

Now follow the next two worked examples and Thevenin's theorem should become very straightforward.

Figure 1.10

Example (3).   Obtain the Thevenin equivalent of the network shown in *Figure 1.10* at the terminals A-B. Hence find the terminal p.d. and the current flowing when a 27 Ω resistor is connected across A-B.

E_{oc} = p.d. across the 12 Ω resistor (and the terminals) with the load removed.

$$\therefore\ E_{oc} = 10 \times \frac{12}{4 + 12} = 7.5\ V$$

Impedance seen looking into terminals A-B with the battery shorted out

$$R_G = \frac{4 \times 12}{4 + 12} = 3\ \Omega$$

The equivalent circuit is shown in *Figure 1.10(b)*.
When $R_L = 27\ \Omega$, the output current

$$I_L = \frac{7.5}{30} = 0.25\ A$$

and the p.d. across the load $= 27 \times 0.25 = 6.75\ V$

Figure 1.11

Figure 1.12

Example (4). Obtain the Thevenin equivalent circuit at terminals A-B of the network shown in *Figure 1.11*.

Dealing first with the parallel part of the circuit, shown in *Figure 1.12(a)*, the open-circuit voltage at terminals C-D will be

$$E_{oc} = 20 \times \frac{2}{2 + 5} = 5.71\ V$$

The resistance seen looking into C-D with the 20 V battery shorted out will be

$$R_G = \frac{2 \times 5}{2 + 5} = 1.43\ \Omega$$

Now this equivalent circuit can be placed in series with the remainder of the network as *Figure 1.12(b)* illustrates. Quite clearly this will finally reduce the circuit to that shown in diagram *(c)* which has an e.m.f. of $(12 - 5.71) = 6.29\ V$ and an internal resistance of $(8 + 1.43) = 9.43$. Notice that the terminal B is positive in this equivalent circuit, and why.

It is good practice to put in arrows to indicate the direction in which the batteries or other sources of e.m.f. are acting as these examples have illustrated.

Try the next two examples on your own and check your solutions before going any further.

Example (5). Find the Thevenin equivalent circuit for the network shown in *Figure 1.13*. Hence find the current that would flow in a 36 Ω load resistor connected across A-B.

Figure 1.13

Figure 1.14

Figure 1.15

Example (6).   Obtain the Thevenin equivalent circuit for the network shown in *Figure 1.14*. What value of load resistor would be required across terminals A-B for a current of 0.5A to flow in the load?

Now here is a further worked example showing how Thevenin's theorem can be applied to a Wheatstone bridge circuit.

Example (7).   In the bridge circuit of *Figure 1.15*, find the current in the centre branch of the bridge and the direction in which it flows.

You will recall that Kirchhoff's laws can be used for the solution of such problems as this, but the resulting simultaneous equations, of which you will require at least three, are rather tedious to work out accurately. We shall apply Thevenin's theorem to the problem and this will be found to simplify matters very considerably.

As the current in the 10 Ω resistor is asked for we treat it as the load resistance connected between our usual terminals A and B, and begin by disconnecting it. Then from *Figure 1.16(a)*:

$$\text{Voltage between C and A} = 24 \times \frac{40}{40 + 475} = 1.864 \text{ V}$$

$$\text{Voltage between C and B} = 24 \times \frac{20}{20 + 250} = 1.778 \text{ V}$$

Hence the p.d. between A and B = 1.864 − 1.778

$$= 0.086 \text{ V } (B \text{ is positive})$$

Figure 1.16

This then is the open-circuit voltage across the load terminals. Next, replacing the battery by its internal resistance which here is zero gives us the circuit of *Figure 1.16(b)*. The resistance seen from the terminals A and B is now clearly

$$\frac{40 \times 475}{40 + 475} + \frac{20 \times 250}{20 + 250} = 36.9 + 18.52 = 55.4 \ \Omega$$

Hence the Thevenin equivalent circuit of the bridge is as shown in *Figure 1.16(c)*. The current through a 10 Ω load resistor connected across A-B will then be

$$I_L = \frac{0.086}{10 + 55.4} \ A = 1.31 \ mA.$$

This current flows in the direction B to A. You will have noted by now that the polarity of the Thevenin equivalent circuit must be such that the current through a connected load resistor will have the *same direction* as would result with the load connected to the original network.

NORTON'S THEOREM

Norton's theorem states that a linear network of generators and impedances with output terminals A and B as shown in *Figure 1.17(a)* can be replaced by a single constant-current generator in parallel with a single impedance Z_G as shown in diagram (b).

The equivalent current source I_{sc} is that current which would flow in a *short-circuit* placed across the terminals of the network. The internal impedance of this source is infinite, but has in parallel with it an impedance equal to the impedance of the network seen looking back into the terminals A-B. This theorem is simply a dual of Thevenin's theorem in that it enables a network to be replaced by a single generator and impedance. In this instance, however, the generator is of the constant-current type and the impedance is in parallel with it, whereas in Thevenin's theorem the equivalent circuit is of a constant-voltage generator in series with the impedance.

In some cases, since the load connected to terminals A and B will now be in parallel with the internal impedance, it is easier to treat this as an admittance Y_G (= $1/Z_G$). You will recall that current divides in a parallel circuit in direct proportion to the branch admittances.

(a)

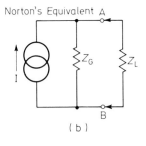

Norton's Equivalent

(b)

Figure 1.17

Example (8). Verify the equivalence of Thevenin and Norton circuits by conversion from one to the other.

The circuits will be equivalent if they both give the same current in, and voltages across, a load resistor connected to the terminals. Referring to *Figure 1.18* which has Thevenin's circuit on the left, we have for the load current

$$I_L = \frac{E_{oc}}{R_G + R_L}$$

Figure 1.18

and the current on short-circuit will be

$$I_{sc} = \frac{E_{oc}}{R_G}$$

Hence the Norton equivalent circuit shown on the right of *Figure 1.18* has a constant-current generator of output E_{oc}/R_G amperes and a resistance R_G in parallel with this generator. *Figure 1.19* shows the conversion of Norton into Thevenin. Here the equivalent Thevenin generator has an open-circuit voltage of I_{sc}/R_G volts in series with a resistance R_G. In any particular problem, therefore, either Norton or Thevenin equivalents may be used, the choice being simply one of convenience.

Figure 1.19

Figure 1.20

Example (9). Deduce the Thevenin and Norton equivalent circuits for terminals A-B in the network of *Figure 1.20*. A 10 Ω resistor is connected across A-B. Use Thevenin's circuit to calculate the load current and Norton's circuit to calculate the load voltage. What is the power in the load?

First the Thevenin equivalent: referring to the circuit, when A-B are open-circuited:

Voltage across A-B $= E_{oc} = 5\dfrac{80}{80 + 20} = 4\text{ V}$

Resistance across A-B $= R_G = 24 + \dfrac{20 \times 80}{20 + 80} = 40\ \Omega$

(a)

(b)

Figure 1.21

The Thevenin equivalent circuit is then as shown in *Figure 1.21(a)*. When a 10 Ω load resistor is connected to A-B, the load current

$$I_\mathrm{L} = \frac{4}{40 + 10} = 0.08 \text{ A} = 80 \text{ mA}$$

Turning now to Norton, if terminals A-B are short-circuited:

$$I_\mathrm{sc} = \frac{4}{40} = 0.1 \text{ A}$$

Hence the Norton equivalent circuit is as shown in *Figure 1.21(b)*. If the 10 Ω load is now connected, the parallel resistors of 40 Ω and 10 Ω reduce to 8 Ω and 0.1 A will flow through this. Hence the voltage across the load is

$$V_\mathrm{L} = 0.1 \times 8 = 0.8 \text{ V}$$

Notice that this solution agrees with Thevenin's circuit conditions: there $I_\mathrm{L} = 0.08$ A and this current in 10 Ω will, of course, develop a p.d. of 0.8 V.

The power in the load can be evaluated as either

$$P = \frac{V_\mathrm{L}^2}{R_\mathrm{L}} \text{ or } I_\mathrm{L}^2 R_\mathrm{L}$$

So

$$P = \frac{0.8^2}{10} \text{ or } 0.08^2 \times 10 = 0.064 \text{ W}$$

ADDING EQUIVALENT CIRCUITS

Figure 1.22

Very often networks are given as, or can be reduced to, a series or parallel combination of Thevenin and Norton equivalent circuits. It then becomes necessary to reduce such equivalent circuits to either a single Thevenin *or* a single Norton equivalent. Which form the reduction takes depends upon whether a series or parallel arrangement is concerned. In *Figure 1.22* for example, the diagram shows a Thevenin circuit of voltage generator E and resistance R_1 in series with a Norton circuit of current generator I and parallel resistance R_2. The best thing to do here is to convert the Norton circuit into a Thevenin circuit. The two voltages are then added together (with regard to sign), as are the two resistances to give a final Thevenin circuit.

Figure 1.23 shows a Thevenin circuit in parallel with a Norton. Here the best thing to do is to convert the Thevenin into a Norton; the resultant currents are then added together (with regard to sign) and the single equivalent to the two parallel resistances calculated. The final circuit is then a Norton equivalent. The next example will illustrate the method.

Figure 1.23

Figure 1.24

Figure 1.25

Example (10).   By conversion to a Norton equivalent circuit, calculate the voltage across the 10 Ω resistor shown in the circuit of *Figure 1.24.*

We start by converting each branch to a Norton equivalent:

For branch A $I_{sc} = \dfrac{2}{3}$ A, $R = 3$ Ω

For branch B $I_{sc} = 1$ A, $R = 4$ Ω

For branch C $I_{sc} = \dfrac{6}{5}$ A, $R = 5$ Ω

Figure 1.25 shows the transformed circuit; the 10 Ω load resistor remains unaffected. From this circuit:

$$\text{Total current } I = \frac{2}{3} + 1 + \frac{6}{5} = \frac{43}{15} = 2.867 \text{ A}$$

$$\text{Total resistance: } \frac{1}{R} = \frac{1}{3} + \frac{1}{4} + \frac{1}{5} + \frac{1}{10} = \frac{53}{60}$$

$$R = 1.132 \ \Omega$$

Then $V_L = I R_L = 2.867 \times 1.132 = 3.245$ V

TRANSFER OF POWER

Figure 1.26

When a generator is connected to a load, power is dissipated in the load. It is frequently necessary to make sure that the greatest possible power is dissipated in the load and not wasted in other parts of the circuit. Since any network containing one or more sources of voltage or current can be reduced to a Thevenin equivalent, our investigation will clearly centre on finding the value of load resistor R_L which will result in the maximum power being dissipated in R_L. We shall consider here only the case where the load is purely resistive.

Figure 1.26 shows a Thevenin equivalent generator with a load R_L connected to its terminals. Clearly, as R_L is varied, the current I will vary and so the power dissipated in R_L, $I^2 R_L$ W, will also vary. It might appear from this that all we have to do is to make I as large as possible, but this is an impossible solution because I can only be at its greatest value when $R_L = 0$ and all the circuit power is then dissipated internally in R_G. As R_L is increased from zero, the total circuit power is distributed between R_L and R_G; we want to find the condition where the power share of the load resistor is a maximum.

Example (11). A battery of e.m.f. 10 V and internal resistance 8 Ω is connected to a load resistor which can be varied from 0 to 16 Ω. Sketch a graph showing the variation in load power as the load is varied between these limits, and deduce the condition which gives the maximum power in the load.

We draw up a table of values of R_L, conveniently in 2 Ω steps, and then calculate the circuit current for each step. The power in the load P_L can then be derived:

R_L	0	2	4	6	8	10	12	14	16	Ω
$R_L + R_G$	8	10	12	14	16	18	20	22	24	Ω
I_L	1.25	1.0	0.83	0.71	0.625	0.55	0.5	0.45	0.42	A
P_L	0	2.0	2.75	3.03	3.125	3.09	3.0	2.83	2.82	W

The graph of R_L against P_L is shown in *Figure 1.27* along with the circuit diagram. From the graph we see that the power rises comparatively rapidly as R_L is increased from zero and reaches a maximum value of 3.125 W when $R_L = 8$ Ω. But the internal resistance of the battery is also 8 Ω; it appears then that we obtain the maximum power in the load when the load resistance is equal to the internal resistance of the source.

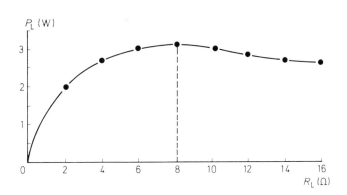

Figure 1.27

Now the showing of a single example like this does not prove the result in general terms. For those who are familiar with elementary calculus, the following proof will show that the result is indeed as our previous example suggested: the maximum power in the load is obtained *when the load resistance is equal to the internal resistance of the generator.*

In a circuit of e.m.f. E, internal resistance R_G and load resistance R_L

$$I = \frac{E}{R_L + R_G}$$

Then load power $P_L = I^2 R_L = E^2 \dfrac{R_L}{(R_L + R_G)^2}$

Differentiating this expression gives us

$$\frac{dP_L}{dR_L} = E^2 \frac{(R_L + R_G)^2 - 2R_L(R_L + R_G)}{(R_L + R_G)^4}$$

For a maximum power, this expression will be zero, therefore the numerator must be zero:

$$(R_L + R_G)^2 = 2R_L(R_L + R_G)$$

$$\therefore\ R_L + R_G = 2R_L$$

and $\qquad R_L = R_G$

This is a very important result and one which will continually turn up in various guises throughout the whole of the course.

DECIBELS AND ATTENUATION

The decibel (dB) is a unit in which power ratios and gain or loss ratios of related quantities such as current and voltage may be expressed in a convenient form. The decibel is actually a one-tenth part of a unit called the Bel (after Alexander Graham Bell) but the Bel is inconveniently large and is rarely used.

The ratio of two powers, P_1 and P_2, say, can be described by finding the logarithm (to base 10) of that ratio. This logarithmic ratio is measured in Bels so that a power ratio is given as

$$\log \frac{P_2}{P_1}$$

Since 1 Bel = 10 dB, this expression becomes

$$10 \log \frac{P_2}{P_1}$$

and this is the form in which the decibel is usually stated.

Example (12).   Express as decibel gain or loss, power ratios of (a) 100 times, (b) 5 times, (c) 0.01 times.

(a)   Gain = 10 log 100
                 = 10 × 2 = 20 dB
(b)   Gain = 10 log 5
                 = 10 × 0.6990 = 6.99 dB
(c)   Gain = 10 log 0.01
                 = 10 × (−2) = −20 dB

In example (b), 6.99 dB would normally be rounded up to 7 dB. In example (c) we have a power loss, indicated by the negative sign. It is of particular importance to notice from this that, if the ratio P_2/P_1 is less than unity, then the logarithm of the ratio will be negative, indicating a power loss or attenuation. So with this convention, a positive sign will correspondingly indicate a power gain. Since from elementary mathematics

$$10 \log \frac{P_2}{P_1} = -\ 10 \log \frac{P_1}{P_2}$$

the numerical answer obtained will be the same *irrespective* of the form in which the ratio is considered, as we see when we compare examples (a) and (c) above. The correct sign to indicate a power loss or gain *must*, however, be obtained from the ratio P_2/P_1.

We can save ourselves work if we take the ratio of powers always to be *greater* than unity, inverting if it is less. By this means we always get a wholly positive characteristic to the logarithms and so avoid the difficulty of having to cope with negative numbers. Whether the answer is a gain or loss is at once determined by the original form of the power ratio. There is never any doubt about the sign of the answer in a particular case, as we now illustrate.

Example (13).   A network has a power output equal to only 1/5th of the input. Find the network loss in dB.
We do this problem the 'fractional' way first.

$$\text{Gain} = 10 \log 0.2$$
$$= 10 \times \overline{1}.3010$$
$$= 10 \times (-1 + 0.3010)$$
$$= 10 \times -0.6990 = -6.99 \text{ dB}.$$

Now to avoid the negative characteristic and the necessity to express the logarithm of 0.2 as a *wholly* negative number, let us take the power ratio concerned as 5 by inverting the original fractional ratio. Then

$$\text{Gain} = 10 \log 5$$
$$= 10 \times 0.6990$$
$$= 6.99 \text{ dB}.$$

But the original power ratio tells us that the network is plainly introducing a power loss, hence

$$\text{Loss} = -6.99 \text{ dB} \quad \text{or } 6.99 \text{ dB down.}$$

Decibels can, of course, be converted back into a power ratio. Let the required ratio be N. Then the reverse process is used to that employed above for expressing power ratios in dB, as the next example illustrates.

Example (14).   Express 6 dB as a power ratio, giving the answer to the nearest integer.

Here $10 \log N = 6$
therefore $\log N = 0.6$
and $N = \text{antilog } 0.6$
                 $= 3.981$

Hence to the nearest integer, a 6 dB power ratio = 4 times.

ADDING UP DECIBELS

With the decibel, if the signal power at the output of an amplifier is 20 times that at the input, the gain is $10 \log 20 = 13$ dB. With two similar amplifiers in cascade (the output of one feeding into the input of the second), the output power would be $20 \times 20 = 400$ times that at the input or $10 \log 400 = 26$ dB, which is 13 *plus* 13 dB.

This illustrates one of the advantages of the decibel: when large ranges of power gains are involved, conveniently small figures replace large ones. Also the net power gains of a number of systems in cascade involve the *product* of their individual power gains but only the algebraic *sum* of their decibel equivalents. Addition is always preferable to multiplication.

An attenuator may be regarded as the converse of an amplifier, and its power loss may be described in similar units. If, say, three stages of amplification having power ratios of P_1, P_2 and P_3 are followed by a cable connection having an attenuation of $-P_4$, then the output level of the system will be $P_1 + P_2 + P_3 - P_4$ dB above the original input level.

> (15)   Express power ratios of (a) 0.005, (b) 10^8 as dB.
> (16)   Express (a) 90 dB, (b) -4 dB as power ratios.

It is clear from our examples above that the decibel is only a relative unit of power level; it is simply a ratio, not an absolute measure. To say that the gain of a system is 6 dB implies that the *ratio* of output power to input power is 4 times, nothing else. We have no idea of how many watts the output actually is. If some standard power level is chosen as a 'zero' or reference level, however, then the absolute power may be expressed in decibels above (or below) that chosen level. For a particular case any reference level might be selected which happens to be convenient, but it is the practice in general, and in particular in telecommunications engineering, to have a power level of 1 mW (0.001 W) as the standard datum. Powers less than 1 mW have negative decibel levels.

With this standard, any power P can be expressed as 10 log $(P/1 \text{ mW})$ dB referred to 1 mW. Hence a power gain of 20 dB (representing, as we have seen from an earlier example, a ratio of 100 times) will, referred to the standard 1 mW as input, represent an output of (1×100) mW = 100 m or 0.1 W. In the same way, a power loss of 20 dB (-20 dB) referred to 1 mW as input will represent an output power of $(1 \times 0.01) = 0.01$ mW or 10 μW. The expression 'dB referred to 1 mW' or 'dB above or below 1 mW' is abbreviated to dBm. Thus

$$20 \text{ dBm} = 20 \text{ dB referenced to } 1 \text{ mW}$$
$$= 20 \text{ dB above } 1 \text{ mW}$$
$$= 100 \text{ mW}.$$

> (17)   The power loss in 1 km of coaxial telephone cable is 2.0 dB. What is the power loss in 10 km of the cable?
> What signal power input is required in London to deliver 10 μW of power to Birmingham? (Take London to Birmingham as 120 *miles*.) Comment on your answer.

CURRENT AND VOLTAGE RATIOS

In general, two powers P_1 and P_2 are compared by noting either the voltage developed across a known impedance or the current through it. If the input and output impedances of an amplifier, say, are equal, the power ratio will be proportional to the square of the voltage (or current) ratio. For since

$$power = I^2 R \text{ or } \frac{V^2}{R}$$

$$\frac{P_2}{P_1} = \left[\frac{V_2}{V_1}\right]^2 = \left[\frac{I_2}{I_1}\right]^2$$

i.e. voltage gain $= 10 \log\left[\frac{V_2}{V_1}\right]^2 = 20 \log \frac{V_2}{V_1}$

or current gain $= 10 \log\left[\frac{I_2}{I_1}\right]^2 = 20 \log \frac{I_2}{I_1}$

In both cases, the equal values of the input and output impedance R cancel out.

It is more usual to work in terms of voltage ratio in practice, even though the input and output impedances of the network may not be equal (which they rarely are). Strictly, this is an inaccurate procedure, but it seems to be an accepted convention. In such usage, of course, the power ratio is *not* equal to the square of the voltage ratio, but the decibel is used to express voltage gain (or loss) and not to compare input and output powers. Thus an amplifier whose output voltage is 40 times the input voltage has a *voltage* gain of 20 log 40 = 32 dB.

Example (18). An amplifier has a voltage gain of 20 at low frequencies and a voltage gain of 50 at high frequencies. What is the relative response at low frequencies to the response at high frequencies, in dB?

We could work out the separate dB gains at low and high frequencies and by subtraction find the response at low frequencies relative to that at high frequencies. It saves time, however, if we write

$$\text{Relative response} = 20 \log \frac{\text{output at low freq.}}{\text{output at high freq.}}$$

$$= 20 \log \frac{20}{50} = -20 \log \frac{50}{20}$$

$$= -20 \times 0.398$$

$$= -7.96 \text{ dB.}$$

Here now is your first set of problems.

PROBLEMS FOR SECTION 1

Group 1

(18) A battery of e.m.f. 2.2 V has an internal resistance of 0.1 Ω. What will be the terminal voltage when a resistor of 2 Ω is connected across the battery terminals?

(19) The terminal voltage of a battery is 10.5 V on open-circuit but this falls to 10.2 V when a current of 2 A is drawn from the battery. Find the e.m.f. and internal resistance of the battery.

(20) When a load resistor of 1 Ω is connected across a battery, the terminal p.d. is 6 V. When the resistor is replaced by one of

2 Ω, the terminal p.d. increases to 6.1 V. What is the e.m.f. and internal resistance of the battery?

(21) When a resistance of 2 Ω is connected to a certain battery, the power dissipated in the resistance is 32 W. When a resistance of 3 Ω is connected, the power dissipated is 12 W. Find the value of resistance which will dissipate the maximum power when connected to this battery, and calculate the value of this maximum power.

(22) Write down Thevenin's theorem. Obtain the Thevenin equivalent circuits for the networks shown in *Figure 1.28*.

(a)   (b)   (c)   (d)

Figure 1.28

Figure 1.29

Figure 1.30

(23) Obtain the Thevenin equivalent of the network shown in *Figure 1.29*. Hence calculate the current that would flow in a 50 Ω resistor connected to terminals A-B.

(24) By finding Thevenin's equivalent of the circuit of *Figure 1.30*, determine the value of load resistor required across A-B for a current of 100 mA to flow in it.

(25) Obtain the Thevenin *and* the Norton equivalents for terminals A-B in the network of *Figure 1.31*. A 100 Ω load resistor is connected to A-B. Using the equivalent circuit as necessary, find (a) the load voltage; (b) the load power.

(26) Obtain the Norton equivalents for the circuits of *Figure 1.28* and *1.29* above.

(27) Obtain the Thevenin equivalent of the network shown in *Figure 1.32*. Hence deduce the Norton equivalent.

(28) A bridge circuit is shown in *Figure 1.33*. Find the current in the centre arm of the bridge.

(29) Repeat problem (22) assuming that the battery has an internal resistance of 1 Ω.

Figure 1.31

Figure 1.32

Figure 1.33

Group 2

Figure 1.34

Figure 1.35

Figure 1.36

(30) A signal generator has its output terminals connected to a variable load resistor R_L. The voltage V_L across R_L for various settings of R_L are given in the following table:

R_L	25	50	75	100	Ω
V_L	33	50	60	67	mV

Determine the e.m.f. and internal resistance of the generator output. What would the short-circuit current be from this generator? What would be the maximum power available in the load?

(31) A battery of e.m.f. 18.2 V and internal resistance $r\ \Omega$ is connected across terminals A-B of *Figure 1.34*, and it is found that the p.d. across the 10 Ω resistor is 10 V. What is the internal resistance of the battery?

(32) In *Figure 1.35* 1 kΩ resistor is connected between the points P and Q; show that a current of 0.93 mA will flow in this resistor.

(33) The following data was obtained from an experiment to find the internal resistance of a group of cells:

R_L	0	1	2	3	4	5	Ω
V_L	0	1.82	2.79	3.40		4.11	V
P_L					3.63		W

Complete the table where necessary.

Plot a graph of power to a base of load resistance and hence determine the value of the internal resistance.

(34) What do you understand by the term dBm? What special advantages does it have in the calculation of power ratios? What powers are represented by (a) 25 dBm, (b) −13 dBm?

Four networks are connected in cascade. If the decibel gains and losses of the individual networks are −7.35 dB, +4.25 dB, +12.8 dB and −2.7 dB, what will be the power output if 0 dBm is applied at the input?

(35) Define the decibel and give two reasons why its use is convenient in transmission work. The input signal to an amplifier varies between 23.5 mW and 1.25 W. Express each power in dB relative to 1 mW and state the change in the level of the signal in dB.

(36) A radio receiver has an automatic gain control system made up of three transistor stages in each of which the gain changes by 3 dB for each 100 mV of control bias applied. A change in the receiver input from 100 μV to 100 mV produces a +4 dB change in the output. Find the corresponding change in the control bias voltage.

(37) In *Figure 1.36* an a.c. source maintains 0.5 V r.m.s. across terminals AB. Calculate, in dB, the reduction in output power (in the load across terminals CD) attributable to the network with the dotted lines.

2 D.C. transients

Aims: At the end of this Unit section you should be able to:
Understand transient behaviour of series connected C-R and L-R circuits.
Explain how current and voltage vary with time in series C-R and L-R circuits.
Define the time constant of series C-R and L-R circuits.
Calculate the component voltage or current at any instant in C-R and L-R circuits which have been connected to or disconnected from a direct current supply.
Explain the effect of circuit time constants on rectangular waveforms and pulse trains.

In alternating current theory, problems are solved by considering the results of applying sinusoidal voltages to circuits containing resistive or reactive elements or combinations of these elements. When the applied voltage is sinusoidal, the voltages produced across the individual elements are also sinusoidal, differing only in magnitude and (for reactances) in phase from the input. We shall be considering such circuit behaviour in later Unit sections.

When a circuit is switched from one condition to another either by a change in the applied voltage or a change in one of the circuit elements, there is a transitional period which may be relatively short or long during which the circuit currents and voltages change from their former values to new ones. After this transitional interval, the circuit settles down to what is known as the *steady state*.

For the present we shall consider what happens when we apply *abrupt* voltage changes to simple circuits containing resistive and reactive elements. Such voltage changes are known as *transients* literally meaning a transition from one particular voltage state to another.

The simplest example is that of a voltage step. This is a waveform which has zero amplitude prior to a time $t = 0$; it then rises instantaneously to some finite level and remains at that level (the steady state) for an indefinite period thereafter. *Figure 2.1* shows such a voltage step function.

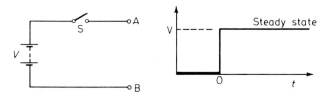

Figure 2.1

We can obviously obtain such a voltage step from a simple battery and switch circuit as the figure shows. Before the switch is closed, the voltage across terminals A and B is zero. As soon as the switch is closed the voltage across A and B rises very rapidly to V volts.

We cannot obtain an *instantaneous* rise in practice since this would imply that the voltage was at two different levels at the same instant, but we can, nevertheless, treat the output at the terminals as being a very good approximation to an ideal step waveform. By the use of sophisticated electronic systems, both voltage and current step functions can be generated which represent the almost perfect condition of an instantaneous rise.

FUNDAMENTAL RELATIONSHIPS

We begin by establishing the relationships between voltage v and current i at any given instant of time for each of the basic elements of resistance, inductance and capacitance, assuming that these are ideal elements.

1. RESISTANCE

For a purely resistive element, current is proportional to voltage. So at any instant of time

$$i = \frac{v}{R} \text{ or } v = iR$$

Let a step function be applied to a resistor. Applying the above equations, the current and voltage waveforms will be as illustrated in *Figure 2.2* at (a) and (b) respectively. The waveforms for current and voltage in a resistive circuit will always be *identical* with the applied voltage, the relative amplitudes being determined only by the value of the resistance.

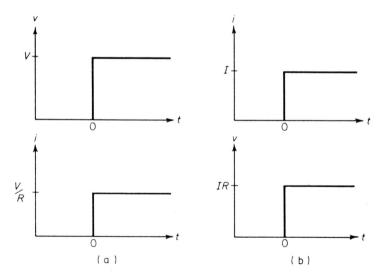

Figure 2.2

2. INDUCTANCE

The property of inductance is a function of the magnetic field associated with current flow in a conductor. If the current is constant, the field is constant, but if the current is changing, the field must also change. This changing field induces an e.m.f. in the conductor which acts in such a direction that it opposes the change in current; Lenz's Law. This induced e.m.f. is proportional to the rate of change of current with respect to time and is expressed as

$$e = L \times \text{rate of change of current}$$

$$= L \frac{di}{dt}$$

which is Faraday's Law.

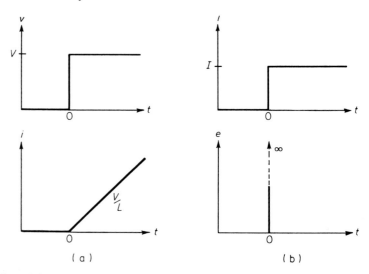

Figure 2.3

For current and voltage step functions applied to an inductor, the situation shown in *Figure 2.3* arises. For the current step, the time rate of change of current, di/dt, is infinite since we assume that the current changes from zero to I amperes instantaneously. So the induced voltage, e, is also infinite for zero time as shown in the diagram at (b). For the voltage step of diagram (a), consider the instant the step is applied to the inductor; then $i = 0$ and $e = V$. Thus at time $t = 0$ (t_o) we have

$$V . = L \frac{di}{dt_o}$$

$$\therefore \quad \frac{di}{dt_o} = \frac{V}{L} \text{ A/sec.}$$

So the current rises at this rate and is represented by a *ramp* waveform, a straight line sloping as shown in the diagram. Unlike the case of the purely resistive circuit, the current and voltage waveforms in an inductor are *not* identical with the applied waveforms.

3. CAPACITANCE

The charge Q on a capacitor and the voltage between its plates are related by the equation

$$Q = CV$$

but $\quad Q = It$

$$\therefore \quad It = CV$$

A small charge dQ due to a current i flowing for a time dt produces a small change of voltage dv,

$$dQ = Cdv = idt$$

$$\therefore \qquad i = C\frac{dv}{dt}$$

When a voltage step is applied to a capacitor, the rate of change of voltage with respect to time, dv/dt, is infinite since we assume that the voltage changes from zero to V volts instantaneously. Hence the current pulse will be infinite for zero time as shown in *Figure 2.4(a)*. For the

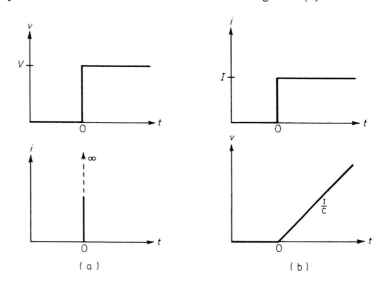

Figure 2.4

current step of *Figure 2.4(b)* consider the instant the step is applied to the capacitor; then $v = 0$ and $i = I$. Then at time $t = 0$

$$I = C\frac{dv}{dt_o}$$

$$\therefore \qquad \frac{dV}{dt_o} = \frac{I}{C} \quad \text{V/sec.}$$

The voltage rises at this rate across the capacitor and is represented by a ramp waveform, a straight line sloping as shown in the diagram at (b).

These three cases are, of course, ideal and theoretical. No circuit element conforms exactly and under all conditions to the ideal concepts of resistance, inductance and capacitance which we have visualised above, though some may do so nearly enough for practical purposes within a more or less restricted range of circumstances. In general, circuits exhibit behaviour which is the result of a mixture of ideal elements and two of these will form the basic investigation into transient behaviour in this Unit Section:

(i) A series arrangement of resistance and capacitance.
(ii) A series arrangement of resistance and inductance.

THE SERIES *C-R* CIRCUIT

Figure 2.5

We will now investigate what happens when a voltage step waveform is applied to a-series arrangement of resistance R and capacitance C. For our purpose, it is sufficient to take the step function as being generated by a simple battery and switch system; so in the circuit of *Figure 2.5* a battery, V volts, is wired in series with a switch S to the series C and R elements. We understand that there is no residual charge on the capacitor before the switch S is operated.

When S is closed the voltage across C does not immediately rise to the voltage level V since a movement of electric charge is necessary and the expression for charge, $Q = It$, tells us that the capacitor needs time to charge. Immediately after switch-on at $t = 0$ a displacement current begins to flow around the circuit. Electrons move into the plate of the capacitor connected to the negative pole of the battery and flow out of the plate connected to the positive pole, a process which leads to the capacitor acquiring charge and hence a rise in voltage across its terminals.

The only opposition to the flow of current at the *instant* the switch is closed is that represented by resistor R. So the instantaneous value of the current at the moment of switch-on is simply that given by the Ohm's Law value of V/R. The capacitor at that instant has no charge and hence no voltage across its terminals; since the sum of v_c and v_r must at all times equal V, and v_c is instantaneously zero, all the applied voltage must appear instantaneously across R. We will indicate this initial value of the current by I_0.

This initial current does not continue unchanged as it would do if only the resistor was present. C begins to charge immediately and the voltage across its terminals rises accordingly. The voltage across R correspondingly falls by an equal amount v_c, so that for a given value of $v_r = V - v_c$. Consequently at any particular time instant after switch-on, the charging current will be *less* than I_0 and will be expressed by

$$i = \frac{V - v_c}{R} = \frac{v_r}{R}$$

So, as the voltage across C rises, both the circuit current and the *rate* of charging falls. Hence C charges progressively more slowly as time passes. Looked at simply, as an increasing number of electrons pack into the negative-connected plate and an equal number flow out of the positive-connected plate, there is an increasing force of repulsion tending to keep out those wanting to enter the negative plate and an increasing force of attraction tending to prevent others leaving the positive plate. The process is rather like packing people into a hall. When the doors are first opened there is a comparatively rapid entry rate; as the hall fills the flow slackens, and when the hall is filled the flow stops altogether.

Likewise, with the passage of time, the capacitor must eventually 'fill up'. Its terminal voltage v_c will then be equal to V, so that v_r will be zero and the circuit current will be zero. Throughout the entire charging cycle, therefore, we can make the following observations:

At switch-on ($t = 0$): $v_c = 0$, $v_r = V$ and $I_0 = \dfrac{V}{R}$

At some instant during the charge: $v_c > 0$, $v_r = V - v_c$ and $i = \dfrac{V - v_c}{R}$

At the completion of the charge: $v_c = V$, $v_r = 0$ and $i = 0$

So the capacitor voltage has risen from zero to V volts, the resistor voltage and circuit current have fallen from V and I_0 respectively to zero. The kind of variation we can expect in the capacitor voltage and the circuit current after switch-on at time $t = 0$ will therefore be as shown in *Figure 2.6*. Both of the curves for v_c and i have the same

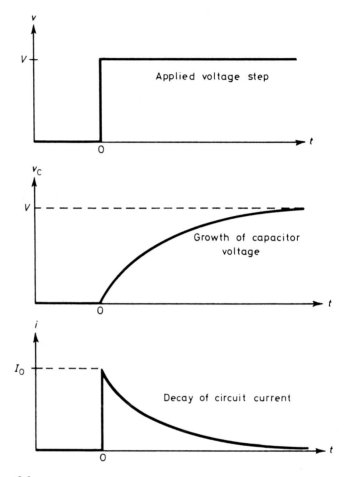

Figure 2.6

mathematical form and we shall derive this a little later on. For the present we can call them the curves of *exponential growth* (for v_c) and *decay* (for i) and keep their general appearance in mind.

Follow this next worked example carefully.

Example (1). A capacitor is connected in series with a 10 kΩ resistor and switched suddenly across a 200 V d.c. supply. What is the initial current and the voltage across C when the circuit current is 5 mA?

At switch-on, the initial current $I_0 = \dfrac{V}{R} = \dfrac{200}{10000}$ A

$$= 20 \text{ mA}.$$

This current decays towards zero as the capacitor charges; when it has fallen to 5 mA, the voltage across R at that instant will be

$$v_r = iR = 5 \times 10^{-3} \times 10000 = 50 \text{ V}$$

But at any instant $\quad v_c = V - v_r$

$$\therefore \qquad v_c = 200\text{--}50 = 150 \text{ V}.$$

Try the next two examples on your own:

Example (2). When a capacitor and series resistor are connected suddenly to a 50 V d.c. supply, the initial current is 100 mA. Calculate the value of the resistor and the current at the instant when the voltage across C is 20 V.

Example (3). A voltmeter whose resistance is 20 kΩ is connected in series with a capacitor and a 100 V battery. What will the voltmeter read (a) at the instant of switch on; (b) at the instant the current is 2 mA; (c) when the capacitor is fully charged?

TIME CONSTANT The curve of *Figure 2.7* represents the rise of voltage across the capacitor. We notice that the rate of increase of voltage is greatest at the commencement of the charge and becomes progressively smaller as the charge proceeds. This rate is indicated by the degree of steepness

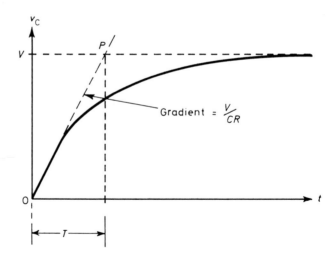

Figure 2.7

of the curve at any point; and this, in the usual way, is measured as the gradient of the tangent drawn to the curve at the point in question. In mathematical form the gradient is dv_c/d_t, where dv_c is the small increment in the capacitor voltage over a small increment of time dt. (*Note.* Strictly this symbolism is for the limit of the ratio $\delta v_c/\delta t$ where the changes are infinitesimally small.)

As before

$$dQ = C dv_c = i dt$$

and so

$$i = C \frac{dv_c}{dt}$$

At the instant the switch is closed, referring to *Figure 2.5*, $t = 0$ and the initial current

$$I_o = \frac{V}{R} = C \frac{dv_c}{dt}$$

So the *initial* gradient of the curve is

$$\frac{dv_c}{dt_o} = \frac{V}{CR} \text{ V/s}$$

If the charge was to continue at this rate indefinitely along the broken line OP in *Figure 2.7*, the time that would elapse before v_c reached its final value V would be T seconds. But from the diagram

$$T = \frac{\text{voltage}}{\text{rate of increase of voltage}} = V \div \frac{V}{CR}$$

$$\therefore \quad T = CR \text{ sec}$$

This product is known as the *Time Constant* of the circuit and it is a very important concept.

Example (4). Can you verify that the product *CR* leads to the dimension of time?
(Hint: express *C* in terms of charge Q, and then in terms of time.)
When you use the *CR* product you must make sure that the correct units are employed. *C* must be expressed in farads and *R* in ohms for the answer to be in seconds. However, if *C* is expressed in μF, the time will be given in μs. It is often easiest to work in μF for *C* and MΩ for *R*, the answer then again being given in seconds.

Example (5). What is the time constant of a 4 μF capacitor and a 100 kΩ resistor? Work the problem first in farads and ohms, and then in μF and MΩ.

Working in farads and ohms, we have

$$T = 4 \times 10^{-6} \times 100 \times 10^3 = 0.4 \text{ s}$$

Alternately, working in μF and MΩ

$$T = 4 \times 0.1 = 0.4 \text{ s}$$

Example (6). A 10 μF capacitor and a 2 MΩ resistor are switched suddenly to a 100 V supply. Find (a) the time constant, (b) the initial current, (c) the initial rate of rise of voltage across *C*.

(a) $T = CR = 10 \ \mu\text{F} \times 2 \text{ M}\Omega = 20 \text{ s}$

(b) $I_o = \dfrac{V}{R} = \dfrac{100}{2 \times 10^6}$ A $= 0.05$ mA

(c) Initial rate of rise of voltage $= \dfrac{V}{CR}$ V/s

$$= \dfrac{100}{20} = 5 \text{ V/s}$$

(7). A series circuit made up of a 50 μF capacitor and a resistance R is to have a time constant of 4 s. What should be the value of R? If the circuit is switched to a 100 V d.c. supply, find (a) the initial current, (b) the rate at which the voltage is rising when the capacitor voltage has reached 30 V.

You may perhaps have had a little difficulty with the last part of the previous problem. You have been asked to find, not the initial rate of increase of capacitor voltage but the rate of increase at some later stage, when the capacitor has already acquired some of its possible charge. Let us look into this problem in a little more detail.

At any point on the charging cycle the voltage across C opposes the applied voltage, and this is a continuing process all the time the charge is taking place. Let the capacitor voltage be at some particular value v' at any instant during the charge, then the current

$$i = \dfrac{V - v'}{R} = C.\dfrac{dv_c}{dt}$$

and so
$$\dfrac{dv_c}{dt} = \dfrac{V - v'}{CR} \text{ V/s}$$

This is clearly *less* than the initial rate of increase given by V/CR. Hence the curve of capacitor voltage against time becomes progressively less steep as time goes on and will constantly approach the limiting condition of a horizontal line as $(V-v')$ approaches zero. Now, referring to *Figure 2.8*, at any particular instant t_1 the capacitor has

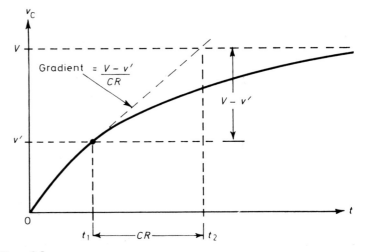

Figure 2.8

still to be charged $(V-v')$ volts. If this charging rate was then to be maintained, the time for the charge to be completed would be $(t_2 - t_1)$ seconds; then

$$t_2 - t_1 = \frac{\text{voltage available}}{\text{rate of increase of voltage}}$$

$$= \frac{V - v'}{(V - v')/\text{CR}} = CR \text{ s}$$

Hence $t_2 - t_1 = T$, the time constant.

This argument must be true for any selected point on the charging curve. Hence at any point on the curve *the time remaining* to complete the charge, if the charge then continued at a constant rate, is CR s. In theory the capacitor can never be completely charged, but after a time interval equal to $5CR$ s the charge is within 1% of its final value.

In *Figure 2.9* we have used this information to obtain an approximate graph of voltage against time. The time constant is the time it would take the capacitor to reach the value of the applied voltage V

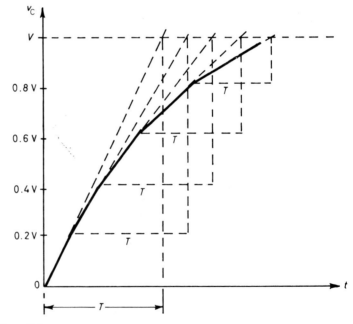

Figure 2.9

if the initial rate of increase could be continued. As we have seen, this statement applies to any instant in the charging cycle, but the final value of the voltage is V in each case. So we can draw a number of horizontal lines each of length equal to CR, at intervals corresponding to equal intervals of voltage. For clarity the intervals have been taken as 0.2 V, but a more accurate curve can be obtained if smaller intervals are chosen.

(8) A 10 μF capacitor is charged from a 100 V d.c. supply through a resistance of 0.5 MΩ. Use graph paper to draw an

approximate curve of the rise of voltage across C for values of time $t = 0$ to $t = 30$ s employing the method outlined above. Take the voltage intervals to be 10 V. From your curve, read off the capacitor voltage after a time equal to CR sec has elapsed, and express this as a percentage of the applied voltage V.

THE EQUATION OF CHARGE

Figure 2.10

To deduce the mathematical expression for the capacitor voltage at any instant calls for some advanced mathematics. If your knowledge of calculus is not up to it, you might miss out the next few lines of working and concentrate on the result we shall obtain at the end.

Let $q = v_c C$ be the instantaneous charge on C at a voltage v_c. Then from *Figure 2.10* the applied voltage V is the sum of v_r and v_c which at any instant are iR and q/C respectively.

$$\therefore \quad iR + \frac{q}{C} = V$$

But $i = \dfrac{dq}{dt}$ so that $\dfrac{dq}{dt}R + \dfrac{q}{C} = V$

Rearranging $\dfrac{dq}{q - CV} = -\dfrac{dt}{CR}$

and integrating $\log_e (q - CV) = -\dfrac{t}{CR} + K$

where K is a constant.

We can evaluate K by knowing the initial conditions: when $t = 0$, $q = 0$, so $K = \log_e (-CV)$

$$\therefore \quad \log_e \frac{q - CV}{-CV} = -\frac{t}{CR} \quad \text{or} \quad \frac{CV - q}{CV} = e^{-t/CR}$$

$$\therefore \quad CV - q = CVe^{-t/CR}$$

$$q = CV(1 - e^{-t/CR})$$

$$= Q(1 - e^{-t/CR}) \tag{2.1}$$

where Q is the final charge on the capacitor. Writing $q = v_c C$, we obtain the expression for the voltage on C at any time t:

$$v_c = V(1 - e^{-t/CR}) \tag{2.2}$$

To acquaint you with the application of this expression, here is a worked example.

Example (9).   A 10 μF capacitor is charged from a 100 V supply through a series resistor of 0.5 MΩ. Calculate the voltage across C for the following intervals after the charge commences. (a) 2 s; (b) 5 s; (c) 10 s.

We calculate the time constant CR: $CR = 10 \times 0.5 = 5$ s.

Here $V = 100$ V, and we require to find values of v_c, given values of t.

(a) $v_c = V(1 - e^{-t/CR})$

For t = 2 $v_c = 100(1 - e^{-2/5})$

$\qquad\qquad = 100(1 - e^{-0.4})$

We need now to find the value of $e^{-0.4}$. It can be proved that e is a constant given approximately by 2.7183. Values of e raised to both positive and negative powers can be found in most books of mathematical tables or it can be evaluated on most pocket calculators; (*You need an e^x button on your calculator. Then, in this case, set your display to −0.4 and press the e^x button.*) By either of these means, we find that $e^{-0.4} = 0.67$. So

$$v_c = 100(1 - 0.67) = 100 \times 0.33$$

$$= 33 \text{ V.}$$

Hence, after a time of 2 sec, the capacitor voltage has grown from zero to 33 V.

(b) Here $t = 5$, so $v_c = 100(1 - e^{-5/5})$

$$= 100(1 - e^{-1})$$

We find that $e^{-1} = 0.368$, so

$$v_c = 100(1 - 0.368) = 100 \times 0.632$$

$$= 63.2 \text{ V}$$

We shall refer back to this particular answer a little further on.

(c) Here $t = 10$, so $v_c = 100(1 - e^{-10/5})$

$$= 100(1 - e^{-2})$$

This time we find that $e^{-2} = 0.135$, so

$$v_c = 100(1 - 0.135) = 100 \times 0.865$$

$$= 86.5 \text{ V}$$

You will agree that, even if this is the first time you have had to work with an exponential equation, the calculations are not very difficult.

The result obtained for part (*b*) of this last example is of very particular interest to us. Notice that the value for time t was equal to the time constant of the circuit, that is, 5 s. If in any example we set $t = CR$ seconds, the term in e *always* evaluates to e^{-1}. Hence we draw an important conclusion: when the capacitor has charged for a time equal to the time constant, *the voltage across it will always have reached 63.2% of the final value V*. This gives us another interpretation of time constant and one which particularly emphasises the choice of words.

So far we have concentrated only on the exponential growth equation. If you glance back at *Figure 2.6* you will see that the circuit current follows an exponential decay curve, and quite clearly, so does the fall of voltage across the resistor. We can easily deduce the mathematical expressions for the circuit current and the resistor voltage at any instant of time from our knowledge of the growth equation (2.2)

above. At any instant

$$v_r = V - v_c$$

then
$$v_r = V - V(1 - e^{-t/CR})$$
$$= V.e^{-t/CR} \qquad (2.3)$$

Also the current at any instant in the resistor, and hence in the circuit as a whole is

$$i = \frac{v_r}{R} = \frac{V}{R} e^{-t/CR}$$

$$\therefore \quad i = I_0 e^{-t/CR} \qquad (2.4)$$

When $t = 0$, $e^0 = 1$ and so $i = I_0$, the initial current.

THE DISCHARGE OF A CAPACITOR

Figure 2.11

Consider *Figure 2.11* where the capacitor is charged through resistor R by the switch connection being made as shown. When the charge is complete the switch is moved to position 2 and the series combination of C and R is short-circuited. The capacitor will then discharge through R and the circuit current will flow in the direction indicated.

By Kirchhoff, the e.m.f. acting in the closed loop is now zero, so the sum of v_c and v_r is *at all times zero*. At the instant the short-circuit is applied, the capacitor voltage is equal to V and the voltage across the resistor is $-V$. As the capacitor discharges, both of these voltages must decay towards zero, and so the curves of capacitor and resistor voltage will be as shown in *Figure 2.12*.

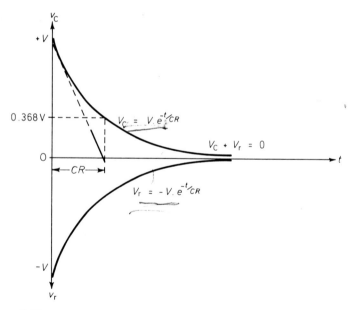

Figure 2.12

Take special note of the fact that although the resistor voltage looks rather like an exponential growth curve, it is a decay curve, the voltage *falling* from its initial value of $-V$ to the zero line. We should expect, therefore, that both curves will have equations of the form given in (2.3) and (2.4) above. This is indeed so, and if the necessary calculations are made, we find that

$$v_c = Ve^{-t/CR} \quad \text{for the capacitor}$$

$$v_r = Ve^{-t/CR} \quad \text{for the resistor}$$

The current in the circuit also decays and is easily calculated since $i = v_r/R$. So

$$i = -\frac{V}{R}e^{-t/CR} = I_0 e^{-t/CR}$$

where I_0 is the initial current. The negative sign tells us that the current during discharge flows in the opposite direction to that which flowed into the capacitor during the charge. As *Figure 2.12* shows, if the capacitor (or resistor) voltage continued to fall at its initial rate, the discharge would be completed in a time equal to *CR* seconds.

For any of the decay equations already mentioned, notice that when $t = CR$, the term of $e^{-t/CR}$ comes to e^{-1}, hence the curve, whether of voltage or current, decays away to $e^{-1} = 0.368$ of its initial value.

Figure 2.13

Example (10). The circuit of *Figure 2.13* is part of an electronic system such that when the voltage across the terminals AB reaches 62.3 V the capacitor *C* is instantly discharged, the applied 100 V supply then being allowed to charge it through *R* as before. Sketch a graph showing the variation of (a) capacitor voltage, (b) circuit current throughout several cycles of the above sequence. Calculate
   (i) the initial current;
   (ii) the current at the instant before the capacitor is discharged, showing this on the graph.
   The circuit time constant is 2 MΩ × 5 μF = 10 s
(a) As the applied voltage is 100 V and the capacitor charges to 63.2 V, the capacitor charges for 10 s before being discharged (since in a time equal to *CR* the capacitor voltage is always 63.2% of the applied voltage). The graph of capacitor voltage against time is shown in *Figure 2.14(a)*.

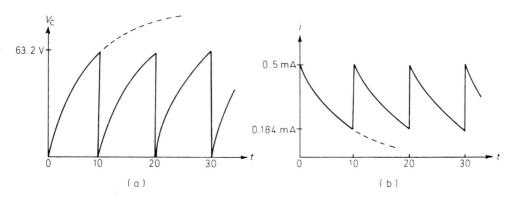

Figure 2.14

(b) The circuit current will decay when the capacitor discharges, but will be restored to its initial value $I_0 = V/R$ each time the

capacitor is discharged. So

$$I_0 = \frac{100}{2 \times 10^6} \text{ A} = 0.5 \text{ mA}$$

At the instant the capacitor is about to be discharged, the voltage across $R = 100-63.2 = 36.8$ V, hence the current at this instant will be

$$i = \frac{36.8}{2 \times 10^6} \text{ A} = 0.184 \text{ mA}$$

The graph of current against time is shown in *Figure 2.14(b)*.

Both of the curves are examples of a particular kind of *sawtooth* waveform. You will be meeting up with waveforms of this sort in your Electronics syllabus work.

(11) In *Figure 2.12* the gradient of the line representing the initial rate of decrease of v_c is $- V/CR$. Prove that this is so.

(12) Sketch, on the same voltage/time axes, three curves representing the rise of voltage across a capacitor C when R has a low. medium and high value of resistance.

(13) Sketch on the same charge/time axes, three curves representing the increase of charge q on a capacitor C when R has a fixed value but C has a low, medium and high value of capacitance.

THE SERIES *L-R* CIRCUIT

Figure 2.15

We turn now to the series circuit made up of inductance in series with resistance. The resistance may be a separate component or it may be the actual ohmic resistance of the wire making up the inductance. When, in the circuit of *Figure 2.15*, the battery is suddenly switched to the inductance, the current will build up to its final possible limit of V/R but it will not do this without the passage of time. We recall that when the current is increasing towards its V/R value, the changing magnetic field induces an e.m.f. in the coil which opposes the increase, and this opposition depends upon the *rate* of increase of the current. Hence time is required for the current to flow in an inductive circuit.

Consider some instant t sec after the voltage is applied; the current has risen to i amp and the voltage across R is then iR volts. The remaining part of V, $(V-iR)$ volts is available to increase the circuit current and the rate at which it will increase will depend upon this available voltage. The induced e.m.f. will be equal to this voltage at all times, hence

$$e = (V - iR) = L\frac{di}{dt}$$

or
$$V = iR + L\frac{di}{dt}$$

At the instant the voltage is applied, $i = 0$ and $V = L\dfrac{di}{dt}$

$$\therefore \quad \frac{di}{dt} = \frac{V}{L} \; A/s$$

This is the initial rate of increase of the current. If the current was to continue at this rate unopposed, it would reach its final value $I = V/R$ in a time given by

$$T = \frac{\text{final current}}{\text{rate of change of current}} = \frac{V/R}{V/L}$$

$$= L/R \; s$$

This situation is analogous to the rise of voltage across a capacitor; hence the quotient L/R is the *time-constant of an inductive circuit.*

(14)   Can you verify that L/R leads to the dimension of time? (Hint: express L in terms of voltage and time by Faraday's Law)

(15)   What is the time constant of an inductance of 10 H which has a resistance of 100Ω?

At any instant during the rise of current in an inductance, the back induced e.m.f. opposes the supply voltage and this is a continuing process all the time the current is rising. The rate of rise of the current gets less and less as time goes on, and the graph of current against time,

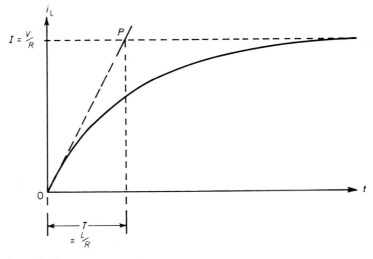

Figure 2.16

instead of following the initial rate line OP in *Figure 2.16* bends over to become more and more horizontal as the final limit of current is approached. Let the current be i, then at any instant

$$L\frac{di}{dt} = V - iR$$

and

$$\frac{di}{dt} = \frac{V - iR}{L} \quad \text{A/s}$$

This is clearly less than the original rate of increase V/L A/s proved above.

At any instant the current rise still required is $(V - IR)/R$, and the rate of rise is $(V - iR)/L$. Hence at *any* instant, the time for the current rise to be completed, if it were to continue at a constant rate is

$$\frac{V - iR}{R} \times \frac{V - iR}{L} = \frac{L}{R} \quad \text{seconds}$$

This is the same time as that found for completion at the initial rate of rise and the argument used must hold for any instant of time. Hence, at any point on the current-time curve, the time remaining for the completion of the rise of current, if the rise then continued at a constant rate, is L/R s. You will have realised by now that the situation and the form of the curve are completely analogous to the charging of a capacitor.

Current in an inductive circuit, like capacitor voltage in a CR circuit rises gradually to its final steady-state value, the rise being rapid if L is small but slow if L is large, assuming a constant value of R. Conversely to the capacitor case, an increase in resistance *reduces* the time constant of the LR circuit. In theory, the current never reaches its final value since a time equal to L/R seconds always remains outstanding to complete the rise, but in practice a time equal to five times L/R brings the current to within 1% of its final steady value.

It is clear that the equation expressing the rise of current in an inductance will be of exponential form and similar in pattern to that derived for the CR circuit. If the necessary calculations are carried out, we find that the current i_L at any instant is given in terms of the final current I, inductance L and resistance R by

$$i_L = I(1 - e^{-Rt/L}) \tag{2.5}$$

If now we set $t = L/R$ seconds, the equation becomes

$$i_L = I(1 - e^{-1}) = I(1 - 0.368)$$

$$= 0.632I$$

So, in a time equal to the time constant, the current will have risen *always* to 63.2% of its final value.

If you have mastered problems associated with CR circuits you should have no difficulty in coping with the present examples. Here are two worked examples to show you the way.

Example (16).   When a coil is connected to a 100 V d.c. supply the final steady current is measured as 0.5 A. At the instant when the current was changing at the rate of 10 A/s the current was 0.2 A. What is the resistance and inductance of the coil?

What was the current in the coil at the instant $t = 0.05$ s?

$$\text{Final current } I = \frac{V}{R} \quad \therefore \quad R = \frac{V}{I} = \frac{100}{0.5} = 200\,\Omega$$

also

$$\frac{\mathrm{d}i}{\mathrm{d}t} = \frac{V - iR}{L}$$

$$\therefore \quad 10 = \frac{100 - (0.2 \times 200)}{L}$$

$$\therefore \quad L = \frac{100 - 40}{10} = 6\,\mathrm{H}$$

For the second part of the question we require the time constant:

$$T = \frac{L}{R} = \frac{6}{200} = 0.03\,\mathrm{s}$$

then

$$\frac{Rt}{L} = \frac{0.05}{0.03} = 1.67 \text{ (for } t = 0.05 \text{ s)}$$

so

$$i = I(1 - e^{-1.67}) = 0.5(1 - e^{-1.67})$$

$$= 0.5(1 - 0.189)$$

$$= 0.405\,\mathrm{A}$$

Example (17). A relay coil having a resistance of 20 Ω and an inductance 0.5 H is switched across a d.c. supply of 200 V. Calculate: (a) the time constant; (b) the initial rate of rise of current; (c) the current at a time equal to the time constant; (d) the current after 0.05 s; (e) the energy stored in the field when the current is steady.

(a)

$$T = \frac{L}{R} = \frac{0.5}{20} = 0.025\,\mathrm{s}$$

(b)

$$\text{Initial rate of rise of current} = \frac{V}{L} = \frac{200}{0.5}$$

$$= 400\,\mathrm{A/s}$$

(c) The current rises to 63.2% of its final value in a time equal to the time constant. Final current $I = V/R = 200/20 = 10$ A

$$\therefore \quad i_L = 0.632 \times 10 = 6.32\,\mathrm{A}$$

(d) After time $t = 0.05$ s,

$$\frac{Rt}{L} = \frac{20 \times 0.05}{0.5} = 2$$

$$i_L = 10(1 - e^{-2}) = 10(1 - 0.135)$$

$$= 8.65\,\mathrm{A}$$

(e) Energy stored $= \frac{1}{2}LI^2$ joules

$$= \frac{1}{2} \times 0.5 \times 10^2 = 25\,\mathrm{J}.$$

DECAY OF CURRENT The last part of the previous example dealt with the energy stored in the magnetic field when the steady state has been reached. The expression for energy was derived in your previous year's work and you may have called it to mind without too much effort.

Suppose a steady current I to be flowing in an inductor; now let the applied voltage V be removed and at the same instant let the coil be short-circuited. The current in the coil does not fall immediately to zero, for the collapse is opposed by the self-induced e.m.f. and this is now in such a direction that it tends to *maintain* the current at its original value. Let the current be iA at a time t seconds after the collapse has begun. Then

$$iR + L.\frac{di}{dt} = 0$$

since there is no external voltage acting on the coil.

When $t = 0, i = V/R$ (its steady value at the instant of short-circuit), and so

$$IR + L\frac{di}{dt} = 0$$

$$\frac{di}{dt} = -\frac{IR}{L} = -\frac{V}{L} \text{ A/s}$$

This is the initial rate of change of current, the negative sign simply indicating that the current is decreasing. Apart from this sign change, the value is the same as that of the initial rate of rise of current discussed earlier. Solving the equation above in a manner similar to that already used for the charge of a capacitor, we find that the current at any instant t during the decay cycle is

$$i_L = Ie^{-Rt/L} \tag{2.6}$$

The curve of this equation is shown in *Figure 2.17* and is the same as the curve of current growth but turned upside down. If the fall con-

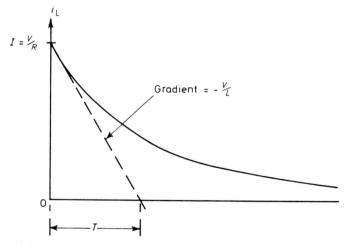

Figure 2.17

tinued at the initial rate the decay would be completed in a time equal to L/R sec, the time constant again. Setting $t = L/R$ in equation (2.6)

above we get

$$i_L = Ie^{-1} = 0.368I$$

Hence in a time equal to the time constant, the current in the inductor has decayed to 36.8% of its initial value.

When an inductive circuit is suddenly interrupted, the induced e.m.f. may be many times greater than the applied voltage and is often sufficient to create an arc at the switch contacts. This arcing is destructive to the contacts and a spark-quench circuit is often wired across the switch terminals. This circuit is made up of a capacitor and a low value resistor in series; the energy of the collapsing magnetic field is then transferred to the electric field of the capacitor, thereafter being rapidly dissipated in the resistive part of the arrangement.

Some devices, i.e. ignition coils, operate on the principle of a high induced e.m.f. across the coil when the current is suddenly interrupted.

DIFFERENTIATING AND INTEGRATING CIRCUITS

Suppose that a voltage pulse having a time variation as shown in *Figure 2.18(a)* is applied to a series CR circuit. There are two possibilities of interest to consider: the time constant of the CR circuit may be short relative to the pulse duration P or it may be long. Suppose firstly that the product CR is very short compared with P.

Then the charging of the capacitor through R will be completed in a fraction of the time P and thereafter V_C will remain at the peak level of the pulse amplitude, $\hat{V}$. When the pulse ends, the capacitor will discharge rapidly through R and V_C will return to zero. *Figure 2.18(b)* shows the voltage pulse as it appears across C. Since $V_R + V_C$ must at all times equal $\hat{V}$, the voltage across R rises instantly to $\hat{V}$ at the onset of the pulse and thereafter decays rapidly to zero as V_C rises to $\hat{V}$. It then remains at zero for the duration of the pulse.

When the pulse ends, the capacitor discharges through R; the voltage across R instantly follows the fall (which is now in the opposite sense to the charge rise) and decays from its negative level back to zero, see *Figure 2.18(c)*. The points of interest to notice here are:

(a) the voltage output across C is a very close approximation to the shape of the input pulse, in fact, the shorter the product CR becomes, the better the approximation.

Figure 2.18

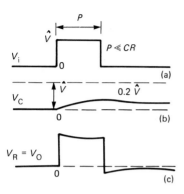

Figure 2.19

(b) the *output* across R consists of two very narrow voltage pulses of opposite sign, one coinciding with the start and the other with the end of the input pulse.

This circuit, in which the product *CR* is very much shorter than *P* and the output is derived from R, is called a *differentiating* circuit. The narrow pulses developed across R are approximately proportional to the time rate-of-change of the input voltage. You may like to refer back to *Figure 2.4(a)* on page 23 and re-read the text there to help you grasp the concept of electronic differentiation.

Suppose now that we change over the positions of C and R and make the product *CR* very large compared with the pulse duration *P*, as indicated in *Figure 2.19(a)*. At the onset of the pulse the voltage across C will now rise very slowly and will have reached a level that is only a fraction of $\hat{V}$ by the time the pulse ends; *Figure 2.19(b)*. From this point on, C will discharge through R, but as the rate of discharge is governed by the voltage available across R (and this is a lot less than $\hat{V}$), the discharge rate will be different from the charge rate. Hence the discharge curve will exhibit a long decay tail as *Figure 2.19(b)* shows. The corresponding variation in the voltage across R is given in diagram (c). The points of interest this time are:

(a) the voltage across R is a close approximation to the shape of the input pulse. In fact, the greater the *CR* product, the better the approximation;

(b) the *output* voltage across C is a low amplitude pulse many times the length of the input pulse.

This form of circuit, in which the product *CR* is very much longer than *P*, is called an *integrating* circuit. The extended output pulse developed across C is approximately proportional to the time-integral of the input voltage.

> *Example (18).*   What would the true differentiated version of a rectangular voltage pulse look like, and how closely does a practical differentiating circuit approximate to it?
>
> For the rectangular pulse shown in *Figure 2.20*, the instantaneous rate of change (or gradient) dV/dt is either infinite or zero. It is infinite on the leading and trailing edges of the pulse where the waveform gradient is vertical, and zero elsewhere where the waveform is horizontal and the gradient zero. A true picture of the differentiated form of the rectangular pulse consequently is as shown in the figure.
>
> The output from a practical circuit has been shown in *Figure 2.18(c)* and although this consists of narrow spikes of voltage, the similarity to the true (and unobtainable) differentiated voltage is clear. For an extremely short time-constant the similarity becomes very marked and the term 'differentiating circuit' is fully justified.

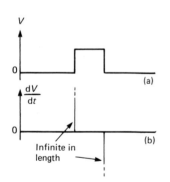

Figure 2.20

APPLICATION TO PULSE TRAINS

Suppose that a succession of rectangular pulses is applied to differentiating and integrating circuits in turn. Let P_1 be the duration of each pulse and P_2 the interval between the pulses.

The result of applying such a pulse train to a differentiating circuit where $CR \ll P_1$ is shown in *Figure 2.21*. The voltage waveforms developed across C and R are similar to those already described, and the output across R is a succession of alternate positive and negative spikes. If the negative spikes are removed by a simple diode connected across R (make a sketch of how you would do this) and the positive spikes are 'clipped' to a predetermined level (how might you do this?), a train of very short duration pulses may be obtained.

Some new points of discussion arise when we turn to the integrating circuit. Again, the general shapes of the voltage developed across C and R are similar to those already described, but this time the long decay tail of the discharging capacitor is not permitted to fall away to zero. As *Figure 2.22(b)* shows, the *mean* level of voltage across C tends to rise with each successive pulse because the capacitor has barely started to discharge before the following pulse turns up. After a number of pulses have passed, a steady state is reached in which the charge acquired by the capacitor during pulse period P_1 is exactly *equal* to the charge lost during interval P_2. This means that the mean current flowing into

Figure 2.21

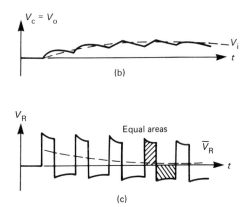

Figure 2.22

C through R is zero when equilibrium has been reached, so that the mean value of V_R is also zero.

The graph at (c) shows the voltage developed across R and at equilibrium the area (representing voltage × time) enclosed above the mean (zero) line during the time P_1 is equal to the area below this line during the time P_2.

The mean output across C, shown as a broken line in diagram (b), is seen to be a long single pulse, albeit with a serrated edge; the circuit has integrated (or summed up) all the separate input pulses into a single pulse. The output across R is a good replica of the input voltage train, but the waveform is balanced about a zero level, unlike the input which is positioned wholly above the zero line. This effect comes about because the presence of the capacitor removes the d.c. component of the input signal. The succession of positive input pulses can be considered to be made up of a steady (d.c.) component of voltage and a purely alternating component of voltage, and only the alternating component appears across R.

In many circuit applications it is necessary to re-insert the steady component if the output has to be taken from R. This process is known as *d.c. restoration*.

Example (19).   The input to the circuit of *Figure 2.23(a)* is the rectangular waveform of *Figure 2.23(b)*. Sketch the output waveform, marking the high and low voltage levels attained and indicating the new zero level.

In the circuit shown, the time constant $CR = 0.01 \times 0.1 = 0.001$ s or 1000 μs, which is long compared with the period between the pulses, 50 μs. Taking the output from across the resistor where the shape of the input waveform will be practically unaffected, the average value of the input is clearly

$$V_{mean} = \frac{P_1}{P_1 + P_2} \cdot \hat{V} = \frac{10}{60} \times 9 = 1.5 \text{ V}$$

and the output wave must then 'balance' itself so that its mean value is zero, that is, the wave must therefore vary between -1.5 V and $+7.5$ V as shown in *Figure 2.23(c)*.

(a)   (b)   (c)

Figure 2.23

ACTIVE CIRCUITS

The C-R circuits just discussed are *passive* differentiators or integrators. *Active* forms of these circuits can be made using operational amplifiers, and these are used extensively in automatic control systems and (in the case of integrators) analogue computers.

Figure 2.24(a) shows the essential arrangement of an operational amplifier used as a differentiator.

From operational amplifier theory (covered in your electronics course) we have a virtual earth at the inverting input terminal and negligible current flows into the amplifier because of its very high input impedance. Hence the input voltage v_i may be considered to be developed across the capacitor C, the output voltage v_o across the

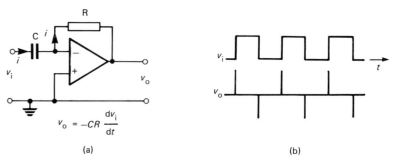

$$v_o = -CR \frac{dv_i}{dt}$$

(a)   (b)

Figure 2.24

resistor R and the input current i flows through C and R effectively in series. The charge on the capacitor is

$$q = Cv_i$$

The charging current, i, is the time rate of change of charge or

$$i = \frac{dq}{dt} = C\,\frac{dv_i}{dt}$$

At the output, voltage v_o must obey Ohm's law and be expressed as $-iR$, hence

$$v_o = -iR = -CR\,\frac{dv_i}{dt}$$

The negative sign appears because the amplifier is used in the inverting mode and the output is antiphase to the input. Thus we see that the output voltage is proportional to the time derivative of the input, and with a 'gain' magnitude of CR. This means that the more rapid the rate of change of the input, the higher the output voltage. A rectangular wave input will give very sharp output pulses corresponding to the rising and falling edges where the input is changing; *Figure 2.24(b)*.

For the active integrator, capacitor C and resistor R are interchanged, *Figure 2.25(a)*. The input voltage V_1 will now attempt to charge the capacitor plate connected to the input through the resistor. Because of the phase inversion taking place in the amplifier, however, the output voltage V_o will try to charge the other capacitor plate in a direction which tends to neutralise the charge on the input plate. As the capacitor charges, in other words, the output from the amplifier must go more and more negative to maintain the charging current constant. But when a capacitor is charged from a constant current source, the rise in capacitor voltage is *linear*, hence with a positive input voltage, the output of the integrator will be a negative-going linear ramp, and conversely.

As for differentiation, negligible current flows into the amplifier terminal and

$$\frac{V_i}{R} = -\frac{dq}{dt}$$

But

$$dq = C\,.\,dV_o$$

therefore

$$\frac{V_i}{R} = -C\,\frac{dV_o}{dt}$$

and

$$dV_o = -\frac{1}{CR}\,V_i\,dt$$

Integrating, we get

$$V_o = -\frac{1}{CR}\int V_i\,dt$$

Therefore the output voltage of this circuit is the integral of the input voltage with a gain magnitude of $1/CR$. The response of the integrator to a negative-going voltage step is shown in *Figure 2.25(b)*.

Both the active differentiator and integrator are important circuit elements. We will be meeting them again in the sections on automatic control systems and digital instrumentation.

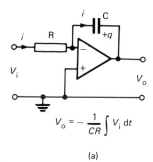

$$V_o = -\frac{1}{CR}\int V_i\,dt$$

(a)

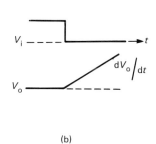

(b)

Figure 2.25

PROBLEMS FOR SECTION 2

(20) A capacitor is connected in series with a 5 kΩ resistor to a 200 V d.c. supply. Find the initial current and the voltage across the capacitor when the current is 20 mA.

(21) When a capacitor is connected to a 25 V supply the initial current is limited to 100 mA by a series resistor. Calculate the value of the resistor and find the charging current when the voltage across C has risen to 15 V.

(22) A 10 μF capacitor is to be charged through a 100 kΩ resistor from a d.c. supply. Find (a) the circuit time constant, (b) the additional series resistor required to increase the time constant to 4 s, (c) the additional parallel resistor required to reduce the time constant to 0.25 s.

(23) A 5 μF capacitor is to be charged to 50 V through a 1 MΩ series resistor. Calculate the gradient of the voltage-time curve at the instants of time when the voltage across C is zero, 10 V, 20 V, 30 V and 40 V.

(24) A welding machine is controlled by a timer which depends upon the charging of an 8 μF capacitor. If the time constant of the circuit is to be variable between 0.5 s and 25 s, find the limits of the value of the resistor to be wired in series with the capacitor.

(25) A 150 V battery is switched suddenly across a circuit consisting of a 20 μF capacitor in series with a 100 kΩ resistor. Write down the expression representing (a) the voltage across C, (b) the current in the circuit, at any subsequent time after the switch is closed.

(26) A coil of resistance 20 Ω and inductance 250 mH is connected to a 20 V d.c. supply. Calculate the initial rate of increase of current and the final steady current.

(27) When a coil is connected to a 20 V d.c. supply the final steady current is 2.5 A. The current was 0.5 A at the instant when the current was changing at the rate of 3 A/s. Find the coil resistance and its inductance.

Group 2

(28) A 50 μF capacitor in series with a 2 kΩ resistor is connected suddenly to a 100 V d.c. supply. Find (a) the initial current, (b) the circuit time constant, (c) the voltage across C when $t = 0.04$ s.

(29) When a capacitor and series resistor are connected to a 110 V d.c. supply the initial current is 110 mA. Find the value of the resistor. What is the circuit current at the instant when the voltage across C is 50 V?

(30) A voltmeter whose resistance is 10 kΩ is in series with a 80 μF capacitor. The combination is switched suddenly across a 100 V supply. What will the voltmeter read (a) at the instant of switch-on, (b) at a time $t = 0.4$ s? What will the circuit current be at the instant the voltmeter reads 40 V?

(31) In *Figure 2.26*, $C = 2$ μF and $R = 0.5$ MΩ. What is the potential at terminals **AB** (a) before switch S is closed, (b) at the instant the switch is closed, (c) 2 s after the switch is closed?

(32) The capacitor and resistor in *Figure 2.18* are interchanged. Calculate the potential at terminals **AB** for each of the three conditions given in the previous question.

Figure 2.26

Figure 2.27

Figure 2.28

Figure 2.29

(33) A 10 μF capacitor is fully charged from a 500 V supply. The supply is then disconnected and a 1 MΩ resistor placed across the capacitor. Calculate (a) the charge on the capacitor at the instant the resistor is connected, (b) the charge on the capacitor at time $t = 10$ s. What will the discharge current be at this instant?

(34) A coil of inductance 0.5 H and resistance 25 Ω is connected to a 25 V supply. Calculate (a) the final current, (b) the time constant, (c) the current at time $t = L/R$ s.

(35) In *Figure 2.27* calculate the steady state values of the current in the coil and in the parallel resistor. If switch S is now suddenly opened, what will be the current in the 30 Ω resistor 0.1 s later?

Group 3

(36) A 10 H coil of resistance 50 Ω is suddenly connected to a 100 V supply. Find (a) the current after 5 s, (b) the time at which $v_R = v_L$.

(37) A constant voltage is applied to a 2 H inductor. At the instant $t = 0$ the voltage across L is 25 V; at the instant $t = 0.025$ s the voltage across L has decayed to 5 V. What is the resistance of the inductor?

(38) In *Figure 2.28* the circuit is in a steady state. Calculate (a) the potential between terminals AB, (b) the voltage to which C is charged, (c) the charge on C, (d) the energy stored in C, (e) the current in the 1 MΩ. The 100 V supply is now suddenly disconnected. In what time will the capacitor voltage fall to 10 V?

(39) A capacitor is fully charged from a 150 V supply, it is then disconnected from the supply and joined in parallel with an uncharged 10 μF capacitor, no charge being lost in the process. The combination is now discharged through a 100 kΩ resistor and the voltage falls to 37 V in a time of 3 s. What is the capacitance of the first capacitor?

(40) A rectangular pulse is applied to an integrating circuit. Sketch the waveforms developed across C and R respectively when (a) the pulse width is greater than the *CR* product, (b) when the pulse width is smaller than the *CR* product.

(41) Define the time-constant of a *CR* circuit. If a square wave oscillating between 0 V and −6 V at a frequency of 500 kHz is applied to the input A of the circuit of *Figure 2.29*, draw a graph of the voltage waveform at B for the following values of C and R: (a) 0.001 μF, 500 Ω, (b) 0.001 μF, 2 kΩ, (c) 0.001 μF, 1 MΩ.

(42) A telephone dial may operate between 7 and 12 pulses per second with a break percentage of 63 − 72%. What is the duration of (i) the minimum pulse break, (ii) the minimum make pulse?

3 Alternating current: series circuits

Aims: At the end of this Unit section you should be able to:
Solve problems involving voltage, current and phase angle in series combinations of inductance and capacitance, taking account of their resistances.
Draw phasor diagrams for series circuits and understand voltage, impedance and power triangles.
Define power factor and identify the active and reactive components of current and power.
State the conditions for series resonance and solve problems relating to series resonance.
Define Q-factor and understand its importance in high and low frequency circuits.

In the previous year's work, you have studied alternating current theory as far as the meaning of peak and r.m.s. values, reactance, impedance and phase angle, and their applications to simple series combinations of resistance, inductance and capacitance. You have also had some practice in drawing phasor diagrams to illustrate the action of the circuits. It is now necessary to extend this theory to more complicated circuits and, in addition, to study the meaning of power dissipation in alternating current theory.

First of all we will revise briefly some of the previous work.

BASIC RELATIONSHIPS Resistance is that property of an electric circuit which opposes the flow of current by absorbing energy. This energy is generally dissipated as heat and the rate of dissipation is proportional to the product I^2R. Reactance is that property which opposes any *change* in existing current or voltage conditions in a circuit and is that quantity which determines the r.m.s. current I which flows when an r.m.s. voltage is applied. Reactance is possessed by inductors and capacitors.

In an inductance, a *change* in the magnitude or direction of the current changes the magnetic field associated with the current and hence changes the flux linking with the turns of the coil; an e.m.f. is then induced in the coil which opposes the change producing it. This opposition to the change in current is known as the inductive reactance, denoted by X and measured in ohms. When an alternating sinusoidal current flows in an inductance, there is a continual change in both magnitude and direction and the reactive opposition increases as the frequency increases, since the rate of change of current is then greater and consequently the self-induced back e.m.f. is greater. We recall that inductive reactance is expressed as

$$X = 2\pi fL$$

where L is in henrys and f is the frequency in hertz.

When a capacitor is connected to an alternating supply, it undergoes a periodic process of charge and discharge, thus appearing to conduct an alternating current. The charge and discharge cycle constitutes an opposition to the flow of current and this constitutes the capacitive reactance of the capacitor, denoted by X_C and again measured in ohms. Capacitive reactance decreases as the frequency increases. We recall that capacitive reactance is expressed as

$$X_c = \frac{1}{2\pi fC}$$

where C is in farads and f is in hertz.

Reactance resists the passage of an alternating current *without* the dissipation of energy. In purely reactive elements, all the energy supplied to the magnetic or the electrostatic fields during alternate quarter-cycles of the input wave is returned to the generator during the succeeding quarter-cycles. Hence the total energy supplied and the power dissipated is, in both cases, zero.

Phase In a purely resistive circuit, the current at any instant is directly proportional to the voltage. Then, if the applied voltage is a sine wave, the waveforms of voltage and current being zero at the same instant, are at their peak values at the same instant, hence voltage and current are in phase. *Figure 3.1(a)* shows the phase relationship and the phasor diagram.

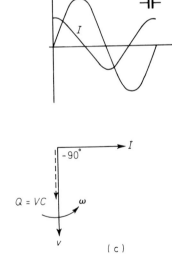

Figure 3.1

In a purely inductive circuit, the self-induced e.m.f. is, by Lenz's Law, in opposition to the applied voltage and proportional to the rate of change of current. So

$$e = -L\frac{\mathrm{d}i}{\mathrm{d}t}$$

where the negative sign simply indicates the effect of opposition. But if the current is

$$i = \hat{I} \sin \omega t$$

the rate of change of current

$$\frac{di}{dt} = \omega \hat{I} \cos \omega t$$

so that the back e.m.f. becomes $e = -L \omega I \cos \omega t$. But this e.m.f. is equal and opposite to the supply voltage. Hence the supply voltage $v = L \omega \hat{I} \cos \omega t$, being a cosine wave, leads the current, which is a sine wave, by 90°. Or, as it is more usually remembered: *in a purely inductive circuit the current lags on the voltage by 90°. Figure 3.1(b)* shows the relationship and the phasor diagram.

In a purely capacitive circuit, the instantaneous charge on the capacitor $q = Cv$ where v is the instantaneous voltage. Let

$$v = V \sin \omega t$$

then
$$q = Cv = VC \sin \omega t$$

but current is rate of change of charge, and so

$$i = \frac{dq}{dt} = \omega CV \cos \omega t$$

Compared with the voltage wave, the current, being a cosine wave, has a lead on V of 90°. Hence, *in a purely capacitive circuit the current leads the voltage by 90°.* The phasor diagram for the capacitive circuit is shown in *Figure 3.1(c).*

It is essential that you keep these basic principles in mind at all times. To refresh your memory on them, work the following assignment problems before going any further.

---

(1)   Calculate the reactance of a coil of inductance 100 mH when it is connected to a 500 Hz supply.

(2)   A coil of inductance 0.28 H has a reactance of 4400 Ω when connected to an a.c. supply. What is the frequency of the supply?

(3)   Calculate the reactance of a 1000 pf capacitor when connected to a 50V 20kHz supply. What current will flow in the circuit?

(4)   A capacitor takes a current of 5 A from a 230 V 50 Hz supply. Calculate the capacitance of the capacitor.

Impedance   The voltage-current relationship for any a.c. circuit containing inductance and capacitance obeys Ohm's Law exactly as it does for d.c. circuits where only resistance is concerned. For this reason such circuits are known as *linear* or *passive* circuits to distinguish them from circuits containing, for example, diodes or transistors, which do not, in general terms, obey Ohm's Law.

In a.c. circuits in addition to resistance we have reactance, and voltages and currents are measured by their r.m.s. values. In real circuits, reactance is never divorced from resistance, particularly so in the case of large inductances where coils with many hundreds of turns of wire may be concerned. So in such circuits there is a *combined* opposition, reactive *and* resistive, to the flow of current and this opposition is known as the *impedance* of the circuit. Impedance is denoted by the symbol Z and is measured in ohms.

Also, the phase angle between voltage and current is no longer exactly zero as it is for pure resistance nor exactly 90° as it is for pure reactance, but lies between these limits, the actual value depending upon the relative magnitudes of the reactive and the resistive elements. Further, as the reactive element depends upon frequency, the phase angle will also be a function of frequency.

A.C. CIRCUIT PROBLEMS

The solution of a.c. circuit problems, both for series and parallel circuits, usually comes down to finding the magnitude and phase angle of the resultant phasor of a number of other phasors set up to represent the circuit conditions. There are several approaches to problems of this sort, but we are concerned in the present Unit Section and in the one that follows with only two of these:

(i) by making a scaled phasor diagram of the circuit currents, voltages or impedances from which the required solution may be obtained by direct measurement of the resultant phasor both as regards magnitude (length) and phase (angle); and
(ii) by the application of simple trigonometry to a phasor sketch diagram of the circuit quantities.

We shall concentrate mainly on methods of calculation by trigonometry but it will be wise to verify the solutions by scaled diagrams wherever possible. Some of your course assessment work will include problems solved by this last method.

Inductance and resistance in series

Figure 3.2

In the circuit of *Figure 3.2* a resistance $R\,\Omega$ is in series with an inductor of reactance $X_L\ (=\omega L)\,\Omega$. The voltage across the resistance, V_R, is in phase with the current I, and the voltage across the inductor, V_L, leads the current by 90°. The supply voltage V is the phasor sum of V_R *and* V_L since we are dealing with a series circuit. Also the current is common to all the component parts of a series circuit, so we can use current as our reference phasor and relate all the voltage conditions to it.

Figure 3.3(a) shows the phasor diagram of voltages; angle ϕ is the phase difference between V and I, and I lags V by this angle. Clearly for such a combination of resistance and inductance ϕ must be postive and lie between 0° and +90°. By Pythagoras we have

$$V = \sqrt{(V_R^2 + V_L^2)}$$

and
$$\tan\phi = \frac{V_L}{V_R}$$

It is usually best to work in terms of resistance, reactance and impedance rather than voltage. Look at the triangle of *Figure 3.3(a)* and note that its sides are made up of the phasors $V_R = IR$, $V_L = IX_L$ and $V = IZ$. Since the current I is a common factor to all these, we can

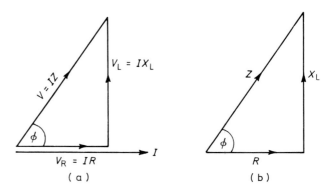

Figure 3.3

draw a similar triangle strictly in terms of R, X_L and Z. This has been done in *Figure 3.3(b)* and gives us what is known as the *impedance* triangle. The angle ϕ is, as before, the phase angle between current and voltage. Again, since this is a right-angled triangle, we can write

$$Z = \sqrt{(R^2 + X_L^2)}$$

so that the current $I = \dfrac{V}{\sqrt{(R^2 + X_L^2)}}$

and $\tan \phi = \dfrac{X_L}{R}$, $\cos \phi = \dfrac{R}{Z}$, $\sin \phi = \dfrac{X_L}{Z}$

The impedance triangle is a very useful diagram in the solution of problems in alternating current circuits. See how it, and the voltage phasor diagram, is used in the following worked problems.

Example (5).   A 250 V 50 Hz supply is connected to an inductive circuit. A current of 2 A lagging on the voltage by $30°$ flows in the circuit. Calculate the impedance, reactance, resistance and inductance of the circuit.
 Figure 3.4(a) shows the circuit with the voltage and impedance triangles at *(b)*. In drawing the voltage triangle, I is the reference phasor, V_R is in phase with I and V_L leads I by $90°$.

$$\text{Circuit impedance } Z = \frac{V}{I} = \frac{250}{2} = 125 \ \Omega$$

From the impedance triangle

$$\cos \phi = \frac{R}{Z} \quad \text{and} \quad \sin \phi = \frac{X}{Z}$$

for $\phi = 30°$ $\cos \phi = 0.8660$ and $\sin \phi = 0.5$

Then   resistance R $= Z \cos \phi = 125 \times 0.8660 = 108.25 \ \Omega$
         reactance X_L $= Z \sin \phi = 125 \times 0.5 \quad = 62.5 \ \Omega$

But $X_L = 2\pi f L$

$$\therefore L = \frac{X_L}{2\pi f} = \frac{62.5}{2\pi \times 50} = 0.2 \text{ H}$$

Figure 3.4

Example (6).   In a series a.c. circuit a pure inductance is placed in series with a 150 Ω resistor. If the current flowing is 0.5 A when the supply is 100 V at 800 Hz, find with the aid of a phasor diagram (a) the p.d. across the inductor, (b) the inductance of the coil, (c) the phase angle between voltage and current.
   Figure 3.5(a) shows the circuit with the voltage phasor diagram at (b). Using the voltages this time, we have $V^2 = V_R^2 + V_L^2$

Now $V = 100$ V   and $V_R = 0.5 \times 150 = 75$ V

$\therefore$ $V_L = \sqrt{(100^2 - 75^2)} = 66.14$ V

Notice that the ordinary algebraic sum of V_R and V_L does *not* come to 100 V.

(b) $X_L = \dfrac{V_L}{I} = \dfrac{66.14}{0.5} = 132.28\ \Omega$

But $X_L = 2\pi f L$ $\therefore$ $L = \dfrac{X_L}{2\pi f} = \dfrac{132.28}{2\pi \times 800} = 0.026$ H

(c) $\cos\phi = \dfrac{V_R}{V} = \dfrac{75}{100} = 0.75$

$\therefore$ $\phi = 41.4°$

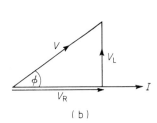

Figure 3.5

Try the next problem on your own.

(7)   A series circuit having a ratio of resistance to reactance at 100 Hz of 4 to 1 draws a current of 1.25 A when connected to a 50 V 100 Hz supply. Calculate the resistance and inductance of the circuit. Find the frequency at which this circuit would take 2 A from a 200 V supply.

Resistance and capacitance in series   As in the case of resistance and inductance in series, the current is limited by the combined effect of resistance and reactance, this being the a.c. impedance of the circuit. Again, the current is common to both circuit elements. The voltage across the resistor, V_R, is in phase with I and the voltage across the capacitor, V_c, lags the current by 90°. The phasor diagram of *Figure 3.6(a)* shows the addition of V_R and V_C to obtain the supply voltage V. From this triangle the phasor magnitudes are $V_R = IR$, $V_C = IX_C$ and $V = IZ$. Since the current is common, the impedance triangle of *Figure 3.6(b)* can be drawn.

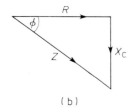

(a)

(b)

Figure 3.6

You should notice that this triangle is similar to that obtained for resistance and inductance in series except that the capacitive reactance X_C is drawn in the direction opposite to that given to X_L. Clearly for such a combination of resistance and capacitance ϕ will be negative, lying between $0°$ and $-90°$. By Pythagoras we have

$$Z = \sqrt{(R^2 + X_C^2)}$$

and so

$$I = \frac{V}{\sqrt{(R^2 + X_C^2)}}$$

also

$$\tan \phi = \frac{X_c}{R} \;,\quad \cos \phi = \frac{R}{Z} \;,\quad \sin \phi = \frac{X_c}{R}$$

Do *not* attempt to memorise these relationships or those which have gone before. Simply keep in mind the phase relationships between voltage and current for the three basic circuit elements and this, together with Ohm's Law, will enable you to work out each problem on its own merits.

Here are two more worked examples to follow through and ma!.e sure that you thoroughly understand these very basic principles.

Example (8). A resistor of 40 Ω is in series with a 15 μF capacitor across a 24 V 400 Hz supply. Calculate (a) the circuit impedance, (b) the circuit current, (c) the phase angle, (d) the voltages across C and R.

(a) We need to know reactance X_C.

$$X_C = \frac{1}{2\pi f C} = \frac{10^6}{2\pi \times 400 \times 15} = 26.53 \ \Omega$$

then

$$Z = \sqrt{(R^2 + X_C^2)} = \sqrt{(40^2 + 26.53^2)} = 48 \ \Omega$$

(b) $I = \dfrac{V}{Z} = \dfrac{24}{48} = 0.5$ A

(c) $\tan \phi = \dfrac{X_C}{R} = \dfrac{26.53}{40} = 0.6633$

$$\therefore \qquad \phi = -33.6°$$

(d) Volts across R = IR = 0.5×40 = 20 V
Volts across C = IX_C = 0.5×26.53 = 13.26 V

Notice again that the ordinary algebraic sum of V_R and V_C does not come to 24 V.

Example (9). A circuit comprising a 500 Ω resistor in series with a capacitor is supplied from an a.c. source whose frequency and output voltage may be independently adjusted. When the frequency is set to 1 kHz, the output voltage is adjusted until the p.d. across the capacitor is 7 V and the current drawn is 20 mA. Draw a scaled phasor diagram to find the output voltage of the source for this condition.

The frequency is now adjusted to 500 Hz. What output voltage will now be needed to give the same circuit current as before ?

Again the reference phasor is current I.

$$\text{Volts across } R = IR = 20 \times 10^{-3} \times 500$$

$$= 10 \text{ V}$$

$$\text{Volts across } C = IX_c = 7 \text{ V and this lags } I \text{ by } 90°$$

The applied voltage $V = IZ$

Figure 3.7 shows the circuit and the scaled phasor diagram. By measurement

$$V = 12.2 \text{ V}, \quad \phi = 35° \text{ lagging } I.$$

When the frequency is halved the capacitive reactance is *doubled*. Hence, if the circuit current is to be the same at 20 mA, the voltage across the capacitor will be *twice* what it was originally i.e. $2 \times 7 = 14$ V. The voltage across R will be unchanged at 10 V. Hence the new output voltage from the source will be

$$V = \sqrt{(V_R^2 + V_L^2)} = \sqrt{(10^2 + 14^2)} = 17.2 \text{ V}$$

Figure 3.7

(10) A circuit comprising a 1 μF capacitor in series with a 300 Ω resistor is connected to an a.c. source of 15 V. If a current of 25 mA flows in the circuit, calculate the supply frequency.

POWER IN A.C. CIRCUITS

The power developed in a d.c. circuit is given by the product of voltage and current. In an a.c. circuit the *instantaneous* power is similarly expressed by the product of the instantaneous voltage and the instantaneous current, so that

$$P = vi \quad \text{W}$$

Since instantaneous values are continually changing, this expression for power is of no practical value. What we want to know is an average value for the power dissipated in the circuit over a period of time. It might at first be thought that the product of the r.m.s. values of voltage and current will give us the result we are looking for, but this is not so. In fact, such a product will give us the power which *appears* to be dissipated in the circuit, and as we shall see, this is not the same as the true power.

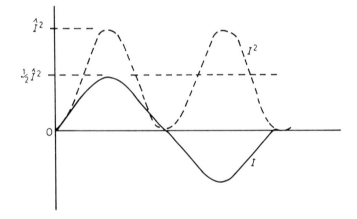

Figure 3.8

If an alternating r.m.s. voltage V volts is applied to a pure resistance R and an r.m.s. current I amperes flows, then $V = IR$. The power dissipated as heat at any instant is $\hat{I}^2 R$ watts and a curve of power plotted against time will be as illustrated in broken line in *Figure 3.8*. The curve is a sine-squared curve having a maximum amplitude $\hat{I}$ and its average value is half of this. The average power consumption in the resistance is therefore

$$P = \frac{\hat{I}^2 R}{2} \quad \text{W}$$

But $\hat{I} = \sqrt{2}\,I$ so that the power dissipated in terms of r.m.s. current is $I^2 R$ watts which is the same as the dissipation for a direct current I. This of course follows from our original definition of r.m.s. values.

When an alternating voltage is applied to a pure reactance, the power consumption is, as we have noted in our earlier work, zero. All the energy supplied during each alternate quarter-cycle of the input waveform is stored in either the magnetic or the electric field of the inductor or the capacitor respectively, and returned to the generator during the succeeding quarter-cycle. So, whenever the current and voltage are 90° out of phase, the power dissipation is zero. Power therefore is dissipated only in the resistive elements of a circuit.

We will now use this fact to find the power dissipation in a circuit where, as always in practice, resistive elements are present and the phase angle between current and voltage is some angle ϕ different from $90°$.

Power factor Let V volts be applied to a circuit of impedance Z as shown in *Figure 3.9*, along with the phasor diagram. The current flowing will be V/Z. leading or lagging on the voltage by phase angle ϕ. Let the voltage phasor be V, then, OI will be the current phasor representing V/Z amperes. This current can be resolved into two mutually perpendicular components:

$$I_R = I.\cos\phi \text{ in phase with } V$$
$$I_x = I.\sin\phi \text{ in quadrature with } V$$

To find the true power dissipation in the circuit, we replace the *real* current V/Z amperes by these separate current components. We can then sketch a *power phasor diagram*, obtained by multiplying the phasors of *Figure 3.9* by V. This is shown in *Figure 3.10*.

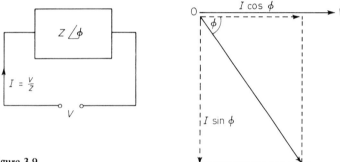

Figure 3.9

Consider first the current represented by $I.\sin\phi$. It is $90°$ out of phase with the applied voltage, hence the quantity $VI.\sin\phi$ represents power which simply supplies the magnetic or electrostatic fields of the reactive elements; it represents power which surges between the generator and the load called *reactive power* and is measured in *volt-amperes reactive*, VA$_r$.

The other current component represented by $I.\cos\phi$ is in phase with the applied voltage, hence the power dissipated is expressed by their product. Hence in the power triangle of *Figure 3.10* the quantity $VI.\cos\phi$ represents the actual power consumed in the circuit. This is called the *true power* and is measured in watts.

So the power dissipated in an a.c. circuit depends not only upon the values of the current and the voltage but also upon the phase angle between them. Only if $\cos\phi = 1$ (which means that $\phi = 0°$ and so current and voltage will be in phase) is the true power actually given by the product VI.

The VI product, which is measured in volt-amperes, is the *apparent power*; it is the result we would get if we simply measured the r.m.s. current and the r.m.s. voltage relating to a particular circuit and multiplied them together to get a power quantity. But the phase angle has been ignored in such a measurement, hence the VI product and the

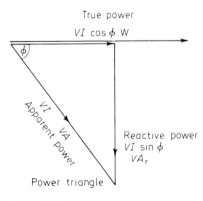

Figure 3.10

true power product $VI.\cos\phi$, will not be the same unless $\phi = 0°$. Most electrical machines have their power ratings expressed in volt-amperes.

The quantity $\cos\phi$ is called the *power factor* of the circuit. Power factor lies, therefore between zero and unity.

The ratio $\dfrac{\text{true power}}{\text{apparent power}} = \dfrac{VI.\cos\phi}{VI} = \cos\phi$

Hence   true power = apparent power × power factor

If the impedance of the circuit is Z, then

$$\cos\phi = \frac{R}{Z} = \frac{R}{\sqrt{(R^2 + X^2)}} = \frac{\text{resistance}}{\text{impedance}}$$

These statements are true only for sinusoidal waveforms. If the waveform is not sinusoidal, the power may still be expressed as $VI.\cos\phi$ but ϕ is not in general the angle of phase difference between current and voltage.

(11) Show that true power can be expressed in the alternative forms

$$I^2 Z \cos\phi \quad \text{and} \quad (V^2/Z) \cos\phi$$

Follow the next example carefully. It illustrates two methods of calculating circuit power.

Example (12).   A coil, when connected to a 10 V d.c. supply, takes a current of 0.5 A but when connected to a 50 V a.c. supply takes a current of 2 A. Calculate the resistance and reactance of the coil and the power absorbed by the circuit under both the d.c. and the a.c. conditions.

Consider first the d.c. condition. To the d.c. supply the coil simply presents a resistance, so

$$R = \frac{V}{I} = \frac{10}{0.5} = 20\ \Omega$$

Since a current of 0.5 A flows in this resistance

$$P = I^2 R = 0.5^2 \times 20 = 5\ \text{W}$$

Now under a.c. conditions the coil presents an impedance Z where

$$Z = \frac{V}{I} = \frac{50}{2} = 25\ \Omega$$

But $Z^2 = R^2 + X_L^2$

∴ $X_L = \sqrt{(Z^2 - R^2)} = \sqrt{(25^2 - 20^2)} = 15\ \Omega$

Now since the current in the circuit is 2 A and the power dissipates only in the resistive part of the circuit

$$P = I^2 R = 4 \times 20 = 80 \text{ W}$$

Alternatively

$$P = VI \cos \phi \text{ where } \cos \phi = \frac{R}{Z}$$

$$= VI \frac{R}{Z} = 50 \times 2 \times \frac{20}{25}$$

$$= 80 \text{ W, as before.}$$

The next example illustrates an important principle.

Example (13). A 240 V induction motor delivers an output power equivalent to 200 W at 80% efficiency. If the power factor is 0.85, what current is taken from the supply? If the motor operated at unity power factor, what would be the reduction in current for the same output?

$$\text{Output power } = 2000 \text{ W}$$

$$\text{Input power } = \frac{2000}{0.8} = 2500 \text{ W}$$

$$\text{Power } = VI \cos \phi \quad \therefore \quad I = \frac{P}{V \cos \phi} = \frac{2500}{240 \times 0.85}$$

$$= 12.25 \text{ A}$$

If $\cos \phi = 1$, the current I would be $\dfrac{2500}{240} = 10.4 \text{ A}$

This example shows us that at unity power factor there is a reduction in the current taken by the motor for the same power output. When machines operate at low values of power factor, they draw more current than is necessary. This means that:

(a) the source of supply has to turn out heavy currents without a corresponding useful power being developed in the load equipment;
(b) the power losses in the supply cables are higher than they need be;
(c) the efficiency of the load equipment is reduced because the losses due to the resistance of the conductors in the load are higher than they need be.

The power factor of a machine is a design feature, and since most machines consist largely of coils wound on iron pole pieces and armatures they are inevitably highly inductive. Hence the phase angle is large so cos ϕ is small and lagging. In the next Unit Section we shall discuss ways of "improving" the power factor of inductive machines by bringing it close to unity and so reduce the necessary supply current. You might like to reason out how this might be done.

Items (a) and (b) in the list above are reduced when the power factors of the various machines connected to the source of supply are all close to unity. It is a matter of economics that the consumption of electricity by a plant should be reduced as much as possible, and this can be done by the owner of the plant improving the power factors of his equipment.

(14) A power line supplies 25 A to a welding transformer. If the line voltage is 240 V and the power factor of the transformer is 0.85, what is the true power consumption?

(15) A coil has an inductance of 40 mH and a resistance of 12 Ω. It is connected to a 200 V 50 Hz supply. Calculate (a) the impedance, (b) the circuit current, (c) the mean power, (d) the power factor.

(16) You are given a capacitor and a resistance which you connect in series across an a.c. supply of known frequency. Draw a circuit showing how you would measure the circuit power factor if you are provided with two a.c. voltmeters and one a.c. ammeter.

L, C AND *R* IN SERIES

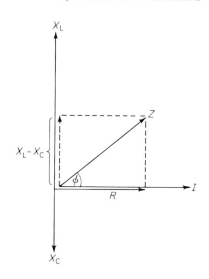

Figure 3.11

As for the series circuits so far discussed, when a circuit is made up of resistive, inductive and capacitive elements all wired in series, the total applied voltage is the phasor sum of the voltages developed across the individual elements. We can perform this addition in the usual way using phasor diagrams and some elementary trigonometry. Also the circuit impedance will be the phasor sum of the separate impedances and since the current flowing is common to all parts of the circuit, the applied voltage is equal to the product of this current and the phasor sum of all the impedances.

Now that we have all three basic elements in the circuit, the phase angle may be positive or negative according to whether the supply voltage leads or lags on the current, and this in turn is dependent upon which reactive element is dominant at the particular frequency concerned. Referring to *Figure 3.11*, we have

$$Z = \sqrt{[R^2 + (X_L - X_C)^2]}$$

and $\tan \phi = \dfrac{X_L - X_C}{R}$

The direct subtraction of one reactance from the other may not at first look like our customary procedure for dealing with phasors, but as the diagram shows, X_L and X_C are in direct opposition to each other and their phasor resultant is clearly the algebraic difference between them.

In the diagram, we have assumed that X_L is greater than X_C but this situation could, of course, be reversed. In the expression for the circuit impedance Z, therefore, our reactive term is represented by this difference. Since the term is squared, it is not important which reactance is subtracted from which. In the expression for tan ϕ, however, the sign of the subtraction is important if we are to avoid confusion over whether ϕ is leading or lagging; if X_L is greater than X_C ϕ will be positive and V will lead I, if X_C is greater than X_L ϕ will be negative and V will lag I.

Usually it is a matter of commonsense to decide which way the angle is acting: if the inductive reactance predominates, clearly I will lag V, and if the capacitive reactance predominates, I will lead V. A particular case occurs when $X_L = X_C$. Here the reactive component disappears completely and the circuit phase angle becomes zero. We will investigate this situation very shortly.

Example (17). A coil of resistance 20 Ω and inductance 0.01 H is connected in series with a capacitance of 4 μF across a 100 V 1000 Hz supply. Calculate (a) the circuit impedance, (b) the circuit current, (c) the phase angle, (d) the power factor.

We calculate first of all the circuit reactances:

For the inductor: $X_L = 2\pi fL$ $= 2\pi \times 1000 \times 0.01$

$$= 62.8 \ \Omega$$

For the capacitor: $X_C = \dfrac{1}{2\pi fC} = \dfrac{10^6}{2\pi \times 1000 \times 4}$

$$= 39.8 \ \Omega$$

Obviously the inductive reactance predominates, so we can expect the circuit current to lag on the voltage, that is, ϕ will be positive. However, we now find the circuit impedance:

(a) $Z = \sqrt{[R^2 + (X_L - X_C)^2]} = \sqrt{[20^2 + (62.8 - 39.8)^2]}$

$$= \sqrt{[400 + 529]}$$

$$= 30.5 \ \Omega$$

(b) Circuit current $I = \dfrac{V}{Z}$

$$= \dfrac{100}{30.5} = 3.28 \ A$$

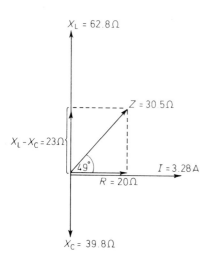

Figure 3.12

(c)   Phase angle: $\tan \phi = \dfrac{X_L - X_C}{R} = \dfrac{62.8 - 39.8}{20}$

$$= \dfrac{23}{20} = 1.15$$

$$\therefore \qquad \phi = 49° \text{ leading}$$

(d)   Power factor $= \cos \phi = \cos 49°$

$$= 0.656$$

This result is illustrated in the phasor diagram of *Figure 3.12*. The diagram is once again an impedance diagram, the applied voltage V being the product of the current I and the total circuit impedance Z.

SERIES RESONANCE

In the *LCR* circuit just discussed, the phase angle between current and voltage depended upon the relative magnitudes of the inductive and capacitive reactances at a particular frequency. The voltage across R is IR volts in phase with the reference current. The voltage across L is IX_L volts leading the current by 90°, and the voltage across C is IX_C lagging by 90°.

The total voltage applied to the circuit V is the phasor sum of these three separate voltages and is represented by a resultant which may lead on, lag on or be in phase with the current, depending respectively upon whether IX_L is greater than, less than or equal to IX_C.

The three possible cases are illustrated in *Figure 3.13*. At (a) the frequency ω is considered to be small, hence $X_L = \omega L$ is small but $X_C = 1/\omega C$ is large. Hence $(X_C - X_L)$ is large capacitively and phase angle ϕ

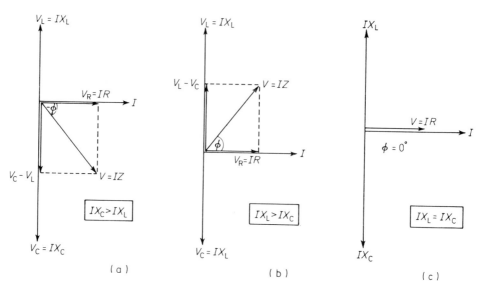

Figure 3.13

is large and negative. At (*b*) ω is considered to be very large, hence ωL is large but $1/\omega C$ is small, Hence $(X_L - X_C)$ is large inductively and phase angle ϕ is large and positive. At (*c*) we consider ω to be such that $\omega L = 1/\omega C$, hence $(X_C - X_L)$ is zero and ϕ is zero. In this circumstance, the voltages developed across the reactances are equal in magnitude and opposite in sign and so cancel out. So the circuit current and voltage are now in phase and so the system behaves as a pure resistance.

When the circuit becomes purely resistive, it is said to be in a state of *resonance*. The frequency at which resonance occurs is called the resonant frequency. The phenomenon of resonance occurs in circuits containing opposite kinds of reactance because both inductive and capacitive elements can store energy during one quarter-cycle of the applied alternative voltage and return it to the generator during the following quarter-cycle. Since the inductance is storing energy when the capacitor is returning energy, and vice-versa, it is possible for the elements to transfer energy from one to the other successively.

The effect can be compared to familiar mechanical systems such as a swinging pendulum, a bouncing ball or a vibrating string. All these systems have a common property: energy of position or state, known as potential energy, and energy of motion, known as kinetic energy. The pendulum has potential energy at the extremes of its oscillations, but no kinetic energy, the motion being instantaneously halted. As the pendulum descends, the potential energy is converted to kinetic energy, the conversion being complete as the pendulum passes its lowest point, for there the velocity is momentarily greatest. Some energy is lost because of air resistance and friction and as a result the pendulum eventually comes to rest. The energy loss in electrical circuits takes place in the resistance of the components and the connecting wires.

Let the frequency of resonance of a series circuit be f_0. Then, since at this frequency $\omega L = 1/\omega C$ we have

$$\omega^2 = \frac{1}{LC} \quad \text{and} \quad \omega = \frac{1}{\sqrt{LC}}$$

but $\quad \omega = 2\pi f_0$

$$\therefore \quad f_0 = \frac{1}{2\pi\sqrt{LC}}$$

We could define resonance as that frequency at which the circuit impedance is a minimum, for since

$$Z = \sqrt{[R^2 + (X_L - X_C)^2]}$$

$$Z = \sqrt{R^2} = R \quad \text{when } X_L = X_C$$

and this must be the smallest possible value for Z.

It is, however, strictly correct to say that resonance occurs when the voltage and current are in phase.

Since $Z = R$ at resonance, the current I_0 at resonance must be at its greatest value:

$$I_0 = \frac{V}{R}$$

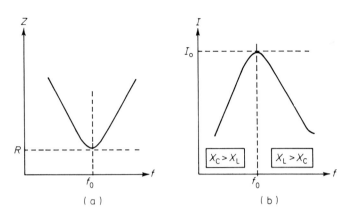

Figure 3.14

Figures 3.14 (a) and (b) show respectively the variation of impedance Z and current I as the frequency is increased through resonance for a series circuit. The circuit is known as an 'acceptor' circuit because it presents the lowest impedance to the flow of current when it is resonant.

Example (18).   A coil of resistance 10 Ω and inductance 100 mH is wired in series with a capacitor of 2 μF to a 50 V, variable frequency supply. Calculate the resonant frequency. What are the voltages across (a) the capacitor, and (b) the coil, at resonance?

$$f_o = \frac{1}{2\pi\sqrt{(LC)}} = \frac{1}{2\pi\sqrt{(0.01 \times 2 \times 10^{-6})}}$$

$$= \frac{10^4}{2\pi\sqrt{2}} = \frac{10^4}{8.886} = 1125 \text{ Hz}$$

At resonance $I_o = \dfrac{V}{R} = \dfrac{50}{10} = 5 \text{ A}$

(a)   Voltage across C:

$$V_C = IX_C = 5 \times \frac{1}{2\pi fC} = 5 \times \frac{10^6}{2\pi \times 1125 \times 2}$$

$$= \frac{5 \times 10^6}{14137} = 354 \text{ V}$$

(b)   Voltage across L:

$$V_L = IZ_L = I\sqrt{(R^2 + X_L^2)}$$

Notice that we have used the coil impedance Z_L, not the coil reactance X_L here. Remember that the resistance is an integral part of the coil, and cannot be separated out from the inductance.

Then $X_L = 2\pi f L = 2\pi \times 1125 \times 0.01$

$$= 70.7\ \Omega$$

and $Z_L = \sqrt{(10^2 + 70.7^2)} = 71.4\ \Omega$

Hence $V_L = 5 \times 71.4 = 357$ V.

which for all practical purposes is the same as the voltage across C

What this example shows us is that the voltages developed across the reactive elements at resonance may be much *greater* than the supply voltage.

CIRCUIT MAGNIFICATION   At resonance the circuit current $I_0 = V/R$ and the voltage across the inductor and capacitor is $I_0\omega L$ and $I_0/\omega C$ respectively. Since $\omega L = 1/\omega C$, these voltages are equal. So

$$V_L = \omega L . \frac{V}{R} \qquad \text{and} \quad V_C = \frac{1}{\omega C}\ \frac{V}{R}$$

and then $\dfrac{V_L}{V} = \dfrac{\omega L}{R}$ and $\dfrac{V_C}{V} = \dfrac{1}{\omega CR}$

These ratios of the voltages across the reactances to the applied voltage are known as the *circuit magnification* or *Q-factor*. We notice from the forms of the ratios that the smaller the circuit resistance R, the greater the Q-factor.

Q-factor may also be defined as

$$\frac{\text{reactance of one kind}}{\text{total circuit resistance}}$$

Hence $Q = \dfrac{\omega L}{R} = \dfrac{1}{\omega CR}$

---

(19)   By noting that at resonance, $\omega = 1/\sqrt{(LC)}$ show that Q may be expressed as

$$\frac{1}{R}\sqrt{\frac{L}{C}}$$

What factors would you take into consideration if you wanted to design a circuit having a very high Q-factor?

A coil of inductance L henrys and resistance R ohms, having no association with a resonant circuit would appear to have a Q-factor which could take any value, depending upon ω. This is true if the coil is to be used over a wide range of frequencies, but in practice an inductance is designed only for a particular frequency range. As ω increases Q will increase provided R remains constant; but resistance depends upon the cross-sectional area of the conductor through which the current flows and at high frequencies (those in excess of some 50 kHz) the current tends to flow in the area nearer the surface of the conductor. This is known as the *skin effect*, and it results in an effective reduction in the cross-sectional area. The relationship between resistance and frequency is not a simple one, but by the use of stranded wire and special methods of winding, the ratio $\omega L/R$ can be made to remain reasonably constant over the frequency range for which the coil is designed.

For inductances using laminated iron cores, such as low-frequency transformers, the Q-factor is quite low, generally of the order of 5 to 20. Coils employed at high radio-frequencies have Q-factors of the order of 100 to 300, the higher values being brought about by the use of ferrite cores. Capacitors, unlike inductors, have very low effective series resistance and so on the whole exhibit much higher Q values than the average coil. In practice, therefore, where both L and C are used in resonant circuits, it is usual to treat the bulk of the circuit resistance as residing in the coil and the total effective Q-factor of the complete circuit approximates to that for the coil alone.

The advantage of high Q's in radio-frequency circuits is that such circuits then exhibit a sharp resonance curve (of I plotted against f) and are capable of discriminating between input signals which have frequencies relatively close together. Such circuits are said to be highly selective; see *Figure 3.15(a)*. Low Q circuits on the other hand have a flat resonance and are not selective in this way, see diagram (b).

We will expand on this aspect of frequency discrimination at the end of the next chapter.

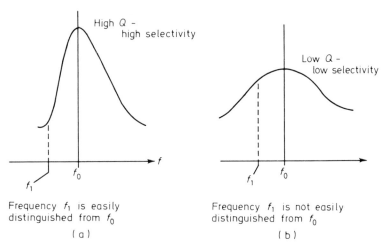

Frequency f_1 is easily distinguished from f_0

(a)

Frequency f_1 is not easily distinguished from f_0

(b)

Figure 3.15

At power frequencies of 50 Hz or so, a high Q circuit is very undesirable. Suppose a capacitor marked as being of 500 V working was used in a series circuit on 240 V mains supplies. This might appear to be adequately rated since the peak voltage of the supply will be 340 V. But at resonance, with a Q factor as low as 5, the voltage across the capacitor will reach some 1200 V and this will most probably lead to dielectric breakdown.

Example (20). For the frequency range, $\omega = 0$ to $\omega = 500$ rad/s, draw on the same pair of axes the reactance-frequency curves for (a) an inductance of 1 H, (b) a capacitance of 4 μF.

From your diagram find the frequency of resonance of a circuit made up of an inductance of 1 H in series with a capacitance of 4 μF.

Inductive reactance is given by $X_L = 2\pi fL = \omega L$. Hence X_L is directly proportional to ω and so the reactance-frequency curve will be a straight line passing through the origin. We require only two points to establish this line, the origin being one of them. For the other, take $\omega = 500$ rad/s, and then $X_L = 500 \times 1 = 500 \ \Omega$. The straight line is shown in the diagram of *Figure 3.16*.

Capacitive reactance is given by $X_C = 1/\omega C$, hence X_C is inversely proportional to ω and the curve this time will be a rectangular hyperbola. We require several points to obtain its shape reasonably accurately. Taking a range of values for ω we can draw up the following table:

ω	200	400	600	800	rad/s
X_C	1250	625	416	312	Ω

The curve is plotted on the axis of negative ohms as we conventionally take capacitive reactance as being negative.

Resonance occurs when the inductive and capacitive reactances are equal in magnitude and opposite in sign. From a study of the diagram this occurs at a frequency of 500 rad/s, or $500/2\pi = 80$ Hz, where on the perpendicular line ABC, AB = BC.

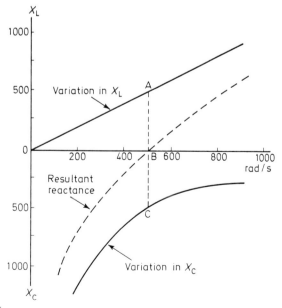

Figure 3.16

PROBLEMS FOR SECTION 3

(21) Complete the following statements:
(a)   The formula for X_L = ...
(b)   The combined effect of resistance and reactance is known as the circuit . . . .
(c)   The formula for X_C = ...
(d)   The current taken by a pure capacitor . . . . the voltage by an angle of . . . .
(e)   Inductive reactance is . . . . to frequency.

(22) An alternating voltage of 100 V and frequency 50 Hz is connected first to a resistance of 50 Ω and then to a pure inductance of 1 H. Calculate the current flowing in each case. The two components are then connected in series across the same supply. What is the current now flowing?

(23) A 1 H inductor having a resistance of 50 Ω is connected in series with a 250 Ω resistor across a 20 V 50 Hz supply. Draw a scaled phasor diagram representing the circuit and use it to find the p.d. across the 250 Ω resistor.

(24) A coil has an inductance of 50 mH and a resistance of 10 Ω. It is connected to a 200 V 50 Hz supply. Calculate: (a) the impedance, (b) the current flowing, (c) the phase angle, (d) the mean power.

(25) A 200 μF capacitor and a resistor of 8 Ω are in series across a 100 V 50 Hz supply. Calculate: (a) the circuit impedance (b) the current flowing, (c) the phase angle.

(26) A 6 μF capacitor is in series with a resistor across a 200 V 50 Hz supply. What must be the value of the resistor if the current is to be limited to 0.5 A?

(27) Define power factor and state why it is so called. Discuss the difference between watts and volt-amperes. A coil of inductance 3 H and resistance 500 Ω is connected to a 50 Hz supply. What is the power factor of the coil at this frequency?

(28) A current of 2 A flows in a series circuit made up of a coil and a capacitor. The voltage across the coil is measured at 225 V and across the capacitor at 60 V. Calculate: (a) the inductance and resistance of the coil, (b) the capacitance, (c) the circuit power factor.

(29) A circuit absorbing 900 W of power is fed from a 200 V supply. If the current drawn is 5.5 A, find the circuit phase angle and power factor.

(30) What is the resonant frequency of a circuit made up of 8 μF in series with a 100 mH inductor.

(31) A capacitor of 4 μF is in series with a resistor of 300 Ω across an a.c. supply. What other factor must be known before the circuit impedance can be found?

This circuit is connected to a 240 V 50 Hz supply. Use phasors to find the circuit current and its phase angle. A 2.5 H coil of resistance 100 Ω is now added in series with the circuit. Find the magnitude and phase angle of the impedance across the supply.

(32) Complete the following statements:
(a)   A resonant circuit has . . . . power factor

(b) A leading power factor indicates a (an) . . . . . circuit.

(c) The object of power factor correction is to bring the circuit phase angle close to . . . .

(d) True power is measured in . . . .

(33) A capacitor is connected in series with a 0.5 H inductor of 20 Ω resistance. When this circuit is connected to a 10 V supply of adjustable frequency, the current is found to reach a maximum at 100 Hz. Claculate for this condition (a) the capacitance, (b) the voltage across the *terminals* of the inductor, (c) the power taken from the supply.

(34) A coil takes 4 A when connected to *either* a 60 V d.c. supply or a 200 V 100 Hz supply. What value of capacitance is required in series with the coil to make the circuit power factor unity?

(35) A circuit comprising a series arrangement of *L* and *C* resonates at a frequency f_o. When *L* is increased by 100 μH, the frequency decreases to $0.5f_o$. What is the value of *L*?

(36) An a.c. supply of 10 V is connected to a series circuit of 100 Ω and 0.16 μF. At what frequency will the phase angle between voltage and current be 45°? If an inductor of 100 mH is now connected in series with the circuit, what will be the frequency at which the phase shift is zero?

(37) Two circuits, A and B, were separately connected to a 200 V 100 Hz supply. Each drew a current of 5 A and consumed a power of 500 W. When connected in turn to a 200 V d.c. supply circuit A drew a current in excess of 5 A but circuit B did not pass any current at all. Explain these effects and calculate the component values used in each circuit.

(38) A test was made on a coil and the following figures were obtained:

Applied voltage = 50 V   Frequency   = 50 Hz
Circuit current = 1.5 A   Power (true) = 10 W

Calculate the reactance and effective resistance of the coil. Explain why the current in this circuit would remain substantially the same if both the applied voltage and the frequency were doubled.

(39) Two single loads A and B are connected across a 240 V 50 Hz supply. Load A takes 500 W at 0.8 power factor leading, load B takes 10 A at 0.6 power factor lagging. Sketch power triangles and from them determine the overall watts, volt-amperes and volt-amperes reactive.

(40) The *Q*-factor of a coil having an inductance of 1 mH is measured at a frequency of 1 kHz and found to be 75. What is the effective resistance of the coil?

(41) An inductor has a *Q*-factor of 45 at a frequency of 600 kHz. What will be its *Q* at 1000 kHz assuming that its resistance is 50% greater at 1000 kHz than it is at 600 kHz?

(42) Power is supplied to a workshop at 440 V and the power lines feeding the workshop have a resistance of 0.2 Ω. If the workshop load is 25 kW at a power factor of 0.7, what power is wasted as heat in the power lines? By how much would this power loss decrease if the load was corrected to have unity power factor?

4 Alternating current: parallel circuits

Aims: At the end of this Unit section you should be able to:
Solve problems involving voltage, current, impedance and phase angle in parallel combinations of resistance, inductance and capacitance.
Draw phasor diagrams for two-branch parallel circuits and use them to determine impedance and phase angle.
State the conditions for parallel resonance and solve problems involving parallel resonance.
Define Q-factor and power factor.
Understand the use of capacitors to improve power factor of single-phase loads.

By this stage we should be thoroughly familiar with the phase relationships between voltage and current for the three basic circuit elements of resistance, inductance and capacitance, and there should be no difficulty in applying them to parallel combinations of these elements.

When resistance, inductance and capacitance are connected in various parallel combinations, problems arising are solved in general in a manner similar to the methods used for parallel resistor circuits but bearing in mind that the branch currents are no longer necessarily in phase. Whereas in series circuits, the total circuit impedance is the *phasor* sum of the individual impedances, in parallel circuits the total circuit impedance is given by the *phasor* reciprocal sum

$$\frac{1}{Z} = \frac{1}{Z_1} + \frac{1}{Z_2} + \ldots\ldots$$

Z_1, Z_2 etc. being the individual branch impedances which of course, must take into account the various phase relationships. *Figure 4.1* shows the general circuit details. There is one other basic difference between series and parallel circuit considerations and that lies in the choice of a reference phasor. In series circuits where, as we have seen, the current is common to all parts of the circuit, we have taken the current as our reference phasor. In parallel circuits the applied voltage V is common to all branches of the circuit; as a consequence we now choose V as our reference phasor and relate the various branch currents I_1, I_2 etc to it in their respective magnitudes and phases. Further, the total circuit current I is the *phasor* sum of the individual branch currents, so that

$$I = I_1 + I_2 + \ldots\ldots$$

These branch currents are, or course, given by the ratio of the applied voltage V (common to all branches) and the branch impedances Z_1, Z_2 etc. Hence

$$I = \frac{V}{Z} = \frac{V}{Z_1} + \frac{V}{Z_2} + \ldots\ldots$$

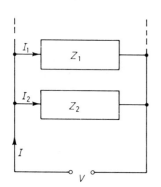

Figure 4.1

from which, by elimination of the common factor V, we arrive at the impedance formula given earlier above.

To sum up: when drawing phasor diagrams for parallel circuits, we draw the applied voltage phasor as reference and set off from it the phasors for the various branch currents, scaled (if necessary) to their proper magnitudes and positioned to their proper phase angles relative to V, lagging or leading as the case may be. In an inductive circuit a lagging current will then appear in the fourth quadrant, i.e. ϕ will be negative. For a capacitive circuit a leading current will appear in the first quadrant so that ϕ will be positive.

The most simple parallel combinations are those of resistance in parallel with either a pure inductance or capacitance, and we shall begin our study with these elementary examples.

RESISTANCE AND INDUCTANCE

Figure 4.2(a) shows the circuit diagram with the branch impedances and currents indicated. The inductance branch is, of course, purely reactive in this instance. From the diagram, the current I_R in R is in

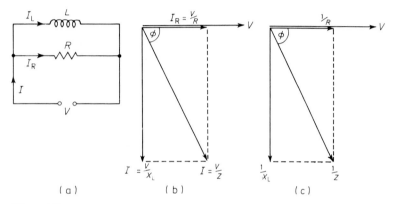

(a)　　　(b)　　　(c)

Figure 4.2

phase with V, and the current I_L in L lags V by $90°$. The phasor diagram is then drawn as shown in *Figure 4.2(b)*; since V is a common factor here, an impedance diagram can be deduced and is shown at (c). From diagram (b) the circuit current

$$I = \sqrt{(I_R^2 + I_L^2)}$$

and the phase angle between the supply current and voltage is

$$\phi = \tan^{-1} \frac{I_L}{I_R}$$

And from diagram (c)

$$\left[\frac{1}{Z}\right]^2 = \left[\frac{1}{R}\right]^2 + \left[\frac{1}{X_L}\right]^2$$

so that

$$\frac{1}{Z} = \sqrt{\left(\frac{1}{R^2} + \frac{1}{X_L^2}\right)}$$

and phase angle

$$\phi = \tan^{-1} \frac{R}{X_L}$$

These are the basic relationships in terms of current and impedance of the parallel arrangement of resistance and inductance. As always, make no attempt to 'memorise' these relationships; draw the phasor diagram and apply Pythagoras and basic trigonometry. The next worked example will illustrate the method to adopt.

Figure 4.3

Example (1).   A coil of inductance 0.5 H is connected in parallel with a 200 Ω resistor across a 50 V 800 Hz supply. Determine (a) the current in each parallel branch, (b) the current drawn from the supply, (c) the phase angle between supply voltage and current.

Figure 4.3(a) illustrates the problem.
(a)   Voltage across both R and L is the applied voltage $V = $ 50 V.

$$\text{Reactance of } L = 2\pi f L = 2\pi \times 800 \times 0.5$$
$$= 2513 \ \Omega$$

$\therefore$ current $I_L = \dfrac{V}{X_L} = \dfrac{50}{2513}$ A $= 0.02$ A (very nearly)

and the phase angle between I_L and V is 90° lagging.

$$\text{Current } I_R = \dfrac{V}{R} = \dfrac{50}{2000} \text{ A} = 0.025 \text{ A}$$

and I_R and V are in phase.

(b)   From the phasor diagram in *Figure 4.3(b)*, the supply current

$$I = \sqrt{(0.025^2 + 0.02^2)} = 0.032 \text{ A}$$

(c)   The phase angle between V and I, using the phasor diagram, is

$$\phi = -\tan^{-1} \dfrac{0.02}{0.025} = -\tan^{-1} 0.8$$

$$= -38.6°$$

Now complete the following problems by yourself.

(2)   An inductive reactance of 32 Ω is connected in parallel with a resistance of value 24 Ω to a 240 V a.c. supply. Find (a) the supply current, (b) the phase angle between the supply current and voltage, (c) the circuit impedance.

(3)   The supply current from a 100 V 500 Hz source to a circuit comprising a 500 Ω resistor in parallel with a pure inductance is found to be 0.25 A. Calculate (a) the current in the inductance, (b) the reactance of the inductance, (c) the value of the inductance in millihenrys.

RESISTANCE AND CAPACITANCE

This parallel arrangement is treated in exactly the same way as the previous case. *Figure 4.4(a)* shows the circuit diagram, with the phasor diagram and impedance triangle respectively drawn at (b) and (c).

Current I_R is in phase with supply voltage V, current I_c leads V by $90°$. As before

$$I = \sqrt{(I_R^2 + I_C^2)}$$

and
$$\phi = \tan^{-1} \frac{I_C}{I_R} = \tan^{-1} \frac{R}{X}$$

You should have no difficulty in following the next example.

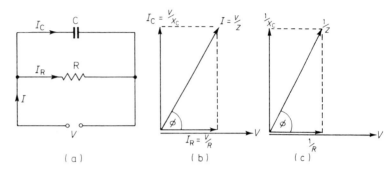

(a) (b) (c)

Figure 4.4

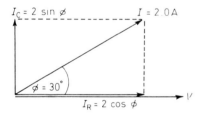

Figure 4.5

Example (4). When a 100 V a.c. supply is connected to a circuit made up of a resistor in parallel with a pure capacitor, the circuit current is 2 A at a phase angle of $30°$ leading the applied voltage. Draw the phasor diagram and calculate (a) the value of the resistance and the capacitive reactance, (b) the circuit impedance.

(a) The phasor diagram is drawn as shown in *Figure 4.5*, knowing that the resultant I (= 2A) leads the voltage V by $30°$. Completing the rectangle to provide the components of I as right-angled phasors now gives us the relative magnitudes of I_R and I_C:

$$I_R = 2 \cos \phi = 2 \cos 30° = 1.732 \text{ A}$$
$$I_C = 2 \sin \phi = 2 \sin 30° = 1.0 \text{ A}$$

From this $R = \dfrac{V}{I_R} = \dfrac{100}{1.732} = 57.7 \ \Omega$

$$X_C = \frac{V}{I_C} = \frac{100}{1} = 100 \ \Omega$$

(b) The circuit impedance is easily calculated:

$$Z = \frac{\text{applied voltage}}{\text{circuit current}} = \frac{100}{2} = 50 \ \Omega$$

(5)   A 1 µF capacitor is connected in parallel with a 1500 Ω resistor to a 40 V 50 Hz supply. Find the supply current and its phase angle relative to the supply voltage.

(6)   A 60 Ω resistor and a 50 µF capacitor are connected in parallel across a 50 Hz. a.c. supply. The current through the resistor is 1.5 A. Calculate the current through the capacitor and the total circuit current.

You should now be ready to tackle parallel circuits where reactance is combined with reactance.

INDUCTANCE AND CAPACITANCE

Although a pure inductance (or a pure capacitance, for that matter) does not exist in practical form, we shall consider the case of a pure inductance L connected in parallel with a capacitor C as an introduction to the real-life circuit where the inductance does possess the bulk of the resistance.

Figure 4.6(a) shows the circuit, with the phasor diagram drawn at (b). Reference phasor V is, as before, drawn horizontally; the current in the inductance, I_L, then lags on this voltage by 90° while the current in the capacitor, I_C, leads the voltage by 90°. Nothing out of the ordinary so far. Since there is no resistance in the circuit, the phasors representing I_L and I_C are in phase opposition, and the resultant current is the difference between I_L and I_C.

As the frequency is gradually increased from zero, I_L will decrease from infinity and I_C will increase from zero. So, depending upon the magnitudes of I_L and I_C the resultant current may lead the voltage, lag the voltage or be zero. In this last condition we are clearly at some frequency where I_L and I_C are equal in magnitude, hence at this frequency the circuit will present zero reactance to the source of supply and become purely resistive. But by supposition the circuit is free from resistance; therefore, under the condition considered, $I_L = I_C$ and the circuit draws *zero current*. Hence we conclude that its *impedance must be infinite*. This is the condition of parallel resonance.

We can calculate the frequency of resonance by considering the circuit impedance. This will be the applied voltage divided by the net circuit current. So

$$Z = \frac{V}{I_L - I_C}$$

where $I = \dfrac{V}{\omega L}$ and $I_C = V \omega C$

(a)

(b)

Figure 4.6

Hence $Z = \dfrac{V}{V/\omega L - V \omega C} = \dfrac{\omega L}{\omega^2 LC - 1}$

But for this to be infinite, the denominator must be zero, therefore

$$\omega^2 LC = 1$$

$$\therefore \qquad \omega^2 = \frac{1}{LC} \quad \text{or} \quad f_o = \frac{1}{2\pi\sqrt{(LC)}}$$

using the symbol f_o for the resonant frequency.

This expression for the parallel resonant frequency is seen to be the same as the one previously calculated for series resonance, but in this case the impedance at resonance is infinite, unlike the series case where, at resonance, the circuit impedance reduces to that of the circuit resistance, and this is normally very small. Also, although the current drawn from the supply is (theoretically) zero, the currents flowing in the inductive and capacitive branches may be very large.

These currents, confined to the parallel loop of the circuit are known as *circulating currents*. Electric charges flow backwards and forwards round the loop and there is a constant interchange of energy between the magnetic field of the inductance and the electric field of the capacitance.

If, as we have assumed, the circuit is free of resistance, there is no dissipation of energy and the oscillatory interchange in the closed loop proceeds indefinitely. This situation must, of course, be theoretical; in practice, some resistance is always present so the circulating currents cannot be maintained without some energy being drawn from the supply.

This practical case will now have to be considered. But try the following problem before going on.

(7)   A 0.02 μF capacitor is in parallel with a pure inductance of 0.25 H. What is the resonant frequency of the circuit? What will be the circuit impedance (a) 500 Hz below resonance, (b) 500 Hz above resonance?

TRUE PARALLEL RESONANCE

In the circuit of *Figure 4.7* let an inductance L henrys having a *resistance R* Ω be connected in parallel with a capacitor C farads. The resistance will now modify the arguments we used in the previous section where it was assumed that the circuit branches were pure reactances.

The current through C leads the applied voltage by 90° and is represented in *Figure 4.8(a)* by the phasor I_C. The current I_L through the inductive branch lags on the applied voltage by an angle χ, say, but χ is not 90° as it would be if there was no resistance in the inductive branch, but $\chi = \tan^{-1} X_L/R$, since we treat this branch as a series combination of L and R. V_R is in phase with I_L and the phasor diagram of this part of the circuit is shown in diagram (*b*).

There is a common phasor V to both diagrams (*a*) and (*b*), so we can combine them as at (*c*) to provide a diagram of the complete circuit. The supply current I is then the phasor sum of I_C and I_L and this makes a phase angle ϕ with the applied voltage.

The relative magnitudes of I_C and I_L will change with frequency, hence ϕ will, with one exception, either lead or lag on the applied voltage. The one exception is when ϕ is zero and I and V are in phase. Analogous to the series circuit, this will be the condition of parallel resonance, this time with the resistance of the inductor taken into account. The diagrams of *Figures 4.9(a)*, (*b*) and (*c*) respectively are for frequencies below resonance, above resonance and at resonance. In this last situation it is seen that the *reactive component* of the inductor current, shown in broken line, is equal to the capacitor current, leaving only the real component of the inductor current as the total current

Figure 4.7

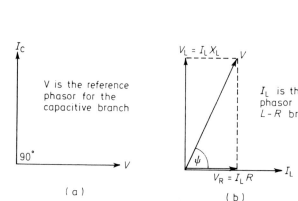

Figure 4.8

which is in phase with the applied voltage. The diagrams are not to scale; at resonance the I phasor is very small since χ approximates closely to $90°$.

From the diagram at (c), we have then

$$I_C = I_L \sin \chi$$

$$\frac{V}{X_C} = \frac{V}{\sqrt{(R^2 + X_L^2)}} \cdot \frac{X_L}{\sqrt{(R^2 + X_L^2)}}$$

$$\therefore \quad X_C X_L = R^2 + X_L^2$$

Let the resonant frequency be f_o, then

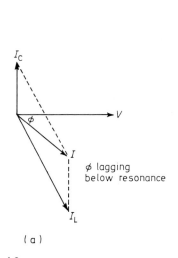

Figure 4.9

$$\frac{2\pi f_o L}{2\pi f_o C} = R^2 + (2\pi f_o L)^2$$

$$\therefore \qquad \frac{L}{C} = R^2 + (2\pi f_o)^2 L^2$$

$$\therefore \qquad f_o = \frac{1}{2\pi} \sqrt{\frac{1}{LC} - \frac{R^2}{L^2}}$$

We see from this result that the presence of resistance in the circuit does now affect the resonant frequency. However, if we set $R = 0$ (or assume that R is very small, the term R^2/L^2 will also be very small), then the expression reduces to

$$f_o = \frac{I}{2\pi\sqrt{(LC)}}$$

which is the result obtained for the series resonant circuit. When R is very small in a parallel circuit, the error introduced by using this simpler formula is negligible.

We have already noted that in a parallel circuit made up of pure reactances the impedance of a parallel circuit in which the inductive branch contains resistance will, while not exhibiting an infinite impedance, at least have an impedance which is very large. We can test this out by again referring to *Figure 4.9(c)*. For here

$$I_C = I. \tan \phi, \text{ since } I_C = I_L \sin \phi \text{ and } I = I_L \cos \phi$$

Let the impedance at resonance be R_D, the *dynamic resistance*.

$$\text{Then} \qquad R_D = \frac{V}{I} = \frac{V}{I_C} . \tan \phi$$

$$= V\left(\frac{X_C}{V} . \frac{X_L}{R}\right), \text{ since } I_C = \frac{V}{X_C} \text{ and } \tan \phi = \frac{X_L}{R}$$

$$\therefore \qquad R_D = \frac{X_C X_L}{R} = \frac{\omega L}{\omega CR}$$

$$= \frac{L}{CR} \ \Omega \qquad\qquad (4.2)$$

As the current and voltage are in phase, this impedance is purely resistive. You should notice that the circuit resistance R affects R_D; as R becomes small, R_D becomes large, tending to infinity as R approaches zero. It can be proved that for R very small, R_D is a maximum at resonance. For this reason a parallel resonant circuit is known as a *rejector* circuit because it offers a very high opposition to the flow of current at the resonant frequency.

Figure 4.10 shows the variation of circuit impedance as the frequency is varied on either side of resonance. This is the response curve of the parallel tuned circuit.

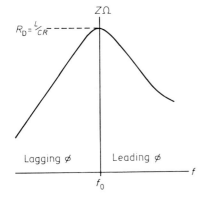

Figure 4.10

Example (8). An inductance $L = 0.05$ H having a resistance $R = 100 \ \Omega$ is tuned to resonance by a parallel capacitor $C = 0.01 \ \mu F$.

Calculate the frequency of resonance (a) taking account of R, (b) ignoring R.

(a)   Taking account of R, we insert the appropriate figures into the expression for resonant frequency:

$$f_\text{o} = \frac{1}{2\pi} \sqrt{\left[\frac{1}{LC} - \frac{R^2}{L^2}\right]} = \frac{1}{2\pi} \sqrt{\left[\frac{10^6}{0.05 \times 0.01} - \left(\frac{100}{0.05}\right)^2\right]}$$

$$= \frac{1}{2\pi} \sqrt{\left[\frac{4 \times 10^{10}}{25}\right]} = \frac{1}{5\pi} \times 10^5$$

$$= 7110 \text{ Hz}$$

(b)   Ignoring R: $f_\text{o} = \frac{1}{2\pi} \sqrt{\left[\frac{10^6}{0.05 \times 0.01}\right]}$

$$= \frac{1}{2\pi} \sqrt{\left[\frac{10^{10}}{5}\right]}$$

$$= 7118 \text{ Hz}.$$

This is a difference of about 1%.

Try this next problem for yourself. Make sure you work in the proper units.

(9)   A circuit comprising a 200 μH coil of resistance 30 Ω is in parallel with a 200 pF capacitor. Find the approximate frequency of resonance and the dynamic resistance.

CURRENT MAGNIFICATION

The currents I_C and I_L circulating in the closed loop of a parallel resonant circuit are, as we noted earlier, very large compared with the current I drawn from the supply. If the circuit resistance is small, so that angle χ in *Figure 4.9(c)* is almost 90°, we can assume that $I_\text{L} = I_\text{C}$, since sin χ is then almost unity. Then since $I_\text{L} = V/\omega L, I_\text{C} = V\omega C$ and $I = V/R_\text{D}$ we have

$$I_\text{L} = \frac{I R_\text{D}}{\omega L} \quad \text{and} \quad I_\text{C} = I R_\text{D} \omega C$$

The ratio $\dfrac{I_\text{L}}{I} = \dfrac{I_\text{C}}{I}$ is the *current magnification* of the circuit, and hence represents the Q-factor of the circuit. So

$$Q = \frac{R_\text{D}}{\omega L} = \omega R_\text{D} C$$

whence $I_\text{C} = I_\text{L} = I Q$

Hence, in a parallel resonant circuit, the currents circulating in the circuit branches may be many hundreds of times greater than the total feed current supplied from the source. You should compare this result with the voltage magnification factor obtained in the case of series resonance.

We can, of course, look at this result as saying that the impedance of a parallel circuit at resonance is equal to Q times the reactance of either branch.

The next worked example will illustrate some points about Q-factor.

Example (10). A circuit consisting of an inductor of 0.05 H and resistance 5 Ω is in parallel with a capacitor of 0.1 μF. Calculate the frequency of resonance. Find for the circuit at this frequency (a) the impedance, (b) the Q-factor.

$$f_o = \frac{1}{2\pi} \sqrt{\left[\frac{1}{LC} - \frac{R^2}{L^2}\right]} = \frac{1}{2\pi} \sqrt{\left[\frac{10^6}{0.05 \times 0.1} - \frac{25 \times 10^4}{25}\right]}$$

$$= \frac{1}{2\pi} \sqrt{\left[\frac{10^9}{5} - 10^4\right]}$$

Clearly the R^2/L^2 term can be neglected compared to $1/LC$; the resistance is only 5 Ω and the simpler expression for f_o could normally be used straightaway.

$$f_o = \frac{1}{2\pi} \sqrt{\left[2 \times 10^8\right]} = \frac{10^4}{\sqrt{2} \, \pi}$$

$$= 2250 \text{ Hz}$$

(a)   At resonance, the impedance $= R_D = \dfrac{L}{CR}$

$$\therefore \quad R_D = \frac{0.05 \times 10^6}{0.1 \times 5}$$

$$= 100 \text{ k}\Omega$$

(b) $$Q = \frac{R_D}{\omega L}$$

$$= \frac{100 \times 10^3}{2\pi \times 2250 \times 0.05} = 141$$

For this last part of the question we need not have used R_D in our Q calculation, for since the Q of the circuit is dominated by the Q of the coil (where the bulk of the resistance resides) we could, of course, have used the general expression for Q

$$Q = \frac{\omega L}{R} = \frac{2\pi \times 0.05 \times 2250}{5}$$

$$= 141, \text{ as before.}$$

SELECTIVITY AND BANDWIDTH

Figure 4.11

Figure 4.12

(a)

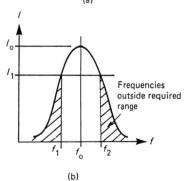

(b)

Figure 4.13

The ability of a resonant circuit, series or parallel, to discriminate between input signals of different frequencies defines it *selectivity*. If a constant voltage is applied to a series circuit and the frequency is varied, the current will become a maximum when the impedance of the circuit is a minimum, that is, when the voltage applied is at the circuit's resonant frequency. We recall that the impedance is then purely resistive and equal to the circuit R. At frequencies above and below resonance, the impedance increases, becoming capacitive below resonance and inductive above, and the circuit current falls from its maximum value of I_0 ($= V/R$) in the manner indicated in *Figure 14.11*. Clearly, the 'peakiness' of this response curve is an indication of the ability of the circuit to pick out one particular frequency (f_0) from some other frequency relatively close by (such as f_1), the circuit currents flowing at f_0 and f_1 being I_0 and I_1 respectively.

The response curve obtained for a parallel resonant circuit is similar, except that this time the impedance is a maximum at resonance and the current drawn a minimum. By using impedance Z, therefore, in place of current I on the vertical axis of *Figure 4.11*, the diagram can be used to illustrate the response of a parallel circuit, and this has been done in *Figure 4.12*. This time the impedance (which is resistive at resonance and equal to L/CR, remember) becomes inductive below resonance and capacitive above. The peakiness of the curve is again an indication of its selectivity.

Ideally we want a resonant circuit to pick out a precise *band* of frequencies centred about the resonant frequency; all other frequencies must be rejected. Such an ideal response curve would be rectangular in shape, with vertical sides and a flat top, rather as shown in *Figure 4.13(a)*. Only those frequencies lying between the limits of f_1 and f_2 would be of interest to us. When we tune into a radio signal, we select first the frequency on which that particular station is transmitting, what is called the *carrier* frequency. The actual voice or music content of the signal then has to be received on a band of frequencies which extends for a certain 'distance' on either side of the carrier frequency. For medium-wave reception, the distance f_1 to f_2 is about 9 kHz. With our ideal response curve, any interference on a frequency such as f_3 outside the limits of our wanted range would not disturb our enjoyment of the programme.

The response curve we actually have, of course, is not rectangular and unless it has steep sides, some frequencies outside the wanted limits of f_1 and f_2 will influence reception; see *Figure 4.13(b)*. The frequency range f_1 to f_2 is known as the *bandwidth* of the system and for high discrimination between what we want and what we don't want the ratio

$$\frac{f_0}{f_2 - f_1}$$

must clearly be large.

Now it might appear at first consideration that the bandwidth of a particular circuit might be anything, being dependent upon the level selected for the current I_1 flowing at frequency f_1 or f_2. And so it would be if the response level I_1 was chosen arbitrarily. But I_1 must obviously always be stated as a definite proportion of the maximum I_o if a meaningful measure of the circuit selectivity is to be obtained.

Let the level I_1 be chosen such that at those points on the response curve, the circuit reactance is equal to its resistance. That is, let $R = X$, then

$$Z = \sqrt{R^2 + R^2}$$
$$= R\sqrt{2}$$

So

$$I_1 = \frac{V}{Z} = \frac{V}{R\sqrt{2}} = \frac{I_o}{\sqrt{2}}$$
$$= 0.707 I_o$$

If, then, we measure frequencies f_1 and f_2 at points where the response has fallen to 0.707 of its peak value at resonance, we obtain a bandwidth figure which, in proportion to the resonant frequency f_o, is a measure of selectivity. We take note of two important points:

(a) A ratio I_o to $0.707 I_o$ corresponds to a *power* ratio of −3 dB. The frequencies f_1 and f_2 are known as the 'half-power points' and the bandwidth of a resonant circuit is always stated with reference to the half-power points.

(b) The phase angle at f_1 and f_2 is $45°$; this follows from the fact that $\tan^{-1} R/X = \tan^{-1} 1$, since $R = X$. Whether the current leads or lags on the voltage by this angle depends upon which side of resonance we consider, i.e. on whether the circuit is inductive or capacitive.

In *Figure 4.13(b)* the capacitance is predominant at f_1;

therefore
$$\frac{1}{\omega_1 C} - \omega_1 L = R$$

and so
$$\frac{1}{C} - \omega_1^2 L = \omega_1 R \qquad \text{(i)}$$

At f_2 the inductive reactance is predominant, and so

$$\omega_2^2 L - \frac{1}{C} = \omega_2 R \qquad \text{(ii)}$$

Adding (i) and (ii):

$$\omega_2^2 L - \omega_1^2 L = \omega_1 R + \omega_2 R$$

and
$$L(\omega_2 - \omega_1) = R$$

Dividing across by ω_0 ($= 2\pi f_o$) we have finally

$$\frac{\omega_2 - \omega_1}{\omega_0} = \frac{R}{\omega_0 L}$$

from which

$$\frac{f_o}{f_2 - f_1} = \frac{\omega_0 L}{R} = Q$$

Thus by choosing this particular response level, we have shown that Q is a direct measure of selectivity.

ACCEPTORS AND REJECTORS

Figure 4.14

A resonant circuit made up of inductance and capacitance in series is known as an acceptor circuit. A resonant circuit made up of inductance and capacitance in parallel is known as a rejector circuit. The essential characteristics are that the acceptor circuit provides an easy path for current at the resonant frequency and a more difficult one for all others, whereas the rejector makes a difficult path for current at the resonant frequency and an easier path for all others.

In radio reception, the required frequency is selected from all others by the use of a rejector circuit connected between the aerial system and earth, see *Figure 4.14*. The circuit is resonated by varying the capacitance and, at the frequency of resonance, when the impedance is a maximum, the greatest voltage is developed across the circuit and applied to the receiver input.

Acceptor circuits have their uses but they are not so often used as rejectors. One use of a rejector is to bypass frequencies which are very close to the wanted frequency and which need to be suppressed. An acceptor can then be connected across a rejector as shown in *Figure 4.15*, where it behaves as a very low resistance to the unwanted signal. It is then known as a 'trap', and the digram illustrates its behaviour in removing part of the frequency spectrum. Its presence does not affect the functioning of the rejector; at the frequency to which the rejector is tuned, the acceptor looks like a capacitance, hence only modifies the actual tuning capacitance of the rejector. Such systems as this are found on fixed tuned circuits, particularly in television receivers.

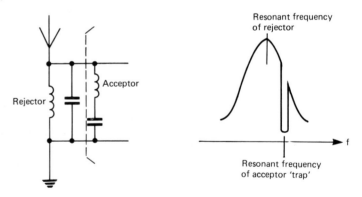

Figure 4.15

POWER IN A PARALLEL CIRCUIT

Consider a parallel combination of reactance and resistance as shown in *Figure 4.16(a)* and the associated phasor diagram at (*b*). Whether the reactance X is an inductor or a capacitor, power will be dissipated only in the resistive branch where the in-phase component of current is $I \cos \phi$. Hence the total *true* power dissipated in the circuit = $V I_R$ = $VI \cos \phi$ watts. As for the series circuit, the power is given by the product of the applied voltage and total current multiplied in turn by the cosine of the phase angle between them.

But the power that is *apparently* being dissipated in the circuit is the product of the applied voltage and the total current only, and this is measured in volt-amperes (VA). Hence

$$\frac{\text{True power}}{\text{Apparent power}} = \frac{VI \cos \phi}{VI} = \cos \phi$$

As for the series circuit, $\cos \phi$ is known as the power factor.

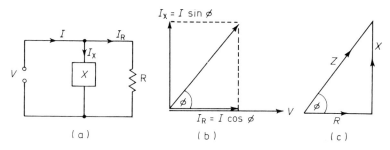

Figure 4.16

From the impedance diagram, *Figure 4.11(c)*, the alternative expression for power factor is clearly

$$\cos \phi = \frac{R}{Z} = \frac{\text{resistance}}{\text{impedance}}$$

For a purely resistive (or a resonant) circuit, $\cos \phi = 1$ since ϕ is zero. This is the case of unity power factor.

Worked examples will perhaps best illustrate the meaning of power factor and how to deal with problems involving power considerations.

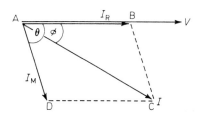

Figure 4.17

Example (11). A 240 V induction motor is connected in parallel with a 100 Ω resistor which can be taken to be non-reactive. The motor draws a current of 3 A and the total circuit current is 4 A. Calculate the power and the power factor of (a) the motor, (b) the complete circuit.

Figure 4.17 shows the circuit and the phasor diagram. The current in the resistor $I_R = V/R = 240/100 = 2.4$ A. This current is in phase with V.

The current in the motor branch, I_M, lags V by an angle θ (which is *not* 90°) and the resultant circuit current I is the diagonal of the parallelogram ABCD. We require to find the cosine of the phase angle ϕ between V and I.

A scaled diagram could be used here, but we will use the *Cosine Rule* from trigonometry — remember, we are not dealing with a right-angled triangle here. Then from triangle ABC:

$$I_M{}^2 = I^2 + I_R{}^2 - 2 I I_R \cdot \cos \phi$$

$$3^2 = 4^2 + 2.4^2 - (2 \times 4 \times 2.4) \cos \phi$$

and from this we find $\cos \phi = 0.665$
This is the power factor of the complete circuit.

Now the power taken by the circuit $= VI \cos \phi = 240 \times 4 \times 0.665$

$= 638.4 \text{ W}$

Power dissipated in the resistor $= I_R{}^2 R$

$= 2.4^2 \times 100$

$= 576 \text{ W}$

Hence the power taken by the motor $= 638.4 - 576$

$= 62.4 \text{ W}$

Now for the motor $\cos \phi = \dfrac{\text{motor power}}{\text{volts} \times \text{motor current}}$

$= \dfrac{62.4}{240 \times 3} = 0.087 \text{ lagging}$

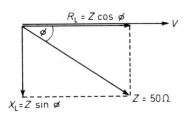

Figure 4.18

Example (12). Two components P and Q are connected in parallel across a 100 V 400 Hz supply. Component P draws a current of 1.5 A at unity power factor, and Q draws a current of 2 A at 0.7660 p-f lagging. Identify and evaluate the two component pieces.

For unity power factor, the component must be purely resistive; for the lagging power factor the component will be inductive. The circuit therefore comprises a resistor R in parallel with an inductor L having some resistance R_L. *Figure 4.18* shows the circuit and phasor diagram.

Resistance of branch $P\!:\!R = \dfrac{\bar{v}}{I_R} = \dfrac{100}{1.5} = 66.7 \ \Omega$

Impedance of branch $Q\!:\!Z = \dfrac{V}{I_L} = \dfrac{100}{2} = 50 \ \Omega$

This impedance is made up of X_L and R_L in series, having a phase angle $\phi = \cos^{-1} 0.7660$; hence $\phi = 40°$. Then from the diagram

$$X_L = Z.\sin \phi = 50 \times \sin 40°$$

$$= 50 \times 0.6428 = 32.14 \ \Omega$$

Hence $L = \dfrac{X}{2\pi f} = \dfrac{32.14}{2\pi \times 400} \text{ H}$

$$= 0.0128 \text{ H} (= 12.8 \text{ mH})$$

You should have no difficulty in calculating that $R_L = 38.3 \ \Omega$.

POWER FACTOR CORRECTION

Parallel resonance can be applied to the problem of power factor correction or improvement, so making generating equipment at mains supply frequencies more efficient. Many industrial loads, particularly motors, are highly inductive and as we have already mentioned in the case of series circuits, this reduces the efficiency of the generating plant. So for reasons of economy it is necessary to make the loading placed on generating equipment as resistive as possible; for inductive loads this can be done by placing a suitable capacitor in parallel with the load. If the system is made resonant in this way, the resistive condition results and the power factor becomes unity or a figure very close to unity.

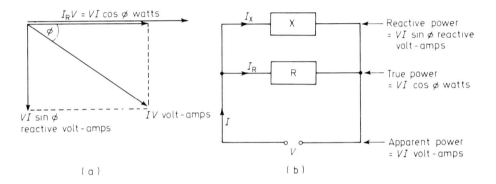

(a)   (b)

Figure 4.19

Calculations on power factor correction are usually made with the various parallel loads described in terms of watts, volt-amperes or reactive volt-amperes. We are already familiar with these terms from the previous Unit section. Suppose an inductive load has a lagging phase angle ϕ, see *Figure 4.19(a)*. Each power phasor is obtained by taking the current phasors for the circuit branches and multiplying them by the common voltage V. Diagram (b) shows how these power components are distributed in the actual circuit elements. If now a capacitor is placed in parallel with the circuit, there will be an additional reactive power leading the voltage by 90°. This will have no effect on the power supplied but it will act in opposition to the existing reactive power component $VI.\sin \phi$ which simply represents power which surges between the generator and the load without doing any useful work. Phase angle ϕ will be reduced to zero when the reactive powers are equal; the true power and the apparent power phasors will then coincide.

The next problem will illustrate power factor improvement.

Example (13). At a full load power of 500 W an induction motor running on 240 V 50 Hz mains supplies, has a lagging power factor of 0.7. Calculate the value of capacitance required in parallel with the motor to raise the overall power factor to unity.

We find first the motor current I:

$$VI.\cos \phi = 500 = 240 \times I \times 0.7$$

$$\therefore \qquad I = 2.98 \text{ A}$$

Capacitor reactive power
- $VI \sin \phi$

$VI \cos \phi$

ϕ reduces as capacitor
reactive power increases

$VI \sin \phi$

Figure 4.20

This current lags the applied voltage by angle ϕ. From *Figure 4.20* the in-phase component of the current is $I \cos \phi = 2.98 \times 0.7 = 2.086$ A, and the reactive component $I \sin \phi = 2.98 \times 0.7141 = 2.13$ A.

To bring the power factor to unity requires the added capacitor to draw a reactive current of 2.13 A *ahead* of the voltage.

Hence
$$X_C = \frac{1}{2\pi f C} = \frac{240}{2.13} = 112.7 \ \Omega$$

$$\therefore \qquad C = \frac{10^6}{2\pi \times 50 \times 112.7} \ \mu F = 28.25 \ \mu F$$

PROBLEMS FOR SECTION 4

Group 1

(14) A 100 Ω resistor is connected in parallel with a 60 μF capacitor across a 200 V 50 Hz supply. Calculate (a) the branch currents, (b) the supply current, (c) the circuit impedance.

(15) A current of 10 A is drawn from a supply of 100 V at a frequency of 50 Hz by a circuit comprising a pure inductor in parallel with a 25 Ω resistor. Calculate (a) the current in the inductor, (b) the reactance of the inductor, (c) the inductance.

(16) A 60 Ω resistor and a pure capacitance are connected in parallel across a 240 V 50 Hz supply. The current taken from the supply is 6 A. Find the capacitance of the capacitor. Verify your worked solution with a scaled phasor diagram.

(17) What value of capacitor should be connected in parallel with a 200 Ω resistor across an 80 V, 50 Hz supply for the phase angle between supply current and voltage to be 45°? What then is the current drawn from the supply?

(18) An alternating supply of 100 V at a frequency of 50 Hz is applied first to a resistor of 50 Ω and then to a pure inductance of 1 H. Calculate the current flowing in each case. The two components are now connected in parallel across the same supply. What current is now taken from the supply?

(19) An inductance of 0.318 H having negligible resistance is wired in parallel with a 5000 μF capacitor across an a.c. supply of frequency 100 Hz. If a current of 0.2 A flows in the inductor, calculate (a) the supply voltage, (b) the capacitor current, (c) the total circuit currrent.

(20) A 100 Ω resistor and a pure inductance L henry are connected first in series and then in parallel to a 1 kHz a.c. supply. Find the value of L for which the phase angle between the supply current and voltage will be the same in each case. Hence calculate this phase angle.

(21) We have seen in the text that the dynamic impedance of a parallel resonant circuit can be expressed as $R_D = L/CR$ Ω. Prove that it may also be expressed as $(\omega L)^2/R$ or as $1/(\omega C)^2 R$.

(22) A coil of inductance 160 μH and negligible resistance is tuned by a parallel capacitor which can be varied from 45 pF to 475 pF. What frequency range will the circuit cover? Would the range be any different if the components were connected in series?

(23) A 10 mH coil has a resistance of 10 Ω. It is connected in parallel with a 0.1 μF capacitor and the applied frequency is adjusted so that the circuit is resonant. What is the circuit Q-factor?

(24) What value of capacitor is required to produce resonance at a frequency of 40 Hz when it is placed in parallel with a 200 mH coil having a resistance of 50 Ω?

(25) Complete the following statements:
(a)   A resistive circuit has . . . . power factor.
(b)   A leading power factor indicates a (an) . . . . circuit.
(c)   The object of power factor correction is to bring the power factor close to . . . . . .

(26) A circuit absorbing 850 W of power is fed from a 200 V supply. If the current drawn is 4.5 A, find the phase angle.

(27) The current taken by an induction motor is 1.2 A when the applied voltage is 250 V. A wattmeter indicates 135 W. What is the power factor and phase angle? (Note: a wattmeter reads true power).

(28) A coil of inductance 3 H and resistance 500 Ω is connected to a 500 V 50 Hz supply. What is the power factor of the coil at this frequency?

(29) An inductor of 0.318 H has an impedance of 200 Ω. It is wired in parallel with a resistance of 200 Ω to a 100 V 50 Hz supply. Find (a) the resistance of the inductor, (b) the total power dissipated in the circuit.

(30) An alternating voltage of angular frequency $\omega = 10^4$ rad/sec is connected to the circuit of *Figure 4.21*. The voltage measured across the 750 Ω resistor is found to be 3 V. Calculate (a) the supply voltage, (b) the total power supplied, (c) the power factor.

It is desired to increase the power factor to unity. What value of capacitor would be required for this and how would it be connected?

(31) A transmitting capacitor has a capacitance of 0.025 μF. It has a power factor of 5×10^{-4} and is carrying a current of 100 A at a frequency of 25 kHz. What power is being dissipated in the capacitor?

(32) The parallel circuit of *Figure 4.22* is connected to a 100 V supply having an angular frequency $\omega = 1000$ rad/s. Calculate the total circuit current and the branch currents. Illustrate your answers by means of a scaled phasor diagram.

(33) A 500 V, 50 Hz motor takes a full load current of 40 A at a power factor of 0.85 lagging. If a capacitor of 80 μF is connected across the motor terminals, show that the power factor will rise to 0.97 and the full load current fall to about 35 A.

(34) Power is supplied to a workshop at 440 V, and the power

Figure 4.21

Group 2

Figure 4.22

lines feeding the workshop have a resistance of 0.2 Ω. If the workshop load is 25 kW at a power factor of 0.7, what power is wasted as heat in the power lines? What would this loss reduce to if the load was adjusted to have unity power factor?

(35)   A circuit is made up of a coil of inductance 180 μH and resistance 10 Ω in series with a capacitor of 300 pF. Calculate (a) the circuit Q-factor, (b) the bandwidth at the resonant frequency.

(36)   A tuned circuit, resonant at a frequency f_o, has two frequencies f_1 and f_2 respectively below and above f_o, at which the current in the circuit is *one-half* the value measured at f_o. Show that

$$f_o{}^2 = f_1 \times f_2 \quad \text{and that} \quad f_2 - f_1 = \frac{\sqrt{3}.R}{2\pi L}$$

5 Transformer principles

Aims: At the end of this Unit Section you should be able to:
State the essential constructional forms of radio-frequency and low-frequency transformers
Explain and use the relationships between input and output currents and voltages and the transformation ratio of the transformer
Draw and understand the phasor diagram of an ideal transformer under no-load conditions
Derive the input resistance of a loaded transformer
Understand the maximum power transfer theorem for resistive loads and sources
Explain iron and resistance losses in a transformer and how these can be minimized by the choice of materials used in the construction.

A transformer is essentially a device in which the magnetic flux produced by a current flowing in one coil is arranged to link with the turns of an adjacent coil. This is illustrated in *Figure 5.1*. An alternating voltage V_1 produces a current I_1 in the coil having turns N_1. This sets up an alternating flux Φ which links with the adjacent coil having turns N_2 and induces an e.m.f. E_2 in this coil. Since the e.m.f. in the second coil is due entirely to the common flux produced by the current in the first coil, the circuits are coupled by mutual induction. This is the fundamental principle of all transformer action.

Transformers take a variety of forms. There are those designed to operate at relatively high-frequencies (radio-frequencies) covering the range from about 100 kHz to possibly as high as 100 MHz. Others are designed to cover the lower range of audio-frequencies from, perhaps, some 100 Hz or so to about 20 kHz. a third group are used exclusively at the power frequency range of 45 to 55 Hz. The physical appearance of each group of transformers varies considerably, particularly between those used at radio-frequencies and those used at power frequency. We will consider briefly the general features of construction of these transformer forms.

Figure 5.1

HIGH-FREQUENCY TRANSFORMERS

In general these consist of two coils wound on a paxolin, polystyrene or some other such insulating material tube, the coil ends being brought out to tags rivetted either to the tube itself or to an attached ring of insulating material rigidly glued to the tube. Unless they consist of only a few turns of wire, in which case they are generally wound as single layers along the length of the tube, the coils are usually "wave-wound". This is a winding system where the coil is built up in criss-cross fashion as illustrated in *Figure 5.2(a)*. This method of winding is not done solely for the sake of neatness; the open type of winding which results reduces the self-capacitance of the coil while at the same time leading to compactness.

The spacing between the coils is relatively large, often two or three centimetres or more. The coils are then said to be *loosely* coupled. On the other hand, *tightly* coupled coils are sometimes seen where the coils are mounted closely side by side or, in some cases, wound one above the other. The coils do not necessarily have the same number of turns.

In transformers of the loosely-coupled kind it is clear that all the flux produced by the energized winding (which we shall refer to as the *primary* coil) does not link with the other (or *secondary*) winding. As the secondary coil is located further away from the primary, so the flux linking with it is reduced, and hence the secondary induced e.m.f. and the mutual inductance decrease.

The proportion of the total flux that links with the secondary is stated as the *coefficient of coupling*, symbol k. For example, if $k = 0.5$, only half the primary flux links with the secondary turns. For reasons which will not immediately concern us here, the value of k is often as small as 0.01 or less.

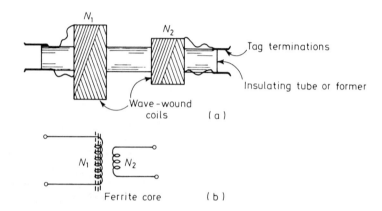

Figure 5.2

Radio-frequency transformers often have an iron-dust (ferrite) core which is used to adjust the coil inductance or modify the coefficient of coupling. In other cases, the coils may be wound directly on to a long ferrite rod where the system acts as the aerial receiving arrangement for portable radio receivers. In nearly all cases, one or both of the coils will be tuned by parallel capacitors to be resonant at one fixed frequency or adjustable over a range of frequencies. As we have already noted above, transformers of this sort are found in circuits which operate within the frequency range 100 kHz to some 100 MHz. The circuit symbol for a r.f. transformer is shown in *Figure 5.2(b)*; if an iron-dust or ferrite core is employed, this is shown as a set of broken lines.

LOW-FREQUENCY TRANSFORMERS   The general construction of transformers designed to cover the audio-frequency range and those to be used on the fixed power frequency of 50 Hz are very similar. The detailed design variations follow from the fact that in the audio-frequency case a range of frequencies has to be catered for at a relatively low power, while at 50 Hz, though the frequency is fixed, considerable power requirements are often the order of the day. In both applications the object is to get as much of the primary flux as possible linking with the secondary coil. This is quite different from the situation found in radio-frequency transformers, and it is not usual to work on low-frequency and power transformers in terms of mutual inductance or coefficient of coupling.

Transformers of this kind consist essentially of two windings wound upon a closed iron magnetic circuit. As before, one of the windings is referred to as the primary and the other as the secondary coil, and the basic arrangement is shown in *Figure 5.3(a)* where again N_1 and N_2 represent the number of turns on the primary and secondary coils respectively.

The closed iron core is used to obtain a high flux and to ensure that the coupling between the coils is as tight as possible. In practice, both coils are usually wound on a centre limb of the core and not on the side limbs as the diagram illustrates for purposes of clarity, but this does not invalidate the principle of operation in any way. The circuit symbol for an iron-cored transformer is shown in *Figure 5.3(b)*; here the iron core is depicted by the solid lines between the coils.

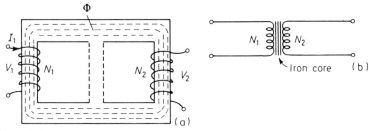

Figure 5.3

TRANSFORMATION RATIO

Referring to *Figure 5.3(a)* again, if an alternating voltage V_1 is applied to the primary coil, both the resulting current I_1 and the core flux Φ will be alternating. The changing flux will link with *both* windings and there will be induced e.m.f.'s in both windings in accordance with Faraday's Laws of induction.

Flux Φ linking with turns N_1 will induce an e.m.f. E_1 proportional to ΦN_1; this is an e.m.f. of self induction. The same flux linking with turns N_2 will induce an e.m.f. E_2 proportional to ΦN_2; this is an e.m.f. of mutual induction. Assuming that all the flux links with both coils, then

$$\frac{E_1}{E_2} = \frac{\Phi N_1}{\Phi N_2} = \frac{N_1}{N_2}$$

So the flux linkages are in the ratio of the number of turns and so also are the induced voltages due to the flux changes. Recalling our earlier work on magnetic induction, we know that the primary induced e.m.f. E_1 is equal and opposite to the input voltage V_1 (back e.m.f., remember?), and clearly the secondary voltage V_2 is equal to E_2. Hence we can write

$$V_2 = \frac{N_2}{N_1} V_1$$

The ratio N_2/N_1 is called the *transformation ratio* of the transformer.

When the secondary has fewer turns than the primary, the ratio is less than unity and $V_2 < V_1$. The transformer is then known as a '*step-down*' transformer. When the secondary has more turns than the primary, the ratio is greater than unity and $V_2 > V_1$. The transformer is now a '*step-up*' transformer. Note that it is to the *voltage* change that these terms apply.

On occasion, a transformer may have an equal number of turns on both primary and secondary. In this case $V_2 = V_1$ and the transformer is known as a 'one-to-one' or 'isolating' transformer, its function being to isolate electrically (from a d.c. point of view) one circuit from another without altering the a.c. conditions. All transformers are isolators in this sense.

In everything we have said above, we have assumed that the transformers are ideal, that is, 100% efficient. In practical transformers this cannot be true and there is always some power loss in the device. The expressions for transformation of voltage are therefore only approximations, although most power transformers have efficiencies above 95%.

We shall next consider the operation of the iron-cored transformer in more detail and return to the differences between fixed frequency power transformers and audio-frequency range transformers later on.

CURRENT TRANSFORMATION

Figure 5.4

In *Figure 5.4* a load resistance R_L has been connected across the secondary terminals of the transformer. The secondary voltage V_2 will now cause a current I_2 to flow through R_L and power will be dissipated in R_L. This power must, of course, originate at the generator connected to the primary terminals. Now since the flux is the same for each winding, the ampere-turns must also be equal, so that $I_1 N_1 = I_2 N_2$ or

$$\frac{N_2}{N_1} = \frac{I_1}{I_2}$$

but

$$\frac{N_2}{N_1} = \frac{V_2}{V_1}$$

so that

$$\frac{I_1}{I_2} = \frac{V_2}{V_1} \tag{5.1}$$

Hence, an increase or step-up in voltage from primary to secondary must be accompanied by a corresponding decrease or step-down in current from primary to secondary, and conversely. The ratio of primary to secondary current is therefore inversely proportional to the turns ratio, that is

$$I_2 = \frac{N_1}{N_2} I_1 \tag{5.2}$$

We can, of course, look at equation (5.1) above in terms of power. $I_1 V_1$ is the power input to the primary, and $I_2 V_2$ is the power output at the secondary into load resistor R_L. So $I_1 V_1 = I_2 V_2$, an obvious relationship since (assuming our transformer is an ideal component) the power input to the primary must be equal to the power delivered at the secondary. Follow the next worked example carefully.

Example (1).   An ideal transformer has 1000 primary turns and 3500 secondary turns. if 250 V is applied to the primary terminals, what voltage will appear at the secondary terminals? if a resistor of 7000 Ω is connected to the secondary, what will be the power dissipated in the resistor, and what will then be the primary current?

$$\text{Transformation ratio} \quad \frac{N_2}{N_1} = \frac{3500}{1000} = 3.5$$

$$V_2 = 3.5 \, V_1 = 3.5 \times 250 = 875 \text{ V}$$

When this voltage is applied to the 7000 ohm resistor, the power dissipated will be

$$\frac{V^2}{R} = \frac{875^2}{7000} = 109.4 \text{ W}$$

This must also be the power into the primary, $V_1 I_1$

$$\therefore \quad I_1 = \frac{\text{power}}{V_1} = \frac{109.4}{250} = 0.44 \text{ A}$$

You should perhaps not need reminding that the voltages and currents in all transformer problems and notes are alternating quantities, stated in their r.m.s. values.

Can you think of an alternative way of solving the above problem?

(2)   An ideal transformer having a primary winding of 1500 turns has a 25 Ω resistor connected across its secondary terminals. A 100 V alternating input produces 75 V across the resistor. Calculate (a) the number of turns on the secondary winding, (b) the current in each winding, (c) the power dissipated in the load.

THE UNLOADED TRANSFORMER

i_m lagging 90° on V_1

V_1 V_2

Flux Φ in phase with i_m and lagging 90° on V_1

Figure 5.5

We now examine the operation of a transformer in rather more detail, although we shall still assume that we have an ideal, loss-free component. Let the transformer of *Figure 5.5* be such a transformer and suppose further that the secondary terminals are left disconnected, so that the transformer is unloaded. Then as far as the input is concerned, the primary winding will appear as a very large inductance and a small current i_m lagging 90° on the applied voltage V_1 will flow when V_1 is connected. This current is known as the *magnetising current*. It will produce an alternating flux Φ in the core of the transformer which is in *phase* with the current and hence also lagging by 90° on the applied voltage.

We can therefore construct a phasor diagram to illustrate this: the relationship between the applied voltage, the magnetising current and the core flux is shown in *Figure 5.6(a)*. Notice particularly that we have taken the flux Φ as our reference phasor, this being the only quantity which is common to both primary and secondary circuit.

The alternating flux produces in the primary winding an alternating back e.m.f. which, in a purely inductive circuit, is at all times equal and opposite to the applied voltage. Since the back e.m.f. must depend upon the magnitude of the alternating flux, it follows that this magnitude is determined *solely* by the magnitude of the applied voltage. This

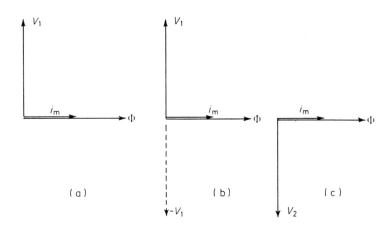

Figure 5.6

is a condition of fundamental importance in the whole of transformer theory: If the applied voltage V_1 is constant, then the flux Φ is constant. This statement is true *irrespective of any other currents* which may be caused to flow in either or both of the transformer windings because of secondary loading or any other reason. *Figure 5.6(b)* now shows us the phasor diagram with the addition of the back e.m.f. equal to $-V_1$.

The alternating flux which threads the primary winding and induces in it the back e.m.f. $-V_1$ links also with the secondary winding, consequently there is induced in the secondary an e.m.f. which is in *phase* with the primary back e.m.f. and *Figure 5.6(c)* shows the phasor representation of this. The magnitude of this secondary e.m.f. is easily calculated, for V_2 is produced by the flux linking with the secondary turns, and as the flux is common to both primary and secondary windings the ratio of the primary induced e.m.f. to that of the secondary must be the same as the ratio of primary to secondary turns. But the primary induced e.m.f. is the back e.m.f. in the primary and this is equal in magnitude but opposite in phase to V_1. Hence the secondary voltage V_2 is such that

$$\frac{V_2}{V_1} = \frac{N_2}{N_1} \quad \text{or} \quad V_2 = \frac{N_2}{N_1} V_1$$

a relationship already derived by an alternative approach in the previous section.

INPUT RESISTANCE

Figure 5.7

When the secondary winding of a transformer is unloaded, the primary impedance is very high and the current which flows is small. When a load is connected to the secondary, the primary current increases and the primary impedance falls. Now the impedance seen at the primary terminals is given by the ratio V_1/I_1 and since I_1 will depend upon the secondary load, so too will the input impedance. The relationship between the magnitude of the secondary load and the effective primary impedance is a very important one in transformer theory and we now investigate it. To simplify things, we will assume that the secondary load is purely resistive, given by R_L.

In *Figure 5.7* let R_L be connected to the secondary terminals and let the primary input be a constant V_1 volts. We have already shown that

$$\frac{V_2}{V_1} = \frac{N_2}{N_1} \quad \text{and} \quad \frac{I_1}{I_2} = \frac{N_2}{N_1}$$

Then, by multiplication of these

$$\frac{V_2}{V_1} \times \frac{I_1}{I_2} = \left[\frac{N_2}{N_1}\right]^2$$

so that

$$\frac{V_2}{I_2} \div \frac{V_1}{I_1} = \left[\frac{N_2}{N_1}\right]^2$$

but $\dfrac{V_2}{I_2}$ = load resistance R_L and $\dfrac{V_1}{I_1}$ = the input resistance R_{in}

$$\therefore \quad \frac{R_L}{R_{in}} = \left[\frac{N_2}{N_1}\right]^2$$

or

$$R_{in} = R_L \left[\frac{N_1}{N_2}\right]^2 \tag{5.3}$$

Now N_1/N_2 which is the inverse of the turns ratio will be greater than unity if $N_1 > N_2$, that is, for a step-down transformer, and less than unity if $N_1 < N_2$, that is, for a step-up transformer. The input resistance of the transformer can therefore be made to suit any required value for a given output load by the proper choice of the turns ratio.

This is an important property of a transformer because it can be used as a resistance transforming device, distinct from its more obvious properties of voltage and current transformation. Stated in words, we say: when a circuit includes a transformer, the resistance of the circuit as seen at the primary terminals is increased or decreased by a factor $[N_1/N_2]^2$. Notice particularly that the resistance ratio depends upon the *square* of N_1/N_2 and not directly upon this ratio as current and voltage ratios do. It helps to keep in mind that the resistance value appears to increase when referred to a winding with a greater number of turns, and to decrease when referred to a winding with a fewer number of turns.

The following worked examples should make things clear for you.

Example (3).   A step down transformer has a turns ratio of 10 : 1. If a resistance of 1 kΩ is connected to the secondary terminals, what effective resistance does the transformer offer at the primary terminals?

In this transformer $N_1 = 10$ and $N_2 = 1$ (strictly in terms of the turns *ratio*), therefore

$$\frac{N_1}{N_2} = 10$$

The secondary load $R_L = 1000 \ \Omega$

Figure 5.8

$\therefore$ primary resistance $R_{in} = \left[\dfrac{N_1}{N_2}\right]^2 R_L = 10^2 \times 1000$

$$= 100 \text{ k}\Omega$$

This result is illustrated in *Figure 5.8*. As far as the circuit connected to the primary is concerned, the transformer and its 1 kΩ load appears as a single 100 kΩ resistor. The secondary load has been 'transferred' or 'reflected' to the primary circuit without in any way modifying the characteristics or behaviour of the circuit; that is, the two circuits shown in the diagram are completely identical as far as the a.c. conditions are concerned.

Example (4). The resistance of a loudspeaker is 9 Ω and it is to be connected to an output transistor in an amplifier which requires a load resistance of 100 Ω. What should be the turns ratio of a transformer used to connect the transistor to the loud-speaker?

This arrangement is a common use for a transformer: as an output transformer connecting an amplifier to a loudspeaker. *Figure 5.9* shows a simplified circuit of this kind.

Using our transformation formula

$$R_{in} = \left[\frac{N_1}{N_2}\right]^2 R_L$$

we have

$$100 = \left[\frac{N_1}{N_2}\right]^2 \times 8$$

$$\therefore \left[\frac{N_1}{N_2}\right]^2 = \frac{100}{8} = 12.5$$

$$\frac{N_1}{N_2} = 3.54$$

Hence we require a *step-down* transformer with a turns ratio of 3.54 : 1.

Figure 5.9

MAXIMUM POWER TRANSFER The previous example raises a very important subject in electrical and electronic principles, i.e. the transfer of electrical power from a generator to a load. In *Figure 5.10*, a generator of e.m.f. E volts and internal resistance r Ω is connected to a load resistor R_L. Current I will flow in the circuit and power will be delivered to the load resistor (where it is required) and to the internal resistance of the generator (where it is not required and is consequently wasted).

What is the relationship between r and R_L for the greatest power to be delivered to the load? We have already proved that this will occur when $r = R_L$, and under this condition it is not difficult to see that the maximum possible power delivered to the load is one-half of the total power supplied by the generator.

Figure 5.10

(a)

This has to look like 50 Ω

(b)

Figure 5.11

Having recalled this important fact, it is now necessary to make the best practical use of it. In most circuits, the internal resistance of the generator and the actual resistance of the load are rarely identical. In the problem above, for example, the load resistance was the 8 Ω of the loudspeaker unit, while the resistance offered by the generator (the transistor amplifier) was 100 Ω. If the loudspeaker is connected directly to the transistor output, only a small part of the available power will be developed in it. By interposing the transformer, the effective resistance of the loudspeaker is increased to 100 Ω and the maximum power is then transferred to it.

Such a process is known as resistance (or impedance) *matching*, so a transformer with a suitable turns ratio affords us a convenient way of reflecting resistance from one circuit to another to maximize the power transfer from a source to load.

Example (5). A generator of e.m.f. 10 V and internal resistance 50 Ω is connected directly to a load resistance of 150 Ω. What power is dissipated in the load? A transformer is now employed to match the load to the generator. Find the necessary turns ratio and calculate the power then dissipated in the load.

Figure 5.11(a) shows the direct connection. The circuit current $I = 10/200 = 0.05$ A, and hence the power dissipated in the load

$$P_L = I^2 R = (0.05)^2 \times 150$$

$$= 0.375 \ W$$

Figure 5.11(b) shows the transformer connected between generator and load. For maximum power in the load, the primary of the transformer must present a resistance of 50 Ω to the generator, that is, a value equal to its own internal resistance. Hence, since

$$R_{in} = \left[\frac{N_1}{N_2}\right]^2 R_L$$

$$\left[\frac{N_1}{N_2}\right]^2 = \frac{R_{in}}{R_L} = \frac{50}{150} = \frac{1}{3}$$

Inverting $\left[\frac{N_2}{N_1}\right]^2 = 3$ or $\left[\frac{N_2}{N_1}\right] = 1.73$

The transformer has to be a step-up transformer with turns ratio 1:1.73. The power in the load will now be

$$P = I^2 R_L = \left[\frac{10}{100}\right]^2 \times 50 = 0.5 \ W$$

This is the maximum possible power.

Try the next problem for yourself. It will illustrate in graphical form how maximum load power occurs when the resistances of the load and generator are equal.

(6)   Assume in the previous problem that R_L can be varied between 100 Ω and 200 Ω in 10 Ω steps. For the direct connection as indicated in (*Figure 5.11(a)*), calculate the circuit current I for each step in the value of R_L and find the corresponding power developed in R_L.

Plot a graph of load P_L (vertically) against R_L (horizontally) and verify that the maximum power is 0.5 W when the value of R_L is equal to 50 Ω.

TRANSFORMER LOSSES AND MATERIALS

When iron cores are used in transformers, two fundamental power losses make their appearance. These losses are
(i)   eddy current losses;
(ii) hysteresis losses.

Eddy current loss results because energy is dissipated as heat in the metal of the core when an alternating current flows in the surrounding coils. The alternating flux, as well as inducing voltages in the coils, produces voltages in the core itself, causing small local currents to circulate in the iron circuit. This loss is reduced by using insulated laminations for the core, so breaking up direct current paths through the material and presenting instead a high resistance to the circulation of such currents. *Figure 5.12* shows the general form of iron core construction for low-frequency and power transformers. For transformers designed for the higher audio-frequencies, the thickness of the laminations is reduced to ensure that the induced voltages do not lead to increased eddy current magnitudes.

At very high frequencies, when it becomes impracticable to make laminations any thinner, core losses are reduced by using iron-dust or granulated iron cores. Such cores are used at radio-frequencies, generally for tuning purposes, and are available for frequencies up to many tens of megahertz. The losses are very small, the binding material between the iron granulations acting as an efficient insulator which breaks up the eddy-current paths to negligible size.

Hysteresis is that property of a magnetic material by which its magnetization depends not only upon the applied magnetizing force but also upon its previous magnetic state. In a magnetic cycle, while the primary current goes through one complete cycle of alternation, the flux density lags behind the magnetizing force; this represents a power loss which appears in the form of heat. You will recall that the area of the hysteresis loop for a particular iron material is proportional to the loss.

Hysteresis loss is reduced by the proper choice of core material. Silicon iron or 'Stalloy' is generally used for low-frequency transformer cores. Iron losses increase as the frequency is raised, but not equally. Hysteresis loss is proportional to the frequency but eddy current loss is proportional to the square of the frequency. The power wasted in iron losses is all supplied by the magnetising current and consequently this current does not lag by exactly 90° on the applied primary voltage as we previously assumed. When transformers are further examined in later parts of the course, factors such as this have to be taken into account.

There is one other fundamental reason for power loss in a transformer, one that is common to all other components as well. This is loss due to the resistance of the windings, referred to as the *copper*

Thin T and U laminations are packed in alternate directions to build up the transformer core

Figure 5.12

Figure 5.13

loss to distinguish it from the iron losses in the core. Resistance losses may be viewed as internal resistances in much the same way as the internal resistance of a cell or generator is considered; as small series resistances incorporated into the otherwise loss-free windings of the transformer. *Figure 5.13* shows the representation of copper losses. Once these are considered, of course, the voltage actually effective on the primary coil is no longer V_1 as we have so far assumed, but less than V_1 by an amount equal to the voltage drop across the series loss resistance R_1. In the same way, the actual voltage appearing at the secondary terminals is less than V_2 by the amount of voltage drop across the series loss resistance R_2. Clearly, since the power loss is expressed by I^2R, the loss increases with the load or the square of the load current.

We can use our resistance-transformation property of a transformer effectively to transfer the copper losses to one winding only, and this often simplifies problems where the copper losses have to be taken into account. The next example will illustrate this.

Example (7). A transformer has a turns ratio of 1 : 5. The resistance of the primary is 2.5 Ω and of the secondary is 7.5 Ω. Find the equivalent resistance of the primary in terms of the secondary, the secondary in terms of the primary, and the total resistance in terms of the primary.

In this problem the ratio

$$\frac{N_1}{N_2} = \frac{1}{5}$$

From *Figure 5.14(a)*, the equivalent resistance of the primary in terms of the secondary = $2.5 \times 5^2 = 62.5\ \Omega$. The equivalent resistance of the secondary in terms of the primary

$$7.5 \times \left[\frac{1}{5}\right]^2 = 0.3\ \Omega$$

This is illustrated in *Figure 5.14(b)*.
The total resistance in terms of the primary

= primary resistance + transferred secondary resistance
= 2.5 + 0.3 = 2.8 Ω

This is shown in *Figure 5.14(c)*.

(a)

(b)

(c)

Figure 5.14

The above example shows us that we can use our transformation relationships in either direction through the transformer (for what is a step-up ratio in one direction becomes a step-down ratio in the other), and also that all the resistances associated with a transformer windings can be transferred entirely to one side of the transformer. As far as the a.c. conditions are concerned, all three diagrams of *Figure 5.14* are identical.

REGULATION AND EFFICIENCY

In most power transformers, the expenditure of energy due to the iron and copper losses is not very great. The efficiency of a transformer is expressed as a percentage:

$$\frac{\text{output power}}{\text{input power}} \times 100\%$$

The input, however, is equal to the output plus the losses, so the efficiency may be expressed as

$$\frac{\text{output power}}{\text{output power + copper losses + iron losses}} \times 100\%$$

$$\frac{\text{power delivered by secondary}}{\text{total power supplied by the primary}} \times 100\%$$

Iron losses are reasonably constant, but copper losses vary as the square of the currents flowing. It can be proved that the efficiency is greatest when the copper losses are equal to the iron losses. To measure efficiency it is convenient to put the transformer on a pure resistive load and measure the power output by means of an ammeter and voltmeter. The input power may be measured by a wattmeter.

As more current is drawn from the secondary of a transformer, the terminal voltage falls because of the increased copper loss. The difference between the secondary p.d. at no load and the secondary p.d. at full load is expressed as a percentage and is known as the *regulation* of the transformer.

$$\text{Regulation} = \frac{\text{No load voltage} - \text{full load voltage}}{\text{Full load voltage}} \times 100\%$$

Regulations of some 1 to 2% are general in well-designed transformers. This is as far as we need to go into transformer theory for the present.

PROBLEMS FOR SECTION 5

Group 1

(8) A transformer has a step-down ratio of 240/12 V. If there are 1600 turns on the primary winding, how many are there on the secondary?

(9) A transformer is to have a voltage ratio of 440/240 V. If there are 315 turns on the secondary winding, find the number of turns required on the primary.

(10) A transformer delivers a load current of 8.5 A. If the primary to secondary turns ratio is 15:2 what is the value of the primary current?

(11) A transformer has a turns ratio of 5:1. A 240 V supply is made to the primary terminals and a pure resistor of 150 Ω is connected across the secondary. Calculate (a) the secondary voltage, (b) the secondary current, (c) the primary current, (d) the power dissipated in the load.

(12) A 240/6 V transformer supplies a number of 6 V 0.5 W filament lamps connected in parallel. Calculate (a) the greatest number of such lamps that the transformer can supply without being overloaded, (b) the primary current under this condition. The transformer is rated at 100 V.

(13) A transformer with a primary coil of 1750 turns has a 50 Ω non-inductive resistor connected across its secondary terminals. A 24 V supply is connected to the primary and 45 V is developed across this resistor. Calculate (a) the transformation ratio, (b) the current in each winding, (c) the power dissipated in the resistor.

(14) A step-down transformer has a turns ratio of 7.5:2. If a resistance of 2 kΩ is connected to the secondary winding, what effective resistance does the transformer offer at the primary terminals?

(15) A loudspeaker of resistance 16 Ω is to be connected to the output terminals of an amplifier which required a load resistance of 200 Ω. What should be the transformation ratio of the transformer?

(16) The primary winding of a 550/110 V transformer has a resistance of 1.5 Ω and a secondary resistance of 0.075 Ω. Calculate the equivalent resistance of the transformer referred to (a) the primary terminals, (b) the secondary terminals.

(17) A generator of e.m.f. 25 V and internal resistance 1 kΩ is connected directly to a load resistor of 50 Ω. What power is dissipated in the load? A transformer is now used to match the load to the generator. Find the required turns ratio and calculate the power now dissipated in the load.

(18) A transformer has primary and secondary winding resistances of 5 Ω and 8 Ω respectively. What will be the secondary terminal voltage (a) on open-circuit, (b) with a load resistor of 500 Ω, if the primary input is 100 V and the transformer ratio is 1:3?

Group 2

(19) A tape recorder head has an internal resistance of 10 Ω and generates an e.m.f. of 1 mV r.m.s. It is connected via a transformer of turns ratio 1 : N to an amplifier which has an input resistance of 100 Ω. Show that the power delivered to the amplifier is given by

$$P = N \left[+ \frac{10}{N} \right]^{-2} \mu W$$

and find the value of N for which thr transfer of power is a maximum.

(20) An e.m.f. of 2 V r.m.s. at a frequency of 800 Hz is applied to the primary terminals of a step-down transformer of turns ratio 5:1. When the secondary is on open-circuit the primary

current is 1 mA and lags the applied voltage by 90°. What is the primary inductance?

When a load resistor is connected to the secondary terminals the primary current is found to increase to 1.4 mA. What is the value of the load resistor?

(21) A 30 μF capacitor of negligible loss is connected to the secondary terminals of a transformer of turns ratio 3:1. What is the equivalent input capacitance seen at the primary terminals? Careful!

(22) A transformer with turns ratio 1:5 is fed from a 100 V 800 Hz supply having an internal resistance of 10 Ω. A coil having a resistance of 100 Ω and an inductance of 70 mH is connected across the secondary terminals. What power is dissipated in the coil?

6 Three-phase circuits

Aims: At the end of this Unit section you should be able to:

Understand the basic principles of the generation of single-phase and three-phase supplies.

Distinguish between delta and star methods of connection for power distribution systems.

Obtain current and voltage relationships for star and delta connections under balanced conditions of load.

Calculate power dissipation in three-phase loads.

Measure power in balanced and unbalanced three-phase loads.

In the previous three Unit sections we have dealt only with single-phase alternating circuits, that is, the source of supply has been a single a.c. generator. It is possible to generate such a single-phase supply by rotating a coil between the poles of a magnet.

In an earlier part of the course you will have learned that when a conductor cuts magnetic flux, an e.m.f. is induced in the conductor. This induced e.m.f. is given by the expression

$$e = B\ell v \quad \text{volts}$$

where B is the field flux density in tesla (T), ℓ is the length of the conductor in metres (m), actively cutting flux, and v is the velocity of the conductor perpendicular to the field flux in metres per second, (m/s).

If the conductor is arranged in the form of a coil (see *Figure 6.1(a)*) mounted on a shaft in such a way that the coil can be rotated between

(a)

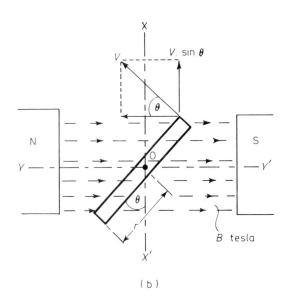

(b)

Figure 6.1

the poles of a permanent or electro-magnet (the *field magnet*), the cutting of flux can be continuous and an e.m.f. will be induced in the side conductors of the coil for as long as the rotation goes on. So that connection to an external circuit can be established, the ends of the coil terminate on brass or copper **slip-rings which rotate with the shaft** but are electrically insulated from it. Two spring-loaded carbon brushes bear against the slip-rings so making continuous connection of the coil (or *rotor*) to the external circuit.

Figure 6.1(b) shows the end view of the coil when the plane of the coil makes an angle θ with a reference axis XOX′ which is in a plane perpendicular to the field. If the coil rotates at N rev/s and the coil radius is r metres, then each side conductor moves a distance $2\pi rN$ m/s and the velocity of the conductors is given by $v = 2\pi rN$ m/s.

For this simple generator we have assumed that the flux density between the pole pieces is uniform, hence the component of velocity perpendicular to the flux is $v.\sin\theta$ as the diagram shows. The e.m.f. generated in each side conductor at any instant is then $B\ell v.\sin\theta$ volts, and the total e.m.f. generated in the coil is twice this:

$$e = 2B\ell v \sin\theta$$

$$= 2B\ell\, 2\pi rN \sin\theta \text{ volts}$$

But $2\pi N$ is the number of radians turned through per second and so equals the angular velocity of the conductors ω radians/s. Hence the instantaneous generated e.m.f.

$$e = 2B\ell\omega r \sin\theta \text{ volts} \qquad (6.1)$$

The peak value of this e.m.f. is $2B\ell\omega r$ volts since the maximum value of $\sin\theta$ is 1, and this will occur when $\theta = 90°$, that is, when the plane of the coil passes through the reference axis YOY′ for it is then instantaneously cutting the flux at right angles. When the plane of the coil passes through the axis XOX′, $\theta = 0$ and the induced e.m.f. is instantaneously zero. For each complete revolution of the coil, therefore, there are two positions giving a peak output and two positions giving a zero output.

The equation for the e.m.f. given in (6.1) above can now be written as

$$e = \hat{E} \sin\theta = \hat{E} \sin\omega t$$

which is the equation of a sinusoidal wave.

POLYPHASE GENERATORS Although the single-phase a.c. generator sketched in *Figure 6.1(a)* is theoretically sound, a number of practical limitations prevent its use. It is much better, for example, to have the field rotate while the coil remains stationary. By this means there is no problem in bringing the generated e.m.f. and the current associated with it out to an external circuit by way of slip-rings or any other kind of sliding contacts. This is particularly important where heavy currents and high voltages are concerned, and if more than a single coil is involved.

Suppose that instead of a single coil, two identical coils are mounted mutually at right angles to each other and rotated in a magnetic field,

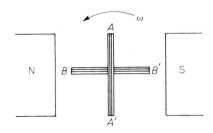

Figure 6.2

see *Figure 6.2*. The e.m.f.'s generated in each of these coils will be sinusoidal in form and will be of the same frequency and peak magnitudes but will differ in phase from each other by 90°. Hence if

$$e_1 = E \sin \omega t$$

then
$$e_2 = E \sin \left(\omega t + \frac{\pi}{2}\right)$$

The phasor diagram and the graphs of the two e.m.f.'s are shown in *Figure 6.3*. This arrangement gives the basic form of a two-phase a.c. generator and the supply is known as *two-phase*.

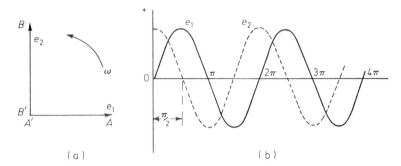

(a)   (b)

Figure 6.3

Suppose now that three identical coils, fixed 120° apart, are rotated in the magnetic field of the generator. The e.m.f.'s generated will again be sinusoidal in form and have the same frequency and peak amplitudes, but will differ in phase from each other by 120°. This time we have a *three-phase* supply. Hence, if

$$e_1 = E \sin \omega t$$

then
$$e_2 = E \sin \left(\omega t - \frac{2\pi}{3}\right)$$

and
$$e_3 = E \sin \left(\omega t - \frac{4\pi}{3}\right)$$

and the phasor diagram and the graphs of the three e.m.f.'s will now be as shown in *Figure 6.4*, (*b*) and (*c*).

(a)

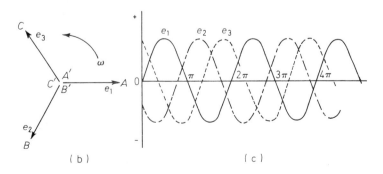

(b)   (c)

Figure 6.4

In the same way it is possible to generate four, six or twelve-phase alternating systems. Such systems are known collectively as *polyphase* systems. Three-phase is the system most commonly used for the generation and transmission of electric power and this will be the concern of the present Unit section.

As we are going to be involved with three voltages, it will be necessary for us to be able to distinguish one from the others at any particular instant of time. The sequence in which the e.m.f.'s are generated depends upon the direction of rotation of the coils. In *Figure 6.4*, the voltage in coil A (e_1) is instantaneously zero but about to begin its cycle. The other two voltages, e_2 and e_3, are part way through a cycle and are instantaneously of negative and positive polarity respectively. This sequence is evident from the phasor diagram where for an anticlockwise rotation the phasors would pass a fixed point in the order e_1 $- e_2 - e_3 - e_1 - e_2$ ..... This can also be seen from the graphical plot where the maximum values occur in the same order. If the coils were rotated in the opposite direction, the sequence would become $e_3 - e_2 - e_1 - e_3$ ....

In order to ensure that the three-phase e.m.f.'s are in their proper positions relative to each other it is necessary to mark the corresponding ends of the coils so that the same direction or sense of voltages is obtained in each winding.

This has been done in the diagrams of *Figure 6.4(a)* and (*b*) where A, B and C represent the start terminals of the coils and A′, B′ and C′ denote the respective finishes. The generated e.m.f.'s will then be correctly displaced by $120°$ when the three starts (or the three finishes) are displaced by $120°$. In practical systems, the phases are distinguished by colour coding the wires conventionally as RED, YELLOW and BLUE phases. The three voltages are known as the phase e.m.f.'s and the order in which they attain their peak amplitudes is the *phase sequence.*

CONNECTION OF PHASES

Figure 6.5

Fundamentally each of the three outputs from a three-phase generator or *alternator* may be independently connected to its own particular load and three completely separate circuits are then obtained. As *Figure 6.5* shows, this arrangement required six wires (or lines) between alternator and loads. If the loads are completely identical, the system is said to be balanced and the e.m.f.'s currents and phase angles will be equal for each output. However, a considerable saving is possible if the phases are interconnected in such a way that six lines are unnecessary.

Referring to *Figure 6.4(b)* it is not difficult to see that the resultant of the three voltage phasors there shown is zero, since the resultant of any two of them will be equal and opposite to the third. Now these phasors may represent currents as well as voltages, hence we may say that the instantaneous sum of the e.m.f.'s or currents in a balanced three-phase system is always zero:

$$e_1 + e_2 + e_3 = 0 \qquad i_1 + i_2 + i_3 = 0$$

It is this property which allows interconnection between the three outputs from the alternator so that only three or four lines are needed.

The two methods of interconnection are known as (a) star or Y, (b) delta or mesh.

STAR CONNECTION By connecting together the starts (or the finishes) of the windings on the alternator as a common point, a star-connected circuit is obtained. This is shown in *Figure 6.6*. The common point of the three windings is called the *neutral* or *star point*, and the line joining the common point of the star-connected loads to this point is the neutral line.

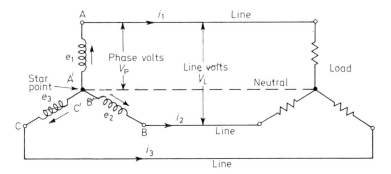

Figure 6.6

Let e_1, e_2 and e_3 be the phase voltages and let i_1, i_2 and i_3 be the respective phase currents. The voltage between any pair of lines is equal to the phasor *difference* between two of the phase voltages. Let the phase voltages be represented by the 120° spaced phasors V_p shown in *Figure 6.7*. Then the line voltages are represented by the sides of the equilateral triangle and the neutral point is at the centre of the triangle. The line-to-neutral voltage has a horizontal projection, V_p. cos 30° or $V_p\sqrt{3}/2$ volts. Since the base length is the sum of two such projections it follows that

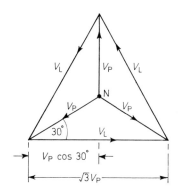

Figure 6.7

$$V_L = 2\ V_p\left[\frac{\sqrt{3}}{2}\right] = \sqrt{3}V_p$$

So the line voltages are equal to $\sqrt{3}$ times the phase voltage. Also, the line current equals the phase current.

We notice the following important points from the phasor diagram of *Figure 6.7*:
 (a) the line voltages are 120° apart,
 (b) the line voltages are 30° ahead of the phase voltages,
 (c) the angle between the line currents and the corresponding line voltages is (30° ± θ), lagging for +θ, leading for −θ.

Example (1). What is the line voltage on a system where the phase voltage is 240 V?

$$V_L = \sqrt{3}.V_p$$

$$= 1.732 \times 240 = 415\ \text{V}.$$

It may have occurred to you that the neutral line is un-necessary if the loads are exactly balanced. For since the line current is equal to the phase current, the three currents meeting at the star-point of the load add together to give the resultant current in the neutral; but for equal currents spaced 120° apart the resultant is zero. Hence there is no neutral current and the neutral line can be removed without in any way upsetting the circuit conditions.

In a real life situation it is not possible that the loads on the system, made up as they are of domestic and industrial demands can be balanced, hence the four-wire system is necessary for the distribution of a.c. supplies. Domestic requirements, heating, cooking and lighting can then be supplied at single phase voltage (usually 240 V) line to neutral, while workshops and industrial plant are supplied at line voltage, $\sqrt{3} \times 240 = 415$ V. This leads to a more efficient use of equipment such as motors and transformers which, by being designed for three-phase operation, constitute balanced loads and give improved performances at higher voltage.

DELTA CONNECTION Connection of coil terminations A to B′, B to C′ and C to A′ results in the alternative form of three-phase connection shown in *Figure 6.8*. This is the delta or mesh connection. Here again the load is assumed to be balanced and this time there is no neutral point or neutral line. The voltage between any pair of lines V_L is this time equal to the voltage across a phase of the alternator, V_p. Hence $V_L = V_p$.

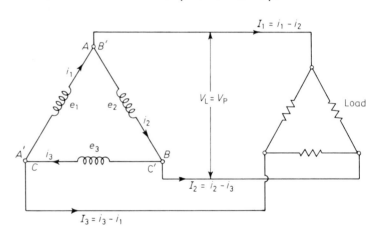

Figure 6.8

The line currents are each made up of two components, one flowing to the load and one flowing from the load. So, for a situation that is very similar to that for line voltages in star connection, the line current equals the phasor difference between two of the phase currents. Then since

$$I_1 = I_2 = I_3 = I_L, \text{ the line current}$$

$$I_1 = i_1 - i_2 = 2I_p \cos 30°$$

$$I_1 = 2 \left[I_p \frac{\sqrt{3}}{2} \right] = \sqrt{3}.I_p$$

and similarly for I_2 and I_3.

So line currents are each equal to $\sqrt{3}$ times the phase current. As for the star connection, you should make a note of the following points:
  (a)   The line currents are $120°$ apart.
  (b)   The line currents are $30°$ lagging on the phase currents.
  (c)   The angle between line current and the corresponding line voltage is $(30° \pm \theta)$.

(2) Sketch a phasor diagram showing line and phase currents for the delta circuit of *Figure 6.8*.

Example (3).   Three non-inductive resistors, each of 100 Ω, are connected (a) in star, (b) in delta to a 440 V three-phase supply. Calculate in each case (i) the phase voltage and phase current, (ii) the line current.

It is necessary in three-phase problems to start with one phase. The 440 V given in the question is the *line* voltage. This is always implied unless the contrary is expressly stated. So V_L = 440 V

For star connection: $V_p = \dfrac{440}{\sqrt{3}} = 254$ V

Since the load resistance is 100 Ω, phase current $= \dfrac{254}{100} = $ 2.54 A

But for star connection $I_L = I_p$

$\therefore$ $I_L = 2.54$ A

For delta connection: $V_p = V_L = 440$ V

For a 100 Ω load $I_p = \dfrac{440}{100} = 4.4$ A

But for delta connection $I_L = \sqrt{3} I_p$

$\therefore$ $I_L = 7.62$ A

(4)   Each phase of a three-phase alternator develops an e.m.f. of 250 V. Find the line voltage for (a) star connection, (b) delta connection. If one of the alternator coils was reversed, what would be the line voltage in star connection?

POWER IN A BALANCED SYSTEM

We consider now the problem of power calculations in balanced star and delta load systems, and to make this a general study we let the load elements be impedances (Z_1, Z_2 and Z_3). Since these impedances are equal in balanced loads, they will carry equal currents, hence the phase power will be one-third of the total power.

The star-connected impedances of *Figure 6.9(a)* carry the *line* currents and the voltage across each is the *phase* voltage. For a phase angle θ between voltage and current in the impedance, the phase power will be

$$P_p = V_p I_L \cos \theta$$

and the total power will be three times this:

$$P_T = 3V_p I_L \cos \theta \tag{6.4}$$

but $\qquad V_L = \sqrt{3}.V_p$

$\therefore \qquad P_T = \sqrt{3}\ V_L\ I_L \cos \theta \tag{6.5}$

        (a)   (b)

Figure 6.9

Turning to the delta-connected load of *Figure 6.9(b)*, the voltage across each impedance is the *line* voltage and the current in each is the *phase* current. Again for a phase angle θ we get

$$P_p = V_L\ I_p \cos \theta$$

and total power $\quad P_T = 3V_L\ I_p \cos \theta \tag{6.6}$

but $\qquad I_L = \sqrt{3}\ I_p$

$\therefore \qquad P_T = \sqrt{3}\ V_L I_L \cos \theta \tag{6.7}$

Since equations (6.5) and (6.7) are identical, the total power in any balanced three-phase load is given by $\sqrt{3}\ V_L I_L \cos \phi$.

For purely resistive loads, $\phi = 0$ and $\cos \phi = 1$, hence $P_T = \sqrt{3}\ V_L I_L$

Example (5).   A balanced three-phase load is connected to a 440 V three-wire system. The input line current is 40 A and the total power input is 15 kW. Calculate the load power factor.

The power factor is, of course, $\cos \phi$

Since $\qquad\qquad P_T = \sqrt{3}\ V_L I_L \cos \phi$

$$15 \times 10^3 = \sqrt{3} \times 440 \times 40 \times \cos \phi$$

$$\therefore \qquad \cos \phi = \frac{15 \times 10^3}{3 \times 440 \times 40}$$

$$= 0.492$$

Example (6). A 415 V three-phase system supplies a balanced load, each arm of which has an impedance of 50 Ω and a phase angle of 36°. Find the line current for star and delta connection, and the total power dissipated.

Working on one phase, in star connection $V = 415$ V

$$V_p = \frac{415}{\sqrt{3}} = 240 \text{ V.}$$

For a load impedance of 50 Ω

$$I_p = \frac{240}{50} = 4.8 \text{ A}$$

but for star connection $I_L = I_p$

$$\therefore \qquad\qquad\qquad I_L = 4.8 \text{ A}$$

For $\phi = 36°$, $\cos \phi = \cos 36° = 0.809$

$$\therefore P_T = \sqrt{3} \, V_L I_L \cos \phi = \sqrt{3} \times 415 \times 4.8 \times 0.809$$

$$= 2790 \text{ W}$$

For delta connection $V_p = V_L = 415$ V

$$I_p = \frac{415}{50} = 8.3 \text{ A}$$

but $I_L = \sqrt{3} I_p$ $\quad\therefore\quad$ $I_L = 14.38$ A

$$P_T = \sqrt{3} \, V_L I_L \cos \phi = \sqrt{3} \times 415 \times 14.38 \times 0.809$$

$$= 8370 \text{ W}$$

This example shows that although the expressions for total power are the same for both star and delta loads, the loads in delta take three times the power of the same loads in star.

(7) Power expressions (6.5) and (6.7) give the *true* power dissipated in the load. Write down the expressions representing (a) the apparent power, (b) the reactive power in the load, stating the appropriate units for these expressions.

MEASUREMENT OF POWER

True power is measured by a wattmeter. A wattmeter is an instrument with a moving voltage (or pressure) coil and a fixed current coil so arranged in relation to each other that the deflection obtained on the

Current coil

Voltage coil

Figure 6.10

i_1

e_1

W_1

e_3 e_2

i_2

W_2

i_3

Figure 6.11

e_1

W_1

Neutral

e_3 e_2

W_2

W_3

Figure 6.12

PROBLEMS FOR SECTION 6

scale of the instrument is proportional to $VI. \cos\phi$. In use, the watt-meter is wired into circuit so that the circuit current passes through the current coil and the circuit voltage is impressed across the voltage coil. *Figure 6.10* shows the general arrangement.

Power in three-phase circuits can be measured by using either two or three wattmeters, depending upon whether the system is three of four-line. The two wattmeter method is illustrated in *Figure 6.11*, the current coils of the meters being placed in series with any two of the three available lines. For a star-connected load

$$\text{Voltage across } W_1 = e_1 - e_3$$

$$\text{Voltage across } W_2 = e_2 - e_3$$

$$\text{Total power} = e_1 i_1 + e_2 i_2 + e_3 i_3$$

Since current i_3 is not passing through a meter, we can eliminate it from these equations. In any balanced system

$$i_1 + i_2 + i_3 = 0$$

$$i_3 = -i_1 - i_2$$

$$\text{Substituting, total power} = e_1 i_1 + e_2 i_2 + e_3(-i_1 - i_2)$$

$$= i_1(e_1 - e_3) + i_2(e_2 - e_3)$$

$$= i_1 \text{ (voltage across } W_1) + i_2 \text{ (voltage across } W_2)$$

But each of these terms represents the wattmeter power readings, hence

$$W = W_1 \text{ reading} + W_2 \text{ reading}$$

This result is equally true for a delta-connected load.

A four-wire star-connected load using three wattmeters is shown in *Figure 6.12*. One meter is placed in each of the lines. Each of these meters will indicate the respective phase power and by a simple analysis similar to that above, the total power is given by

$$W = W_1 \text{ reading} + W_2 \text{ reading} + W_3 \text{ reading.}$$

It is important to note that the readings obtained are *not* necessarily identical. For the two-wattmeter method and a balanced load W_1 reading is always greater than W_2 reading unless the power factor is unity when the readings will be equal.

(8)   A conductor of effective length 25 cm moves with a velocity of 50 cm/s at right-angles to a field of flux density 0.75 T. Find the e.m.f. generated in the conductor.

(9)   An e.m.f. of 1.5 V is induced in a conductor which moves with a velocity of 3 m/s at right angles to a field of flux density 0.5 T. What is the effective length of the conductor?

(10)   A conductor of length 0.25 m moves at a velocity of 250 cm/s in a field of flux density 0.4 T. It the path of the conductor makes an angle of 35° to the direction of the flux, what is the induced e.m.f.?

(11)   A rectangular coil of length 40 cm and breadth 20 cm and containing 1000 turns of wire rotates in a uniform field of

flux density 15 mT about an axis in the plane of the coil joining the middle points of the two short sides. If the coil rotates at a uniform rate of 10 revs/s, show that the generated e.m.f. can be expressed as $e = 24 \pi \sin \theta$ volts.

(12) What is the line voltage on a three-phase supply where the phase voltage is 120 V?

(13) Three non-inductive resistors, each of 100 Ω are connected (a) in star, (b) in delta, to a 500 V three-phase supply. Calculate in each case (i) the phase voltages and phase currents, (ii) the line currents.

(14) In the previous example, calculate the total power dissipated in the load for each connection.

(15) In a three-phase system a balanced load draws a line current of 20 A at a line voltage of 500 V. What is the apparent power supplied to the load. If the true power was 15 kW, what is the power factor of the load?

(16) A three-phase balanced load dissipates 25 kW at a power factor of 0.8 leading. If the line voltage is 440 V, calculate the line current.

(17) A balanced three-phase load dissipates 24 kW at a power factor of 0.928. If the current carried by each line of a three wire supply cable is 36 A, what is the line voltage at the load?

(18) Three coils of resistance 40 Ω and inductance 95.5 mH are connected (a) in star, (b) in delta, to a 400 V, 50 Hz three-phase supply. Calculate for each case the line current and the total power absorbed.

(19) Three capacitors, each of 300 μF, are connected in star to a 500 V 50 Hz three-phase supply. Calculate the line current.

(20) Three equal resistors form a load in star connection fed from a three-phase supply. Prove that the power is reduced by one-half if any one of the resistors is disconnected.

(21) A three-phase alternator has a rating of 25 kVA at 480 V. Find the full load currents for both star and delta connection.

7 Electrical machines

Aims: At the end of this Unit section you should be able to:
Describe the construction of a d.c. machine and explain the action of commutation.
Distinguish between shunt- and series-wound machines.
Sketch and explain the machine characteristics for d.c. motors and generators.
State the e.m.f. and torque equations.
Explain the need for a d.c. motor starter.
Understand the principles of motor speed control.
Define and calculate the efficiency of a machine.
Explain the principle of the stepping motor.

Electric motors and generators are, in general terms, rotating machines in which conversion takes place between mechanical and electrical forms of energy. If electrical energy is supplied to a machine and mechanical energy is taken from it, the machine is a *motor*. If the interchange of energy is in the opposite direction, the machine is a *generator*.

We have already encountered the simple a.c. generator (alternator) in the previous Unit Section as well as in the work of the previous year. We shall be mainly concerned in this section with the characteristics of d.c. machines, though a particular kind of a.c. motor is included in the syllabus and will be dealt with at the appropriate time. Motors and generators will operate from, or produce, either alternating or direct current supplies, depending upon their design.

THE D.C. GENERATOR   The simple alternator described in the previous Unit Section becomes a d.c. generator by the replacement of the slip-rings by a split ring automatic switch or *commutator*. The constructional form of a d.c. generator is in almost every case that of a fixed field magnet (or magnets) with the e.m.f. induced in rotating conductors. A unidirectional output can then be obtained if the rotor winding is switched over at the correct times to reverse one or other of the alternate half-cycles then being generated.

The ends of the rotating coil are connected therefore one to each half of the split ring commutator as shown in *Figure 7.1(a)*, and the e.m.f. is collected from two carbon brushes so positioned that the contacts change from one half of the ring to the other at the instant the e.m.f. is about to change is polarity, that is, when the coil is vertical (as drawn) and the instantaneous e.m.f. is zero. The voltage across the brushes consequently pulsates as it follows each half-cycle of induced e.m.f. but never *reverses* its direction as it did for the slip-ring alternator. You will recognise that the output waveform is now of a rectified a.c. type, being made up of a mean d.c. component on which is superimposed an alternating ripple, see *Figure 7.1(b)*.

No practical d.c. generator is made up of a single rotating coil and

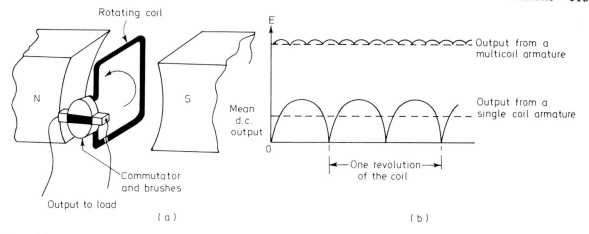

Figure 7.1

a simple split-ring commutator. To obtain a smooth output voltage it is necessary to reduce the amplitude of the alternating ripple component, and this can be done by increasing the number of segments on the commutator along with the numer of coils on the rotor. The output is then taken from each coil not over at 180° rotation period but over only a small angle where the coil position is such that the instantaneous induced e.m.f. is at its maximum. The upper line in the graph of *Figure 7.1(b)* shows the form of the d.c. output from a multi-segment commutator machine.

A practical d.c. generator also has more than a single pair of field poles. Such poles are arranged N, S, N, S alternately around the stator, each pole piece carrying a field coil for magnetic excitation and a shaped extension to distribute the flux evenly around the surface of the rotor. *Figure 7.2* shows the general constructional details of a medium sized, four pole d.c. generator. The stator consists of a yoke, usually of cast steel, to which are bolted the four field magnets. The field windings are wound around the field pole pieces and are con-

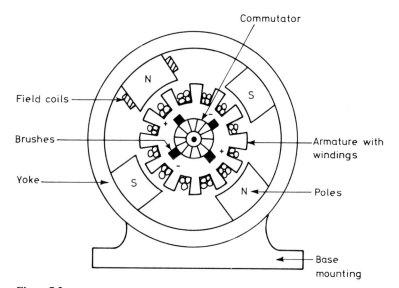

Figure 7.2

nected in series in such a direction that adjacent poles exhibit opposite polarities as mentioned above.

The rotating coils are wound in slots cut lengthwise along the outer
surface of a laminated iron cylinder called the *armature*, and are term-
inated on to commutator segments at one end of the armature. Each
segment is insulated from its neighbour by a strip of mica, the whole
assembly forming a cylinder concentric with the armature and the
central shaft. The brushes which bear on the commutator are usually
of graphitic carbon which has a high resistance to keep sparking to a
minimum, keeps the commutator relatively clean, and by being comparatively soft does not wear or groove the commutator but adapts
readily to its shape. *Figure 7.3* shows the general design and you will
be able to examine a generator or motor armature in the course of
your practical work. The number of slots and commutator segments
are always equal, but the number of brushes is determined by the
electrical characteristics required of the machine. It is always an even
number and brushes of the same polarity are connected in parallel.

Figure 7.3

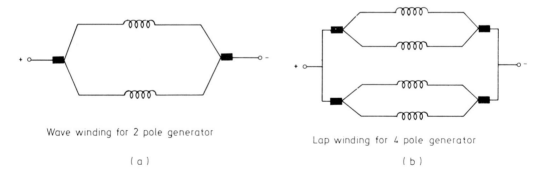

Wave winding for 2 pole generator

(a)

Lap winding for 4 pole generator

(b)

Figure 7.4

There are two ways of winding the conductors on an armature and
these govern the magnitude of the generated e.m.f. However the armature is wound there is always a number of conductors in series between
the brushes, each conductor generating its own e.m.f. in the same
direction. The e.m.f. between the brushes at any instant is the sum of
the instantaneous e.m.f.'s in these conductors just as the e.m.f. of a
number of cells in series is the sum of their individual e.m.f.'s. There
will also be a number of such series systems of conductors in parallel

between the brushes. Each series system produces the same e.m.f. and is unaffected by the number of parallel paths; but as in a series-parallel arrangement of cells, the internal resistance of the armature winding is decreased and its current-carrying capacity is increased, by increasing the number of such parallel paths.

The winding methods are known as (a) wave or two-circuit winding, and (b) lap or multiple-circuit winding. In wave winding, see *Figure 7.4(a)*, there are *two paths in parallel* irrespective of the number of poles, each path supplying half the total current output. Two sets of brushes only are necessary, though it is usual to fit as many sets of brushes as the machine has poles. Wave wound generators produce high-voltage, low-current outputs.

In lap winding there are as many paths in parallel as the machine has poles. The total current output divides equally between them and there are as many sets of brushes as the machine has poles. Lap wound generators produce high-current, low voltage outputs. *Figure 7.4(b)* shows the arrangement of a lap winding.

THE GENERATOR EQUATION

Let Z = the total number of conductors on the armature, Φ Wb be the flux per pole, p the number of pole *pairs* and N the armature speed in revolutions per minute (r.p.m.). Then the e.m.f. generated by the armature is equal to the e.m.f. generated by *one* of the parallel paths. Each conductor passes $2p$ poles per revolution and so cuts $2p\Phi$ Wb of magnetic flux per revolution. Hence the flux cut by each conductor per second is

$$2p\Phi \times \frac{N}{60} \text{ Wb}$$

and so the generated e.m.f. per conductor is

$$E = \frac{2p\Phi N}{60} \text{ volts}$$

For Z conductors and a parallel paths, the effective number of conductors generating an e.m.f. is Z/a and the e.m.f. equation becomes

$$E = \frac{2p\Phi N}{60} \times \frac{Z}{a} = \frac{2p}{a} \frac{\Phi ZN}{60} \text{ volts}$$

But angular velocity $\omega = 2\pi N/60$ rad/s, hence

$$E = \frac{pZ}{\pi a} \Phi\omega \text{ volts} \tag{7.1}$$

This equation is known as the *generator e.m.f.* equation.

For a wave-wound armature the number of conductors in series per path is $Z/2$ and so

$$E = \frac{Z}{2} \frac{2p\Phi N}{60} = \frac{p\Phi ZN}{60} \text{ volts}$$

Again, substituting for angular velocity ω, this becomes

$$E = \frac{pZ}{2\pi} \Phi\omega \text{ volts} \tag{7.2}$$

For a lap-wound armature the number of conductors in series per path is $Z/2p$ and this time

$$E = \frac{Z}{2p} \cdot \frac{2p\Phi N}{60} = \frac{\Phi ZN}{60} \text{ volts}$$

$$= \frac{Z}{2\pi} \Phi\omega \text{ volts} \qquad (7.3)$$

Notice that the general generator e.m.f. equation (7.1) converts to (7.2) and (7.3) directly since for wave-winding there are just two parallel paths, hence $a = 2$, and for lap-winding there are as many parallel paths as there are poles, hence $a = 2p$.

Examples can be worked either in terms of angular velocity ω rad/s or in terms of revolutions per minute (or per second). Keep in mind that $\omega = 2\pi N/60$ rad/s where N is the speed in r.p.m.

Now follow the next two worked examples through carefully.

Example (1).　A 4-pole wave-wound machine has an armature wound with 520 conductors which rotates at an angular velocity of 105 rad/s. If the flux per pole is 15 mWb, what is the generated e.m.f.?

For 4 poles, $p = 2$; for wave-winding, $a = 2$; $Z = 520$ and $\omega = 105$. Then from equation (7.2)

$$E = \frac{pZ}{2\pi} \Phi\omega = \frac{2 \times 520 \times 15 \times 10^{-3} \times 105}{2 \times \pi}$$

$$= 260 \text{ V}$$

Example (2).　A 4-pole lap-wound armature has 320 conductors and is driven at 900 r.p.m. to generate an e.m.f. of 240 V. What is the flux per pole of the machine? What is the angular velocity of the armature?

For a lap-wound machine $E = \dfrac{\Phi ZN}{60}$ volts

Transposing $\Phi = \dfrac{60E}{ZN} = \dfrac{60 \times 240}{320 \times 900} = 0.05$ Wb

Angular velocity $= \dfrac{2\pi N}{60} = \dfrac{2\pi \times 900}{60} = 94$ rad/s.

This example could of course have been worked by first finding ω and then using the formula of (7.3). You should try this as a verification of the solution given above.

GENERATOR CHARACTERISTICS

When the characteristics is no load across the armature terminals the generator is said to be on open-circuit. The e.m.f. (E) generated in the armature conductors will be present at the output terminals as the open-circuit voltage. The open-circuit characteristic (O.C.C.) of a generator is a graph showing the relationship between the generated e.m.f. and the field current at a given speed. This graph can be plotted by set-

Separate
d.c.
supply

I_F

E

V

Field   Armature

Figure 7.5

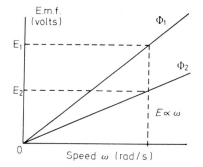

E.m.f.
(volts)

Φ_1

E_1

Φ_2

E_2

$E \propto \omega$

0

Speed ω (rad/s)

Figure 7.6

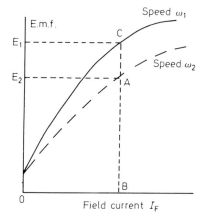

E.m.f.

Speed ω_1

E_1

C

Speed ω_2

E_2

A

B

0

Field current I_F

Figure 7.7

ting up the machine as shown in *Figure 7.5*, the field coils being ener-gised from a separate and adjustable supply.

From the generator equation (7.1) above

$$E = \frac{pZ}{\pi a}\,\Phi\omega$$

and since $pZ/\pi a$ is constant for a given machine, $E \propto \Phi\omega$. This is the e.m.f. expressed in terms of the variables Φ and ω.

The flux per pole Φ is controlled by the field current I_F and when the field current and flux are constant, $E \propto \omega$. Hence a plot of e.m.f. E against angular velocity ω is a straight line passing through the origin, as shown in *Figure 7.6*. If the field current is reduced from, say, I_1 and I_2 another *straight line* characteristic is obtained with a reduced slope and hence smaller values of E at each speed setting.

Now with the speed constant, suppose the e.m.f. to be varied by adjustment of the field current and hence pole flux Φ. Then $E \propto \Phi$ and since $\Phi = BA$ and the pole area A is constant, $E \propto B$. But the flux density B is produced by a magnetizing force H At/m due to the field current I_F, hence $E \propto I_F$ provided that the magnetic circuit does not saturate.

A graph of e.m.f. E plotted against I_F is seen to be similar to the B–H curve for the magnetic circuit of the machine. This open-circuit characteristic is sketched in *Figure 7.7*. You will notice that a small e.m.f. is generated at zero field current. There is always some residual flux in the magnetic circuit due to previous magnetisations and when the generator is driven at speed the armature windings cut this flux and generate a small e.m.f.

(3)   Why do the characteristics flatten out at high values of I_F?

If the generator armature velocity is reduced from ω_1 to ω_2 a similar magnetisation curve is obtained with reduced values of e.m.f. at each setting of field current. Since $E \propto \omega$ when Φ is constant

$$\frac{E_2}{E_1} = \frac{\omega_2}{\omega_1}$$

hence, as shown in the diagram

$$\frac{AB}{BC} = \frac{\omega_2}{\omega_1}$$

$$\therefore \quad AB = BC \times \frac{\omega_2}{\omega_1}$$

and the O.C.C. at any other speed may be drawn in relation to the O.C.C. at speed.

THE GENERATOR ON LOAD   When a load is connected across the armature terminals, a load current I_L A will flow and the terminal voltage will fall from its open-circuit value E to some lower value, due to the voltage drop which now occurs in the armature winding resistance.

If the armature resistance is R_A the voltage drop across it will be $I_A R_A$ (since $I_A = I_L$) and this is subtracted from the generated e.m.f. Hence the terminal voltage V is given by

$$V = E - I_A R_A \tag{7.4}$$

Example (4).   Calculate the terminal voltage of a generator which develops an e.m.f. of 100 V and has an armature current of 20 A on load. The armature resistance is 0.28 Ω.

$$V = E - I_A R_A$$
$$= 100 - (20 \times 0.28)$$
$$= 100 - 5.6 = 94.4 \text{ V}$$

Example (5).   A generator has an armature resistance of 0.8 Ω and when connected to a load of 50 Ω passes a current of 5 A. What is the terminal voltage and the generated e.m.f.? A current of 5 A in a 50 Ω load represents a p.d. of 5 × 50 = 250 V. This is the terminal voltage of the machine. Transposing equation (7.4) to make E the subject, we get

$$E = V + I_A R_A$$
$$= 250 + (5 \times 0.8)$$
$$= 254 \text{ V}$$

TYPES OF GENERATOR

The d.c. generator we have discussed above is a *separately-excited* machine having field magnets whose windings are energised from an external and entirely separate d.c. supply. The provision of such a separate supply is obviously a disadvantage and such machines are used only in special applications. There is no reason why the field magnets should not be energised from the generator output itself, and machines in which this takes place are known as *self-excited* generators. Such generators may take one of three types:

(a) Shunt-wound generators in which the field windings are connected in *parallel* with the armature output;

(b) Series-wound generators in which the field windings are connected in *series* with the armature output;

(c) Compound-wound generators which have a mixture of shunt and series windings designed to combine the advantages of each.

The shunt generator

This type of machine is shown in *Figure 7.8*. Because of the residual flux mentioned earlier, a small current flows in the parallel field windings as soon as the machine is started up. This small current increases the pole flux and there follows a rapid build up in both the field and the generated e.m.f. It is advantageous to keep the shunt current (I_F) as small as possible, getting the ampere-turns for the required flux from a large number of turns. Hence the field windings have a relatively high resistance in these machines, being wound with many turns of relatively fine wire.

Now the voltage across the field coils for different values of field current is given by the straight line graph connecting V and I_F for the particular value of winding resistance R_F. Let this *field resistance line*

Figure 7.8

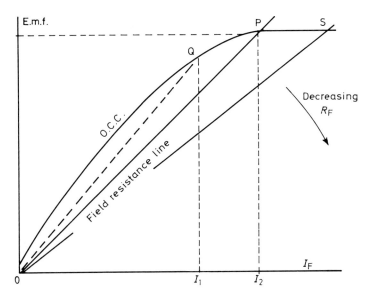

Figure 7.9

as it is called, cut the O.C.C. at a point *P*, see *Figure 7.9*. Then the open-circuit e.m.f. of the generator will build up to this value indicated by the intersection of the magnetising curve and the field resistance line at *P*, and at this point (neglecting the armature resistance) the voltage required across the field is equal to the armature e.m.f. Conditions are then stable.

You will have noticed that a series *regulator* resistance *R* is shown in series with the field windings. If this resistance is increased, the effective value of R_F increases, hence the slope of the field line becomes steeper, point *P* moves down the curve to *Q* and the generated e.m.f. becomes *less*. If the resistance is decreased, R_F decreases, the slope of the field line becomes less and point *P* moves further up the curve to *S*, so *increasing* the generated e.m.f. subject to the saturation conditions of the magnetic circuit materials.

Example (6). A shunt generator supplies a load of 10 kW at 250 V through cables of resistance 0.1 Ω. If the resistance of the armature is 0.03 Ω and of the field coils 75 Ω, calculate the terminal voltage and the generated e.m.f.

$$\text{The current in the load} = \frac{\text{power}}{\text{voltage}} = \frac{10000}{250}$$

$$\therefore \qquad I_L = 40 \text{ A}$$

Volts drop in the cables = 40 × 0.1 = 4 V

Hence the terminal voltage = 250 + 4 = 254 V.

$$\text{The field current } I_F = \frac{254}{75} = 3.387 \text{ A}$$

∴   armature current $I_A = I_F + I_L = 3.387 + 40$

$= 43.387$ A

Volts drop in the armature $= 43.387 \times 0.03 = 1.3$ V

∴   generated e.m.f. $= 254 + 1.3 = 255.3$ V

(7) *Figure 7.10* shows the O.C.C. for a certain shunt generator. Sketch lightly in pencil two field resistance lines for values
of 150 Ω and 200 Ω. What is the open-circuit e.m.f. of this generator for each of these values of field resistance?

(8) In *Figure 7.10* the dotted line represents the field resistance line for 300 Ω. Check that this is so and deduce what would
be the result of running the machine up in this situation.

(9)   A shunt generator has an armature resistance of 0.3 Ω
and a field resistance of 150 Ω. What is the generated e.m.f. if the
machine supplies a load with 10 A at a terminal p.d. 200 V?

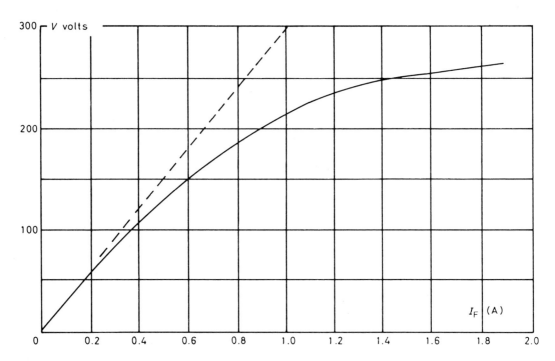

Figure 7.10

It is important when solving problems of this sort not to try and
remember formulae. You require only applications of Ohm's law.
    The load characteristic of a shunt generator is the plot of terminal
p.d. V against load current I_L for a given value of armature velocity ω.
A typical curve is shown in *Figure 7.11*.

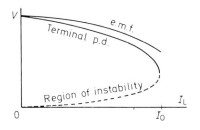

Figure 7.11

The terminal p.d. is greatest when the load current is zero as only the field windings are drawing current from the armature. As the load current increases, the armature volts-drop increases and the terminal p.d. (along with the voltage across the field coils) decreases. The net effect is a gradual and continuing fall in the output voltage. If the external current becomes so large that the machine is overloaded, the terminal p.d. falls off rapidly and difficulty is experienced in getting a field current large enough to produce an e.m.f. which will maintain the terminal voltage. When this adjustment becomes impossible, at current I_0 in *Figure 7.11*, the terminal p.d. and the load current fall to zero and the machine shuts down. This situation should never be allowed to happen in practice.

(10) How do you think the load characteristic of a separately-excited generator would compare with the self-excited case shown in *Figure 7.11*?

The series generator In this form of generator, shown in *Figure 7.12(a)*, the field coils are wired in series with the armature and so carry the full load current when the machine is operating. The resistance of the coils must, as a consequence, be small and relatively few turns of heavy gauge wire are used to provide the required ampere-turns. If the output terminals are on open-circuit the load current is zero and so the field coils carry no current. Hence the field magnets will not excite and the terminal p.d. is very small, only the residual flux generating an e.m.f. in the armature.

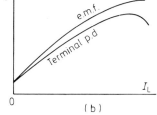

Figure 7.12

The load characteristic of a series generator is shown in *Figure 7.12(b)*. Unlike the shunt generator characteristic which falls, the field flux and hence the terminal p.d. of the series machine rises along a smooth curve as the armature (and load) current increases, but bends over at high values of load current as the poles go into magnetic saturation.

Series generators are little used in practice.

The compound generator This type of generator has field magnets excited partly by high resistance shunt coils and partly by low resistance series coils, the connections being made so that the fields produced are additive.

The two possible methods of connection are shown in *Figure 7.13*, diagram (a) being the short-shunt and (b) being the long-shunt form of connection. The object of this kind of mixed winding is to give a substantially constant terminal p.d. irrespective of the load current being drawn.

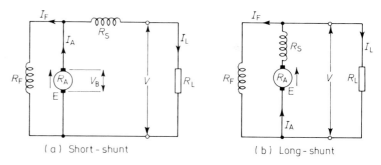

Figure 7.13

When the load current increases, the armature volts-drop increases; this would normally result in a drop in terminal voltage as we noticed for the shunt generator above. The inclusion of the series winding, however, gives an additional field flux in proportion to the current being drawn and so provides a boost to the output voltage which compensates for the increased armature volts-drop. We are, in fact, combining the shunt and series generator characteristics to give either a practically level characteristic or a very slowly rising one. The former is called a *level-compounded* machine and the latter an *over-compounded* machine. These two forms of load characteristic are shown in *Figure 7.14*.

Any calculations for problems involving compound generators are, as usual, simply based on Ohm's law. For the short-shunt generator of *Figure 7.13(a)*

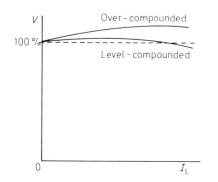

Figure 7.14

$$\text{Volts drop in the series coil} = I_L R_A$$

$$\text{Voltage at the brushes } V_B = V + I_L R_A$$

$$\text{But} \qquad I_A = I_L + I_F$$

$$\therefore \text{ volts drop in the armature} = R_A(I_L + I_F)$$

$$\text{and the generated e.m.f. } E = V_B + R_A(I_L + I_F)$$

(11) Now derive a similar expression for the generated e.m.f. of the long-shunt generator shown in *Figure 7.13(b)*.

THE D.C. MOTOR

In their basic form, d.c. motors and generators are identical and it is only in the direction of energy flow that the essential difference is found. A motor rotates and produces mechanical energy (torque) when given a certain terminal polarity; a generator gives the same electrical polarity when mechanically driven in the *opposite* direction.

The reason for this reversal of direction is that the electric motor depends for its action on the principle that when a current is passed through a conductor which lies in a magnetic field, the conductor is acted on by a force $F = BI\ell$ newtons which tends to move it in a direction perpendicular to itself and to the direction of the field: Fleming's Left Hand Rule. This movement in the field in turn generates an e.m.f. which, in accordance with Lenz's law and the generator e.m.f. equation, opposes the change producing it, i.e. it is a back e.m.f. acting in opposition to the applied voltage and therefore in accordance with Fleming's

Right Hand Rule. This back e.m.f. consequently has the same values as if the machine was running as a generator, i.e. $E \propto \Phi \omega$ and so is proportional to the angular velocity ω. As regards type of armature and field windings, we have exactly the same classification for motors as for generators.

The current I_A which flows in the armature is due to the resultant of these two opposing voltages. If V = applied voltage and E_b = the back e.m.f. then:

$$I_A = \frac{V - E_b}{R_A}$$

$$\therefore \quad I_A R_A = V - E_b$$

$$E_b = V - I_A R_A \tag{7.4}$$

The back e.m.f. determines the armature current and makes the d.c. motor a self-regulating machine. The speed of the motor automatically adjusts itself so that the electrical power required to drive the current through the armature is equal to the mechanical power given out through the shaft to the load. When a load is put on a motor a certain torque is demanded from the motor. This torque is controlled by the armature current and so the motor increases its armature current until it can provide the torque asked for. For any given load condition the motor adjusts its speed so that the back e.m.f. induced in the armature is equal to the supply voltage minus the d.c. volts drop $I_A R_A$ in the armature coils.

As we have noted above, $E_b \propto \Phi \omega$, where Φ is the pole flux and ω the angular velocity of rotation. Combining this relationship with (7.4) above, we get

$$V - I_A R_A \propto \Phi \omega \tag{7.5}$$

and this is a fundamental relationship from which the behaviour of any type of d.c. motor can be determined. As the armature volts-drop $I_A R_A$ is usually very small compared with V, equation (7.5) can be simplified to

$$V \propto \Phi \omega \quad \text{or} \quad E_b \propto \Phi \omega$$

so if there is a change in operating conditions the new values may be calculated by proportion, that is:

$$E_{b_1} \propto \Phi_1 \omega_1 \quad \text{and so} \quad E_{b_2} \propto \Phi_2 \omega_2$$

Dividing we have

$$\frac{\omega_1}{\omega_2} = \frac{E_{b_1}}{E_{b_2}} \times \frac{\Phi_2}{\Phi_1}$$

Try this next example to see whether you have grasped the prinicple of this proportional relationship.

(12)   A motor runs at an armature velocity of 150 rad/s when the armature e.m.f. is 240 V. Find its speed when the flux per pole is reduced 10% if at the new speed the e.m.f. is 235 V.

Torque   The torque T newton-metres (N-m) which a motor can exert is clearly related to the motor power. If the armature radius is R metres and the tangential force F ($= BI\ell$) newtons causes the armature to rotate at angular velocity ω rad/s, then the torque $T = FR$ N-m and the work done by the force in one revolution $= 2\pi FR$ N-m. Therefore the work done by the force in $1s = 2\pi FR\,(\omega/2\pi) = FR\omega = \omega T$ joules, and the power developed

$$P = \omega T \text{ W} \tag{7.6}$$

since 1 W $= 1$ J/s.

Considering the armature input power as VI_A W, we may multiply (7.4) above by I_A and then

$$E_b I_A = VI_A - I_A^2 R_A$$

Looking at each of these terms in turn we deduce

(a) VI_A is the power available for producing motion, the input power.

(b) $I_A^2 R_A$ is the power wasted in the armature (and brush) resistance.

(c) $E_b I_A$ is the armature power.

$I_A^2 R_A$ is the *copper loss* of the motor; $E_b I_A$ is known as the gross power of the motor, but the whole of this power is not available for doing useful work, some of it being required to overcome iron and friction losses. Neglecting these other losses for the moment

$$\text{Gross power} = E_b I_A = \omega T \text{ W}$$

$$\text{Torque } T \quad = \frac{E_b I_A}{\omega} \text{ N-m}$$

But

$$E_b \propto \Phi\omega$$

$$T \propto \frac{\Phi\omega I_A}{\omega} = k\Phi I_A$$

where k is a constant.

Example (13). A d.c. motor takes 10 A from a 240 V supply. The machine losses amount altogether to 300 W. If the machine runs at a speed of 100 rad/s, what is the output torque?

$$\text{Input power} = 240 \times 10 = 2400 \text{ W}$$

$$\text{Output power} = 2400 - 300 = 2100 \text{ W}$$

$$\text{Power} = \omega T \quad = 100T \text{ W}$$

$$\therefore \qquad 100T = 2100$$

$$T = 21 \text{ N-m}$$

Motor characteristics   Like generators, motors are classified according to their method of excitation and may be of the shunt, series or compound wound variety. The shunt and series types are those which concern us here.

The shunt-wound motor

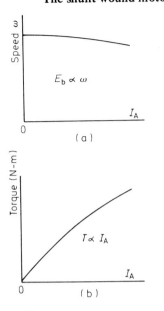

(a)

(b)

Figure 7.15

For a given terminal voltage this type of motor maintains an almost constant speed over a wide range of load torques. Like the shunt generator, the field windings are connected in parallel with the armature (and the input terminals) and are wound with many turns of fine gauge wire. Now $E_b \propto \Phi\omega$ and as Φ is constant the speed is directly related to E_b which, from equation (7.4) is $V - I_A R_A$. Since V is constant, as I_A increases so E_b must decrease, hence ω must decrease, and the motor slows down. The plot of speed against armature current is drawn in *Figure 7.15(a)*.

The torque-current characteristic can be deduced by a consideration of the proportionality $T \propto \Phi I_A$. As more torque is demanded, the armature current increases to provide it and this can continue up to the safe working limit of the armature capacity. For a constant Φ, torque is directly proportional to I_A, hence the characteristic of T against I_A is a straight line passing through the origin. In practice the line bends slightly as *Figure 7.15(b)* illustrates.

(14) Explain why the curve departs from a straight line in this way.

The shunt motor is used on steadily running constant-speed loads, such as printing or weaving machine drives.

The series-wound motor

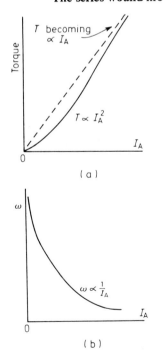

(a)

(b)

Figure 7.16

The d.c. series-wound motor has a wide speed range and a large starting torque and finds considerable employment. The speed varies substantially with load variations. As the field coils are in series with the armature winding they are wound with a few turns of heavy gauge wire which carry the full armature current. The field flux depends upon the armature current, and provided that the iron of the pole pieces is unsaturated, $\Phi \propto I_A$ as we have already noted. The gross armature torque is proportional to ΦI_A and $\Phi \propto I_A$. Hence $T \propto I_A^2$. This means that if the armature current is forced to increase by an excessive load slowing up the motor, a proportionally larger increase in torque is obtained to establish equilibrium again.

A typical plot of torque against armature current is shown in *Figure 7.16(a)*. The current does not follow the square-law shape at high current values as the poles gradually approach saturation and the field flux cannot then increase rapidly as I_A^2, hence the torque becomes more nearly proportional to I_A.

The speed characteristic of a series motor can be deduced by considering the fact that $E_b \propto \Phi\omega$. Assuming that E_b is constant then, if the armature and field drops are small, $\omega \propto 1/I_A$ as long as the poles are unsaturated. The curve of ω against I_A is shown in *Figure 7.16(b)* and approximates to a rectangular hyperbola. The characteristic of high torque and low speed at high values of armature current is ideal in traction systems where considerable friction has to be overcome to get a vehicle moving from rest. Care has to be taken, however, that the load is not suddenly removed as the speed will immediately rise to a possibly dangerous level in an attempt to reduce the armature current by raising the back e.m.f.

Example (15). The armature of a d.c. motor has 300 uniformly spaced conductors. The armature diameter is 20 cm and the conductors are each 20 cm long. If the starting current taken by the motor is 15 A, giving a flux density if 0.5 T in the gap between pole and rotor, calculate the starting torque provided by the motor.

$$\text{Force on each conductor} = BI\ell \text{ N}$$

$$= 0.5 \times 15 \times 20 \times 10^{-2} = 1.5 \text{ N}$$

$$\text{Total force on 300 conductors} = 300 \times 1.5 = 450 \text{ N}$$

$$\text{Torque} = \text{force} \times \text{arm of torque} = 450 \times 10 \times 10^{-2}$$

$$= 45 \text{ Nm}$$

Speed control and starting

From the proportionality $E_b \propto \Phi\omega$, since $E_b = V - I_A R_A$ then

$$\omega \propto \frac{V - I_A R_A}{\Phi}$$

From this we see that the speed may be controlled by varying

(a) The pole flux Φ.
(b) The resistance in the armature circuit, R_A.
(c) The applied voltage V.

We shall be interested in the effect of adding resistance to the armature and field circuits to modify I_A and Φ respectively.

In *Figure 7.17(a)* a resistor R has been added in series with the armature of a shunt-wound motor. At any particular load and armature current value I_A the extra resistance will cause a greater armature volts-drop and consequently a smaller value for $V - I(R + R)$. Hence the motor speed will be reduced when Φ is constant. A disadvantage of this method is that for a given value of R, a change in load torque will lead to a change in speed. A further disadvantage is the relatively large power loss in resistor R.

In *Figure 7.17(b)*, a resistor R has been added in series with the field windings. The effect of this is to reduce the pole flux Φ and so lead to an increase in speed. However, if the load torque is constant, then ΦI_A must be constant so that a decrease in Φ results in an increase in I_A. As a result the motor must be made larger and consequently costs more than it would if no speed variation were required. The method is, however, very simple and is an efficient way of controlling speed above a minimum value obtained with full field current. The next example illustrates this.

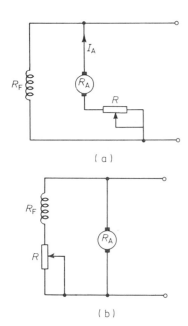

Figure 7.17

Example (16). A shunt motor connected to a 240 V d.c. supply, runs at 1600 rad/s on no-load at an armature current of 1.0 A. If the armature resistance is 2 Ω, calculate the speed of the motor on load when the armature current is 8 A. By what percentage would the field have to be reduced in order to restore the speed to its original value?

We have the proportionality $\Phi\omega \propto V - I_A R_A$
∴ since Φ is constant, the ratio of the speeds will be

$$\frac{\omega_2}{\omega_1} = \frac{V - I_{A_2} R_{A_2}}{V - I_{A_1} R_{A_1}}$$

∴ for $\omega_1 = 1600$ rad/s

$$\frac{\omega_2}{1600} = \frac{240 - (8 \times 2)}{240 - (1 \times 2)} = \frac{224}{238}$$

∴

$$\omega_2 = 1600 \times \frac{224}{238} = 1506 \text{ rad/sec}$$

Now as we have noted in the text $E_b \propto \Phi\omega$ or $\omega \propto E_b/\Phi$
A reduction in flux Φ will consequently increase the speed, so

$$\frac{\omega_2}{\omega_1} = \frac{\Phi_2}{\Phi_1} = \frac{1506}{1600} = 0.94$$

Hence the percentage decrease in Φ will be about 6%.

Speed control of series-wound motors can be brought about by the methods illustrated in *Figure 7.18(a)* and *(b)* which depend upon a variation in Φ and V respectively.

In diagram *(a)* a variable resistor known as a *diverter* is connected in parallel with the series field winding; in this way any part of the main current may be passed through the field coils. Increasing the diverter resistance strengthens the field and the motor slows down; and conversely.

In diagram *(b)* the diverter is placed across the armature. For a given load torque, a reduction in I_A because of a reduction in the diverter resistance leads to an increase in Φ and a reduction in speed.

A method commonly used in fan and cookery mixer motors is shown in *Figure 7.18(c)*. The field coils are regrouped to provide a series of fixed speeds. Alternatively, the field coils are sometimes tapped so that the number of turns in circuit can be varied.

Variation of the applied voltage by a series resistor R is shown in *Figure 7.18(d)*. Increasing R reduces the applied voltage and hence the speed falls. The method leads to a considerable waste of power in the series resistor.

(c)

(d)

Figure 7.18

Starting

At the moment of switching on a motor there is no back e.m.f. and the current that results is given by $I_A = V/R_A$. Once running, the back e.m.f. limits the current to $(V - E_b)/R_A$. To reduce the starting current to a safe value as the back e.m.f. builds up, a starter resistor is included in the armature circuit and this limits the current to about 1.5 times the normal full load value. This current, with a full pole strength of field, gives a good starting torque. *Figure 7.19* shows the basic shunt motor starter connections. As the motor e.m.f. rises the resistance is progressively cut out by moving the starter arm across the contacts.

Figure 7.19

LOSSES AND EFFICIENCY

The losses which occur in generators and motors are of the same kind, that is (a) copper losses, (b) iron losses, (c) friction losses.

Copper losses are the armature copper loss, the field windings copper loss and the loss due to the brush contact resistance at the surface of the commutator. These are all known as I^2R losses.

Iron losses mainly involve eddy-current loss in the armature and pole pieces, and the hysteresis loss in the armature.

Friction losses include the brush friction, bearing friction and air resistance against moving parts (windage), particularly when cooling fans are incorporated.

The energy changes and losses which occur in the transformation of electrical energy into mechanical energy are shown in *Figure 7.20*. This

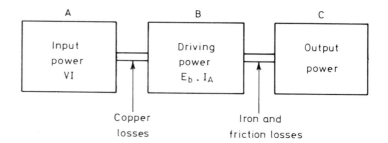

Figure 7.20

is the motor case. Changing this diagram round end to end will provide the appropriate representation of the generator case. The copper losses are represented between sections A and B and the iron and frictional losses between sections B and C. We define

$$\text{Electrical efficiency } \eta_e = \frac{B}{A} \times 100\%$$

$$\text{Mechanical efficiency } \eta_m = \frac{C}{B} \times 100\%$$

$$\text{Overall efficiency } \eta_c = \frac{C}{A} \times 100\%$$

In the absence of any other indication, the efficiency stated is taken to be the overall or *commercial* efficiency η_c. Notice that

$$\eta_c = \frac{C}{A} = \frac{\text{output power}}{\text{input power}} = \frac{\text{output}}{\text{output + losses}}$$

Example (17). A 240 V series motor draws a current of 35 A. The armature resistance is 0.1 Ω and the field resistance is 0.075 Ω. If the iron and friction losses are equal to the copper losses at this load, calculate the commercial efficiency.

Total resistance of motor = 0.175 Ω

$$E_b = V - I_A R_A = 240 - (35 \times 0.175) = 233.88 \text{ V}$$

Input power = 240 × 35 = 8400 W

Armature power $E_b I_A$ = 233.8 × 35 = 8185.8 W

Copper losses = 8400 − 8185.8 = 214.2 W

Iron losses = 214.2 W

Total losses = 2 × 214.2 = 428.4 W

Output power = input power − losses
= 8400 − 428.4 = 7971.6 W

$$\eta_c = \frac{7971.6}{8400} \times 100 = 95\%$$

STEPPING MOTORS

A stepping motor does not rotate smoothly and continuously in the manner of those motors already discussed, but 'steps' from one fixed position to the next in a sequence of discrete movements. The angular extent of the steps can be within a range covering up to 30°, so in a sense such a motor can be thought of as a 'digital device'. It is, indeed, usually operated under digital control, that is, with pulsed and not continuous input signals. Such motors are used in robotics, as head positioners in floppy disc drives, in computer controlled X-Y plotters and in teletype printers, to name only four common applications: anywhere, that is, where incremental and not continuous movement is called for.

An elementary form of stepping motor can be made using an escapement mechanism to advance the movement in discrete steps and many of this form are in use, but modern stepping motors work on the principle that various combinations and phasings of the fields and the interaction between these fields and the rotor field within the motor will cause the rotor to move forwards (or backwards) a defined number of degrees. The number of steps and the speed of rotation are respectively determined by the number of pulses and the frequency of the control signal. A 1.8° step angle is common, so giving 200 steps per revolution, and up to 800 steps per second can be achieved.

Figure 7.21 shows a possible arrangement of a stepping motor connected to an external control system. Suppose the coils to be energised in a particular way with switches Q_1 and Q_2 closed (ON), and the rotor held in a certain position: then changing to switches Q_1 and Q_4 causes the motor to move through a certain angle, say clockwise. A further change to Q_3 and Q_4 will move the rotor through a further clockwise step, after which, with Q_2 and Q_3 closed, the next step occurs. After this the sequence repeats and the motor will continue to step in a clockwise direction as long as the switching cycle continues. To get the motor to step in an anticlockwise direction, the switching sequence is reversed. *Figure 7.22(a)* shows the sequence we have discussed written in tabular form.

It might appear at first that this sequence is haphazard and arbitrary, but this is not so. The control must be precisely programmed. In the present example, for instance, if the switching sequence is interpreted in terms of control logic, where ON = 1, OFF = 0, a pattern becomes evident, see *Figure 7.22(b)*. To move from step 1 to step 2, the initial pattern 1100 is moved one place to the left, and thereafter each step is accomplished by rotating the pattern one more place to the left. For a reversal of the motor, the pattern is shifted sequentially to the right.

The sequence can be controlled by wiring the switches (which are, of course, electronic switches using bipolar or FET devices) to the output of a ring counter* initially loaded with the binary sequence 1100. Each step is then controlled by clocking the counter. Clockwise or anticlockwise control can also be introduced by the counter. Alternatively, the switches may be controlled by a microcomputer which is programmed to operate the required step sequence. A suitable control chip for experimental purposes is the SAA1027.

Step	Q_1	Q_2	Q_3	Q_4
1	ON	ON	OFF	OFF
2	ON	OFF	OFF	ON
3	OFF	OFF	ON	ON
4	OFF	ON	ON	OFF
5	ON	ON	OFF	OFF

Anticlockwise sequence

(a)

Clockwise sequence

Step	Q_1	Q_2	Q_3	Q_4
1	1	1	0	0
2	1	0	0	1
3	0	0	1	1
4	0	1	1	0
5	1	1	0	0

(b)

Figure 7.22

*See *Electronics 2*

PROBLEMS FOR SECTION 7

Group 1

(18)   Fill in the missing words or quantities:

(a) Motors convert . . . . . energy into . . . . . energy.

(b) Efficiency of a machine is defined as . . . .

(c) In a lap winding there are as many parallel paths as there are . . . .

(d) In a wave winding there are . . . . parallel paths.

(e) At a constant speed, generated e.m.f. $E \propto$ . . . .

(19)   A four-pole wave-wound machine has 420 conductors and is driven at 800 r.p.m. to generate an e.m.f. of 200 V. What is the flux per pole of the machine?

(20)   A six-pole generator has a wave-wound armature and is driven at an angular velocity of 42 rad/s. Calculate the number of conductors if the machine produces an e.m.f. of 240 V with a pole flux of 0.04 Wb.

(21)   A generator runs on load with an armature current of 75 A and a generated e.m.f. of 400 V. Determine the terminal p.d. given that the armature resistance is 0.2 Ω.

(22)   A 50 kW, 250 V d.c. generator has an armature circuit resistance of 0.15 Ω. What is the generated e.m.f. on full load?

(23)   Find the value of the back e.m.f. of a motor working from 220 V d.c. mains when the armature current is 10 A. Take the armature resistance to be 0.5 Ω.

(24)   A d.c. shunt motor runs at an angular velocity of 188 rad/s when connected to a 100 V supply and in the unloaded condition the armature current is 0.5 A. If the armature resistance is 3.5 Ω find the speed of the motor when it is loaded and the armature current is 2 A.

(25)   A 460 V motor runs at an angular velocity of 157 rad/s with an armature current of 120 A. If the armature resistance is 0.4 Ω, calculate the percentage change in the pole flux needed to obtain a velocity of 262 rad/s when the current is 125 A.

(26)   What power is needed to drive a 150 kW generator when it is delivering its full rated output, if the machine has a full load efficiency of 91.5%?

Group 2

(27)   Fill in the missing words or quantities:

(a)   Motor torque $T \propto I_A \times$ . . . . .

(b)   Angular velocity $\omega \propto E$ . . . .

(c)   The e.m.f. induced in the armature of a motor . . . . . . the supply voltage.

(d)   The armature power EI_A is called the . . . . . . power.

(28)   The open-circuit characteristic of a d.c. machine is given in the following table:

Generated e.m.f. (V)	100	176	218	240	256	266
Field current (A)	0.2	0.4	0.6	0.8	1.0	1.2

If the machine is used as a shunt generator, find (a) the field circuit resistance to give an open-circuit e.m.f. of 245 V, (b) the open-circuit e.m.f. when the field circuit resistance is 310 Ω.

(29)   Explain why a d.c. series-connected motor has a high starting torque. The armature of a d.c. series motor has 400

Figure 7.23

uniformly spaced conductors. The radius of the armature is 12.5 cm and the conductors are each 25 cm long. If the motor draws a starting current of 10 A, giving a flux density in the gap of 0.5 T, calculate the starting torque.

(30) A 240 V shunt motor runs at 600 r.p.m. when the armature current is 10 A. If the armature resistance is 2 Ω find the speed when a 4 Ω resistor is placed in series with the armature. Assume that Φ and I_F remain unchanged. Why is this method of control inefficient?

(31) *Figure 7.23* shows a shunt motor connected to a 100 V supply. Calculate the speed of this motor when a 2.5 Ω resistor is connected in series with the field winding, assuming that the load remains unchanged and that the flux is proportional to the field current.

(32) A d.c. generator with a 120 Ω shunt field resistance is feeding a load of 20 Ω. The armature resistance is 2.5 Ω and the frictional losses in the generator are equivalent to an additional shunt load of 100 Ω across the output terminals. What is the overall efficiency of the generator?

(33) A d.c. motor operating from a 400 V supply is driving a d.c. shunt wound generator having a field resistance of 125 Ω. This generator is supplying a current of 12 A at 250 V to a heater system. Calculate the fraction of the total power available at the brushes that is dissipated in the field winding. If the overall efficiency of the generator is 75% and the efficiency of the motor alone is 70%, calculate the current and power taken by the motor from the 400 V supply.

8 The induction motor

Aims: At the end of this Unit section you should be able to:
Understand the operation of a three-phase alternator.
Describe how a polyphase supply can produce a uniformly rotating field.
Describe the induction motor and explain its principle of operation.

All the machines described in the previous Unit Section were direct current machines. They have also been the type of machine in which the field has been stationary and the armature has rotated. From a consideration of the basic laws governing the operation of machines however, there is no reason why the field should not rotate, and if a stationary system of coils, suitably wound and disposed, is supplied with alternating current, a uniformly rotating field of constant intensity is indeed produced. This principle is used in the design of several forms of a.c. motors.

If we go back to *Figure 6.4* on page 92, we recall that the three-phase a.c. generator was considered as an arrangement of three identical coils, fixed 120° apart, rotating in a uniform magnetic field; and the observation was made that although the system was theoretically sound, a number of practical limitations prevented its use in that particular form.

One of these limitations is the problem of getting the generated power out of the rotating coils and into the external cables. The use of slip-rings is impracticable where very high currents are concerned and armature insulation is difficult to achieve at high voltage levels. By changing over the field and armature, this problem can be overcome.

In *Figure 8.1* a rotating magnet (the rotor) is turning between fixed coils (the stator coils). As the magnet rotates at a uniform angular velocity, each pole passes a coil in turn. This relative motion of field and coils is exactly similar in its effect with the case where the field is fixed and the coils move past it, hence first a positive e.m.f. and then a

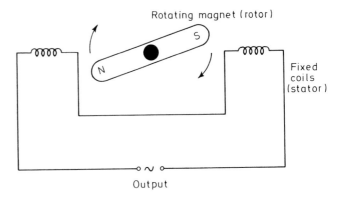

Output

Figure 8.1

negative e.m.f. is induced in each coil. One cycle of e.m.f. is produced for each complete revolution of the magnet and hence the generated frequency is a function of the speed of rotation.

In a practical generator, an electromagnet would be used as the rotor instead of the permanent magnet shown and this would be energised by direct current from an outside source by way of slip-rings. Such rings could be used here where the power requirement of the rotor would be small and constant. The stationary armature or stator coils on the other hand, in which the required e.m.f. is generated, can have direct connections to the external circuit.

A practical form of three-phase alternator is shown in *Figure 8.2*. This has six poles (but a much greater number are commonly used) and these are wound alternately right- and left-handed, similarly wound poles being placed 120° apart. The pole pieces are usually built up from steel stampings and either bolted or dovetailed to the outer frame. This

Figure 8.2

form of construction is known as *salient* pole, the pole pieces projecting as shown and shaped to produce a sinusoidal distribution of the flux in the air gap; the induced e.m.f. is then also sinusoidal. The interconnections between the pole windings are not shown in the diagram for the sake of clarity, but these may be arranged in either star or delta form.

GENERATED FREQUENCY The direction of the induced e.m.f. as the field sweeps round will depend upon the direction in which each pole is wound, and the e.m.f. generated in each coil will complete one cycle as the field moves past one pair of poles.

If ω is the speed in rad/s and p is the number of pole pairs, then $f = p\omega/2\pi$ Hz. Alternately, if N is the speed in rev/min, then $f = pN/60$ Hz. N is the *synchronous* speed of the alternator and is the speed at which the machine must be driven if the required frequency is to be generated. For power generation, 50 Hz is the standard frequency in the UK, although 60 Hz is common in the USA and some other countries. The problem of distribution is eased when the frequency is low, but it must not be so low that flicker is noticed in any lighting.

> (1) Can you think of another disadvantage of a very low frequency?
> (2) Calculate the required speed (in rev/min and in rad/s) of an a.c. generator having (a) 2 poles, (b) 4 poles, (c) 6 poles, for a 50 Hz output frequency.

THE ROTATING FIELD

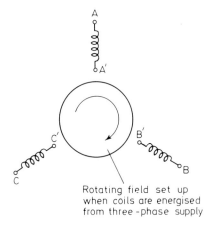

Rotating field set up when coils are energised from three-phase supply

Figure 8.3

In *Figure 8.3* the stator system of a three-phase alternator has been re-drawn in a form which simply shows the appropriate coils spaced at 120° intervals around the stator frame. The rotor has been removed and we are interested only in the field generated within the stator when the coils are *supplied* with three-phase a.c. Just as the rotation of the magnetic field of the rotor in the alternator generates the three-phase supply, so when such a supply is applied to the stator system, we should expect a rotating field to be produced.

Let the stator coils of *Figure 8.3* be energised with three-phase a.c. as shown in *Figure 8.4*. This diagram illustrates the current in the coils, but the pattern can be interpreted as the flux waves set up by the stator windings. The total flux at any instant is the phasor sum of the separate fluxes at that instant. Consider the conditions at intervals of one-sixth of a cycle:

At instant 1: the field of poles AA′ is zero, the fields of poles BB′ and CC′ are equal. Hence the resultant lies midway between poles BB′ and CC′.

At instant 2: the field of poles CC′ is zero, the fields of poles AA′ and BB′ are equal. Hence the resultant lies midway between poles AA′ and BB′.

At instant 3: the field of poles BB′ is zero, the fields of poles AA′ and CC′ are equal. Hence the resultant lies midway between poles AA′ and CC′.

And so on.

By taking intermediate instants of time to those shown, intermediate positions of the maximum field strength can be found which will lie between those marked. If you give the diagram a bit of thought, you should be able to deduce that in each case the resultant flux Φ is constant and equal in magnitude to 1.5 Φ (the maximum flux due to any one phase), and that the field rotates at the same frequency as that of the applied alternating current.

If the supply frequency is f Hz then clearly the field rotates at a speed of $N = 60f/p$ rev/min where p is the number of pole pairs. Increasing the number of poles *reduces* the speed. The speed of field rotation is again known as the synchronous speed.

> (3) In a manner similar to that used in *Figure 8.4*, draw phasor diagrams for the rotating field of a 2-pole, 2-phase stator.

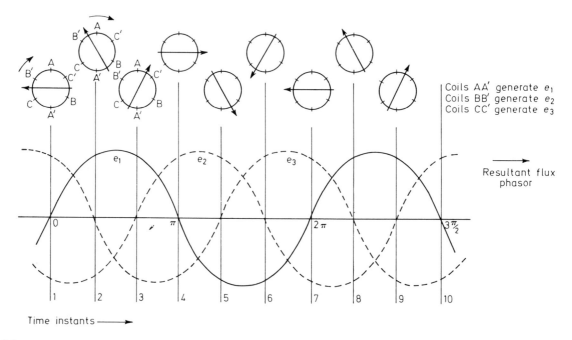

Coils AA′ generate e_1
Coils BB′ generate e_2
Coils CC′ generate e_3

Resultant flux phasor

Time instants ⟶

Figure 8.4

Hence deduce that the resultant flux is equal to the maximum flux Φ due to any one phase. Write down an expression for the synchronous speed in this case.

THE INDUCTION MOTOR

The induction motor depends for its operation on a rotating field of the kind referred to above. The stator of the motor is basically the same as that of the alternator described previously and is wound for two, four, six poles, etc, depending upon the speed required. The salient pole construction is, however, not used. Instead the stator is in the form of a cylinder, the coils being wound in slots cut in the cylinder walls. As always, the iron used is laminated to reduce iron losses and the windings are uniformly distributed, one third of the stator surface being

Laminated steel rotor with embedded copper or aluminium conductors

Copper ring connecting conductors together at each end of rotor

Figure 8.5

devoted to each phase. The windings are usually brought out to six terminals so that the machine may be either star or delta connected.

The most widely used form of rotor for low power machines is the so-called *squirrel cage* rotor. This is illustrated in *Figure 8.5*. It is built up from low hysteresis steel laminations and has longitudinal slots into each of which is placed a single bar of copper or aluminium conductor. Two thick conducting rings of copper are rivetted to each end of the rotor and the conductor ends are brazed or welded to these, shorting all the conductors together and forming a cage from which the name of the rotor is derived.

The advantage of this kind of rotor is that there are no external connections to be made. Slip-rings, commutators or brushes are not required. When the rotor is centralised in the stator cylinder so that the air gap between the conductors and the poles of the stator is small, the assembly forms an induction motor, and the rotor will turn when the stator coils are energized from a three-phase supply.

ROTATION AND SLIP

Figure 8.6 shows one conductor on the rotor in the gap of an induction motor. As the rotating field passes, the conductor is cut by the flux and an alternating e.m.f. is induced between its ends. As this conductor is connected to another conductor spaced one pole pitch away, a current will·flow in this closed loop and the conductor will experience a force tending to move it out of the field and hence to turn the rotor. The direction of this turning force *relative to the field* will be *opposite* to that of the field. It is important to grasp this point and the diagram should help you do it.

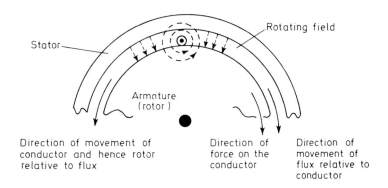

Figure 8.6

In the diagram it has been assumed that the induced e.m.f. and the current are acting out of phase; therefore the direction of the force acting on the conductor will be such that the rotor will tend to turn clockwise (Fleming's Left Hand Rule, remember?). The rotor will consequently by dragged in the direction of the field movement.

At switch-on, the frequency of the induced e.m.f. will be the same as that of the supply, but as the speed of the rotor increases the relative motion between field and rotor becomes less and the frequency of the e.m.f. decreases. The motor can clearly never run at the speed of rotation of the field (the synchronous speed) because the relative motion would then be zero and no e.m.f. would be induced in the conductors.

For this reason the induction motor is known as an *asynchronous* machine.

With no load on the rotor shaft, the torque required has only to be sufficient to overcome the bearing friction and the speed of rotation is very close to that of the field. The motor is then running at practically the synchronous speed. Let N rev/min be the synchronous speed of the field and let N_r be the actual speed of the rotor. Then

$$\text{Slip speed } N_s = N - N_r$$

$$\text{The ratio } \frac{\text{synchronous speed} - \text{actual speed}}{\text{synchronous speed}} = \frac{N - N_r}{N}$$

$$= \frac{N_s}{N}$$

is called the slip s and is usually expressed as a percentage.

The no-load slip will normally be of the order of 99% of synchronous speed corresponding to a slip of 0.01 (1%), and the full-load slip will be of the order of 0.05 (5%). We can express the slip ratio in another way:

$$\frac{N_s}{N} = \frac{60 f_s / p}{60 f / p} = \frac{f_s}{f}$$

and here f_s is the slip frequency; it is the frequency of the rotor e.m.f. when running at slip s.

(4)   What is the slip at standstill?
(5)   What is the rotor frequency in terms of slip s and the supply frequency f?

Example (6). The frequency of the supply to the stator of a 4-pole induction motor is 50 Hz and the rotor frequency is 2 Hz. What is the slip and at what speed is the motor turning?

$$\text{Slip } s = \frac{f_s}{f} = \frac{2}{50} = 0.04 \ (4\%)$$

$$\text{Synchronous speed } N = \frac{60 f}{p} = \frac{60 \times 50}{2} = 1500 \text{ rev/min}$$

$$\text{But rotor speed } N_r = N(1 - s) \text{ since } s = \frac{N - N_r}{N}$$

$$\therefore \quad N_r = 1500 \,(1 - 0.04) = 1440 \text{ rev/min}$$

The speed of an induction motor tends to decrease as the load is increased in order that the increase in the speed of the rotor conductors *relative to the field* (the slip) can generate a current large enough to cope with the additional load, i.e. lead to an increased torque. The load may be increased until the slip is such that the maximum torque is reached; beyond this point the slip approaches unity and the machine stops. It can be proved that the slip (or speed) at which the maximum torque is developed depends upon the rotor resistance.

The squirrel cage motor is ideally suited to drives where an approximately constant speed is required at relatively low power. For higher powers a wound rotor is employed. The rotor conductors here form a three-phase winding wired internally in star. The free ends are brought out to three slip-rings from which external contact is made by carbon brushes in the usual way.

PROBLEMS FOR SECTION 8

(6)   The frequency of the e.m.f. in the stator of a 4-pole induction motor is 50 Hz and that in the rotor is 2.5 Hz. What is the slip and at what speed is the motor running?

(7)   A 4-pole induction motor runs from a 50 Hz supply at a speed of 1450 rev/min. What is the frequency of the rotor current and the percentage slip?

(8)   A 6-pole induction motor is connected to a 50 Hz supply and runs at a speed of 970 rev/min. What is the percentage slip?

(9)   An 8-pole, three-phase induction motor has a full load slip of 0.025 when used on 50 Hz mains. Calculate (a) the synchronous speed, (b) the rotor speed, (c) the rotor frequency.

(10)   Show that the rotor frequency at slip s is given by sf, where f is the supply frequency.

(11)   Show that the rotor e.m.f. is given by sE, where E is the e.m.f. in the stationary motor.

(12)   A three-phase alternator has six poles and runs at 1200 r.p.m. Its output is connected to a 4-pole induction motor which runs at a speed of 1730 rev/min. What is the percentage slip in the motor?

(13)   Do you think it is possible to have an induction motor operating on single-phase a.c.?

(14)   An induction motor operating on a 50 Hz supply has a stator field which rotates at a speed of 375 rev/min. How many stator poles are there?

(15)   A 4-pole, three-phase induction motor has a stator field which rotates at a speed of 1494 rev/min. What is the supply frequency exactly? If the supply frequency now increases by 0.6 Hz, find the new speed of the motor.

(16)   A 6-pole 50 Hz induction motor drives a pump which requires a speed of 40 rev/min for proper operation. If the motor slip is 3%, what gear ratio is necessary between the motor and the pump?

9 Methods of measurement

Aims: At the end of this Unit section you should be able to:

Understand the fundamental principles of error due to instruments and observations.

Appreciate the loading effects and frequency characteristics of some basic instruments.

Recognise that a complex wave is made up of fundamental and harmonic components and explain the effect of amplifier deficiencies on the reproduction of complex waves.

Use a cathode-ray oscilloscope to measure frequency and phase shift.

Under the principles of digital instruments.

Understand the a.c. bridge method of measuring inductance, self-resistance and Q-factor of coils.

The only way to learn about measuring instruments and how to make intelligent measurements is to do practical work in a laboratory. This Unit section deals only briefly with a few basic instruments and the more general measurements to which they can be applied. It is assumed that you are familiar with the various types of analogue (pointer) instruments used for the basic measurement of current, voltage and resistance, and understand the methods of shunt and multiplier resistance additions to such instruments to make them adaptable to a variety of such measurements.

Much of the work of this section will be on the effect of errors introduced by these instruments as well as the errors introduced by observations made from these instruments. In addition, mention will be made on the use of the cathode-ray oscilloscope as a frequency and phase shift measuring device, and the application of bridge measurements to inductive impedances.

TAKING MEASUREMENTS   Looking at the scale of a voltmeter or an ammeter and making a note of what the pointer indicates may seem a simple enought procedure, but the *accuracy* of the observation may be affected in a variety of ways. The most important of these are:

(a) *Calibration errors or faults in the instrument.* No instrument, however sophisticated or expensive, is perfect and what the pointer indicates on the scale is probably not the exact value of the current or voltage present in the circuit being tested. Most good measuring instruments are stated to be within a certain degree of accuracy by the manufacturers. Errors of this sort can be minimised by choosing an appropriate *method* of taking the measurements in which the calibration errors are eliminated.

(b) *Systematic errors or errors of method.* These are errors introduced by the actual method of measurement employed. For example, when an ammeter is introduced into a circuit, the additional resistance, be it ever so small, changes the condition of the circuit in which the current is being measured. These errors can be minimized by using the correct instruments and making the correct method of measurement to suit the circuit conditions.

(c) *Observational or human error.* These errors depend upon the person carrying out the experiment. For example, different people will all read the pointer position on a scale slightly at variance with one another. These errors can be considerably reduced by having a number of readings taken by a number of people; the mean value is then accepted as the correct result. Repeated observations by *one* person do not lead to the same figure as an individual's errors are more likely to be all in the same 'direction'.

Uncertainty can often be checked by deliberately offsetting some quantity and noting when the difference is just perceptible. For example, when using a metre bridge, the experiment depends upon finding a balance point along the slide wire which gives a zero reading on a galvanometer. The uncertainty here may be found by moving the slide wire contact until the galvanometer is just deflected off zero and noting the distance from this position to the 'optimum' position of balance.

(1) In using a bridge system of the sort just mentioned, would the calibration error of the instrument used have any effect on the result?

Figure 9.1

Example (2). A resistor of value about 30 Ω is to be measured by the method shown in *Figure 9.1*. The voltmeter V has a f.s.d. of 100 V and resistance 100 kΩ, and the ammeter A has a f.s.d. of 5 A and resistance 1.55 Ω. Both meters are stated to have an accuracy of ± 2%. In the experiment the voltmeter reads 90 V and the ammeter reads 3 A. Ignoring observational errors, find the probable limits between which the value of the resistor actually lies.

When the voltmeter reads 90 V, the true voltage can lie between 92 V and 88 V. Likewise for the ammeter, the true current can lie between 3.1 A and 2.9 A. Hence the observed value of resistance will lie between

$$\frac{92}{2.9} = 31.724 \ \Omega \quad \text{and} \quad \frac{88}{3.1} = 28.387 \ \Omega$$

But these values include the resistance of the ammeter in series with *R*. Hence the probable value of *R* lies within the range

$$30.174 \ \Omega \quad \text{and} \quad 26.837 \ \Omega$$

As the circuit is connected, the voltmeter resistance is so high compared with *R* that its shunting effect can be ignored.

(3) The probable limits are given above with three decimal places. Would this be justified in such an experiment with the data as given?

(4)   Would any greater accuracy be obtained if the voltmeter was connected as shown by the broken line in *Figure 9.1*?

EFFECT OF INSTRUMENT LOADING

Figure 9.2

Figure 9.3

When instruments are connected into a circuit, the circuit conditions are changed. Hence the readings given by the instruments, irrespective of the accuracy of the instruments themselves, are not identical with the actual currents and voltages which were acting in the circuit before the instruments were inserted. This, of course, is systematic error. To reduce the error, the instruments must conform to certain requirements.

The circuit for measuring current is shown in *Figure 9.2*. The actual current in the circuit is $I = V/R$ (that is, the current before the ammeter is included); but the current indicated by the ammeter after its inclusion will be *less* than this because the ammeter resistance is now placed in series with R. So the indicated current is $I = V/(R + R_m)$, and this is less than the actual current by a factor

$$\left[1 + \frac{R_m}{R} \right]^{-1}$$

It follows that the actual current and the indicated current will be equal only when R_m is zero. The internal resistance of an ammeter should therefore be negligible in comparison with the circuit resistance R.

The circuit for measuring voltage is shown in *Figure 9.3*. Here a voltmeter V is being used to measure the p.d. across resistor R_2. The actual voltage across R_2 is

$$V_2 = V \; \frac{R_2}{R_1 + R_2}$$

but the voltage indicated on the meter will be *less* than this because the voltmeter resistance R_m is itself in parallel with R_2 and effectively reduces its resistance. So the indicated voltage is

$$V_2 = \frac{VR_2}{R_1 + R_2 + \dfrac{R_1 R_2}{R_m}}$$

and this is less than the actual voltage by a factor

$$1 + \frac{R_1 R_2}{(R_1 + R_2) R_m}$$

It follows from this that the actual voltage and the indicated voltage will be equal only when $R_1 R_2/R_m$ is zero, that is, if R_m is infinitely large. The internal resistance of a voltmeter should therefore be very high in comparison with the circuit resistance across which it is placed.

MEASUREMENT OF ALTERNATING QUANTITIES

Alternating currents and voltages can be measured directly by a moving-iron meter, or a moving-coil meter may be used in conjunction with a suitable rectifier.

In the previous year of the course we noted that the moving-iron meter will give a direct indication of r.m.s. current. Since the torque produced in these instruments is proportional to I^2, moving-iron meters read r.m.s. values automatically and their scales are accurate for both a.c. and d.c. inputs. This, together with their robust form of construction, are two of the advantages of this kind of meter, but set against these they have the disadvantages of relatively poor sensitivity and a much heavier power consumption than the moving-coil meter. Moving-iron instruments are particularly suitable for measurement at 50 Hz mains frequency where the additional power consumption and low sensitivity are not important factors.

On the other hand the sensitive and relatively fragile moving-coil instrument is a magnetically polarised device and the direction of pointer movement depends upon the direction of current flow through the instrument. If it is connected directly to an alternating supply, the pointer remains at zero, the suspension being unable to follow the rapid reversals of current in the coil. The meter, in fact, indicates the average value of the sinusoidal input which is zero. If alternating quantities are to be indicated, the meter must be used in conjunction with some sort of rectifier, and *Figure 9.4* shows two methods.

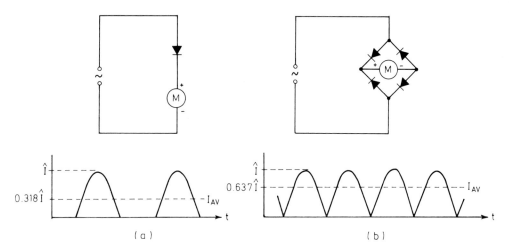

Figure 9.4

In diagram (*a*) a single diode is used in series with the meter. The circuit allows current to flow in one direction only and the meter current waveform is as shown below the circuit. Now the deflection of the moving coil is proportional to the *average* torque acting on the coil, since torque is proportional to current. You will recall that the average value of a sine wave is $2/\pi$ of the peak value or $0.637\hat{I}$. Since every alternative half-cycle is missing in the rectified wave, however, the average falls by a further one-half, hence the meter reading becomes

$$\frac{1}{2} \times \frac{2}{\pi} \times \hat{I} = 0.318\hat{I}$$

The meter is normally scaled to indicate direct current and when used on alternating supplies we should expect it to provide us with the r.m.s. value. In proportion to the r.m.s. value which is $0.707\hat{I}$, the average value of $0.318\hat{I}$ is $0.707/0.318 = 2.22$. Hence the reading of a meter calibrated in terms of direct current has to be multiplied by a factor of 2.22 to indicate the r.m.s. value of the alternating current.

The use of a single rectifier is rarely entertained at low frequencies (power and audio ranges) because the circuit to which the instrument is connected will be asymmetrically loaded. At low input voltages the non-linear relationship between voltage and current in the rectifier leads to a very distorted scale calibration. The most common arrangement is shown in *Figure 9.4(b)*; here the rectifier is a bridge circuit and current is passed alternately by one or other pair of diodes which lie opposite each other. As a result, full-wave rectification occurs and current flows always in the same direction through the meter for every half-cycle of input. The average value of a full-wave rectified current is $0.637\hat{I}$, hence the deflection obtained is twice that of the half-wave rectifier instrument. Hence the reading of a meter calibrated on direct current has this time to be multiplied by the factor $0.707/0.637 = 1.11$. You may remember that this ratio is called the *form factor* of a sinusoidal wave.

This method of a.c. measurement is satisfactory up to some 100 kHz in frequency. Because the scale is calibrated in sinusoidal r.m.s., however, the reading will be *incorrect* when *non-sinusoidal* quantities are measured.

ERRORS AND LIMITATIONS

It might appear at first sight that all we should have to do to turn our basic rectifier instrument into a multi-range meter giving a wide variety of alternating voltage and current measurements would be to add the appropriate multiplier and shunt resistors in series or in parallel with the rectifier respectively, just as would be done for a direct-current multimeter. Unfortunately, such a simplified approach will not work satisfactorily in practice, particularly in the case of current range shunting.

We shall now look briefly at the limitations of moving-iron and moving-coil instruments in respect of range extension and frequency limits when a.c. measurement is concerned.

Shunts are rarely used with moving-iron meters. The deflecting torque depends upon the number of ampere-turns on the coil and for practical design reasons this is usually of the order of 200–300. This kind of figure can be achieved either by having a small number of turns carrying a large current or a large number of turns carrying a small current. In the former case the wire must be of heavy gauge and so the resistance of the coil will be low; this kind of winding is consequently suitable for ammeters. Current ranges are thus possible from a lower limit of about 0.1 A up to 100 A or more, and the need for shunts is eliminated. The many-turn coil is suitable for voltmeter use, the resistance of the coil itself often being high enough to do away with the necessity of series multiplier resistors. For higher voltage ranges than some 50 V or so, an additional series multiplier is usually necessary.

The shunting of moving-iron meters, even if necessary, is rendered very difficult for a.c. measurement by the fact that the coil presents an appreciable inductance as well as resistance, hence as the frequency increases at a given voltage, the current flowing through the meter decreases. It is not sufficient simply to place a purely resistive shunt across the meter coil, since the value of the shunt will be unaffected by frequency but the impedance of the coil will increase with frequency. In theory, the shunt must be *inductive also*, so that the ratio of shunt and coil impedances keep in step as it were, despite changes in

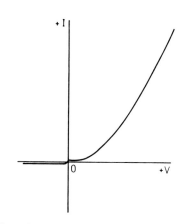

Figure 9.5

frequency. Such a shunt is difficult to design. As a result, moving-iron meters are rarely shunted to provide a range of current indications (tapping the coil is a better solution), and they are rarely ever used at frequencies much in excess of some 200 Hz.

Voltage multipliers, on the other hand, present few problems as a non-inductively wound multiplier resistor is unaffected by frequency. A multimeter or switched-ranged moving-iron voltmeter is therefore perfectly feasible.

When a moving-coil meter is used with a rectifier the deflection remains directly proportional to the alternating current but *not* to the alternating voltage. This is because no rectifier is ideal; it does not behave as a perfect on-and-off switch.

The graph of *Figure 9.5* shows a typical current-voltage characteristic for a meter rectifier. The curve at the lower end of this characteristic shows that Ohm's law is not being obeyed; current is not proportional to voltage. This means that if the meter is used with this rectifier to measure a *voltage* across its terminals, the movement of the pointer will not be uniform (for equal voltage changes) at the lower end of the scale; and the smaller the voltage, the more marked the effect will appear.

For large voltages the effect is not important, because a large value multiplier resistance is then included in series with the meter and this effectively swamps out any variations in the rectifier resistance.

If the voltage drop across the rectifier and meter at f.s.d. is known, this can be subtracted from the required f.s.d. (as in the case of d.c. multipliers) to give the required voltage drop in the series resistor. This value of resistance is then easily calculated as

$$R_s = \frac{\text{required voltage drop}}{\text{required alternating current for f.s.d}}$$

$$= \frac{\text{required voltage drop}}{1.11 \times \text{meter f.s.d. current on d.c.}}$$

In multi-range meters the low voltage a.c. scale is often separately calibrated.

Although, apart from the introduction of errors on the low voltage ranges, and a.c. voltmeter can be used with series multipliers without complication, the measurement of alternating current cannot be undertaken by simple parallel shunting as was the case for d.c. The problem this time is not that of inductance as it was for the moving-iron meter but that of the variation of rectifier resistance.

As the rectifier resistance varies with current the multiplying factor of a parallel shunt would also vary and the meter would require separate scales for each current range, a confusing and not very practicable proposition. For this reason it is usual to employ current transformers in conjunction with rectifier type a.c. meters, the ratio of the windings providing the required scaling so dispensing with the need for ordinary resistor shunts.

Figure 9.6 shows a suitable circuit. The transformation ratio can be calculated from $T = N_1/N_2$. For a 1 mA meter, for example, a secondary alternating current of 1.1 mA will give f.s.d., hence to read 10 mA primary current the required ratio is $1.11/10 = 1 : 9$. In practice a transformer with a fixed secondary is used, the primary being tapped at 1 turn, 10 turns and so on to provide easily switchable current ranges.

Figure 9.6

You will find a current transformer inside an Avometer.

The frequency range of rectifier meters lies roughly between 15 Hz and 100 kHz. Below 15 Hz the pointer oscillates visibly and above some 100 kHz the shunting effect of stray capacitance in the wiring seriously affects the accuracy. In any event, the accuracy is limited by the characteristics of the rectifier and is not better than $1\frac{1}{2}$–2% in most cases.

TOTAL ERROR

The theory of errors is a complicated one and beyond the scope of the present course, but the following notes cover a few of the more common examples which are likely to turn up in electrical experiments where instrument errors are concerned.

When a number of observations are made they will all generally show some deviation from the true value and it is necessary to be able to estimate how large the overall error is likely to be.

(i) *The sum of a number of readings.* The limit of the accuracy of the sum of a number of readings is equal to the sum of the limits of accuracy of the individual readings.

This can be proved as follows: call the readings Q_1, Q_2 and Q_3 and let their limits of accuracy be ΔQ_1, ΔQ_2 and ΔQ_3 respectively. The sum has then a *greatest* value given by

$$(Q_1 + \Delta Q_1) + (Q_2 + \Delta Q_2) + (Q_3 + \Delta Q_3) = (Q_1 + Q_2 + Q_3)$$
$$+ (\Delta Q_1 + \Delta Q_2 + \Delta Q_3)$$

and a *smallest* value given by

$$(Q_1 - \Delta Q_1) + (Q_2 - \Delta Q_2) + (Q_3 - \Delta Q_3) = (Q_1 + Q_2 + Q_3)$$
$$- (\Delta Q_1 + \Delta Q_2 + \Delta Q_3)$$

Hence the greatest departure from the true value is

$$\pm (\Delta Q_1 + \Delta Q_2 + \Delta Q_3)$$

which is the sum of the limits of accuracy of the individual readings.

Figure 9.7

Example (5). In *Figure 9.7* the voltage V is being determined by measuring V_1, V_2 and V_3. Meter V_1 indicates 10 V ± 5%, meter V_2 indicates 40 V ± 2% and meter V_3 indicates 20 V ± 3%. What are the limits between which V probably lies?

$$\text{Clearly } V = V_1 + V_2 + V_3$$

With the given indication percentage errors we get

$$V_1 \text{ indicates } 10 \text{ V} \pm 0.5 \text{ V}$$
$$V_2 \text{ indicates } 40 \text{ V} \pm 0.8 \text{ V}$$
$$V_3 \text{ indicates } 20 \text{ V} \pm 0.6 \text{ V}$$

Hence the extreme limits for V are

$$(10 + 40 + 20) \pm (0.5 + 0.8 + 0.6) = 70 \pm 1.9 \text{ V or } 70 \pm 2.7\%$$

(ii) *The difference between two readings.* The limits of the accuracy of the difference between two readings is equal to the sum of the limits of accuracy of the individual readings.

This can be proved in a manner similar to that in (i) above. Let the readings again be $Q_1 \pm \Delta Q_1$ and $Q_2 \pm \Delta Q_2$. Then for $Q_1 > Q_2$, the greatest possible difference between them is

$$(Q_1 + \Delta Q_1) - (Q_2 - \Delta Q_2) = (Q_1 - Q_2) + (\Delta Q_1 + \Delta Q_2)$$

and the smallest difference will be

$$(Q_1 - \Delta Q_1) - (Q_2 + \Delta Q_2) = (Q_1 - Q_2) - (\Delta Q_1 + \Delta Q_2)$$

Hence the greatest departure from the true value is

$$\pm (\Delta Q_1 + \Delta Q_2)$$

Example (6). In *Figure 9.8* current I_3 is evaluated by measurement of currents I_1 and I_2. If meter I_1 indicates 10 A $\pm 2\%$ and meter I_2 indicates 4 A $\pm 1\frac{1}{2}\%$, what are the extreme values of current I_3 likely to be?

$$\text{Clearly } I_3 = I_1 - I_2$$

Now

$$I_1 \text{ indicates } 10 \text{ A} \pm 0.2 \text{ A}$$

$$I_2 \text{ indicates } 4 \text{ A} \pm 0.06 \text{ A}$$

Hence the limits for I_3 are

$$(10 - 4) \pm (0.2 + 0.06) = 6 \pm 0.26 \text{ A} \text{ or } 6 \text{ A} \pm 4.3\%$$

Here is one to do (and think about) for yourself.

---

(7) Refer again to *Figure 9.8*. If the indication of meter I_2 was 9 A $\pm 1\frac{1}{2}\%$, meter I_1 remaining as before, what would be the probable limits for current I_3? What does the result of this calculation reveal about this circuit arrangement?

Figure 9.8

(iii) *The powers of measured quantities.* If the power of a measured quantity Q is involved in calculations, the percentage error in the calculation of Q^n is n times the percentage error in Q.

Many formulae involve the square or the cube of certain quantities, and it is particularly important that such quantities are measured with the best care possible. Suppose, in an experiment, electrical power dissipation crops up. The current in a resistor is measured as 0.75 ± 0.02 mA, a percentage error of about 2.7%. Now the formulae for power is $I^2 R$ and this introduces the square of the measured quantity. The error in I^2 is then

$$(0.75 \pm 0.02)^2 - 0.75^2 \simeq \pm 0.03$$

and the percentage error in I^2

$$= \frac{0.03}{0.75^2} \times 100 \simeq 5.4\%$$

So the percentage error in I^2 is seen to be *twice* the percentage error in I. This will always be true, and in general, if a power of a quantity is involved, the percentage error in Q^n is n times the percentage error in Q. Hence Q must be measured to a high degree of accuracy. This is true when n is fractional i.e. the error in the root of an observation.

(8)   The formula for the resonant frequency of a series circuit is given by

$$f = \frac{1}{2\pi \sqrt{LC}}$$

If a final accuracy for the frequency of ± 2% is required, what must be the limit of the sum of the percentage deviations in L and C?

(9)   The ratio of two voltages or two currents is to be measured in a circuit. Is it better to take the two readings separately on one meter or to use two separate meters? Give your reasons.

(10)   Prove that the percentage error in the product of a number of measurements is equal to the sum of the percentage errors in the individual measurements.

THE OHMMETER

Any device used for the measurement of the d.c. resistance of passive components is known as an ohmmeter. The most simple form of ohmmeter is shown in *Figure 9.9* and this method of resistance measurement is used in many multimeters for the 'Ohms' ranges. A variable resistor (usually found on the front panel of multimeters) is simply connected in series with the meter movement and an internal battery. In operation, the terminals A-B are first of all short-circuited and the 'Ohms Adjust' control is set to give a full scale deflection on the meter. The unknown resistor R_x is then connected to A and B and the meter indicates a reading less than f.s.d. Hence f.s.d. corresponds to zero ohms and half-scale deflection is obtained when $R_x = R$. The Ohms scale, in other words, reads 'backwards'. The scale is calibrated in ohms but is not linear, the higher resistance values being crowded into the lower part of the scale. You should examine an Avometer to see how the scale is calibrated. Mid-scale readings are the most precise; readings which fall into the first 5 per cent or so of the scale length are usually difficult to judge with any great degree of accuracy.

An alternative circuit is shown in *Figure 9.10*. Again with the test terminals A and B short-circuited, R is adjusted to give a full scale

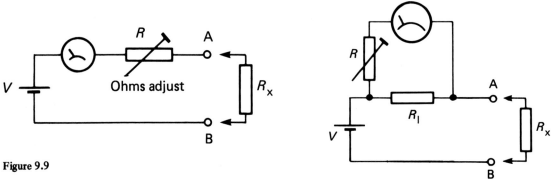

Figure 9.9

Figure 9.10

deflection on the meter which is now essentially a voltmeter. When the unknown resistor is connected, the voltage indicated is that across R_1. Assuming that the meter resistance is large compared with R_1, the voltage indicated by the meter will be

$$\frac{R_1}{R_1 + R_x} \times \text{f.s.d.}$$

Again, f.s.d. corresponds to zero ohms, half-scale when $R_x = R_1$. Scales can be changed by switching in different values of R_1; mid-scale readings of typically 100 Ω, 1 kΩ and 10 kΩ can then be accommodated. For very large resistance values, 1 MΩ and above, it is usual to increase the battery voltage V. In the Avometer, for example, a 1.5 V battery is used for the two lower resistance ranges (usefully up to about 200 kΩ) and a 15 V battery for the higher (up to 20 MΩ) range. The mid-scale values are 20 Ω, 2 kΩ and 20 kΩ respectively.

Some precautions are necessary when using an ohmmeter of this sort. Resistance measurements must not be made on circuits which are in active operation; any voltages present will not only invalidate the reading on the scale, they might well damage the meter itself. It is also necessary to bear in mind that the voltage from the internal battery can lead to problems. When a high value resistance is connected across the test terminals, the voltage across it will approximate closely to that of the internal battery; look at *Figure 9.9* again and take R_x to be very much greater than R and the meter resistance. Then practically the whole of V will appear across R_x. Now if a diode is being checked on the ohmmeter (for forward and reverse resistance readings) two points must be observed:

(a) a *positive* voltage appears at the *negative* terminal of the meter and a *negative* voltage at the *positive* terminal. Hence a good diode conducts (has a small resistance) when its *cathode* end is connected to the positive test terminal of the meter;

(b) when the diode is reversed it will show a very high resistance and the internal battery voltage will appear across it. This could be 15 V on the high Avometer range. Although most diodes will stand this reverse voltage, the base-emmiter junctions of transistors will not. It is always advisable to check transistor junctions on the lowest resistance range where 1.5 V is unlikely to be exceeded as a reverse voltage.

THE ELECTRONIC VOLTMETER

The usual difficulty with analogue instruments is that they disturb circuit conditions when they are connected, and we have discussed this aspect earlier. The greatest source of inaccuracy arises from the measurement of voltage across large resistances. Further, the conventional a.c. meter using a bridge rectifier has an upper frequency limit and is inaccurate with small inputs.

By using an amplifier between the test input terminals and the meter itself, it is possible to provide an extremely high input resistance which draws negligible power from the system under observation, make measurements of very small quantities such as microvolts and microamperes, and extend the frequency range on a.c. to many megahertz. Such an instrument is known as an electronic multimeter.

Looking at a typical voltmeter based on this technique, *Figure 9.11(a)* and *(b)* illustrate the basic form. An input attenuator is switched to the appropriate voltage range required and the input, reduced to the proper level, is then applied to a d.c. amplifier. If the input device of this amplifier is a field effect transistor, an input impedance of hundreds of megohms is possible. Of course the input attenuator degrades this, but the attenuator can, nevertheless, be made up from much higher resistance values than could be used in an ordinary multimeter, so keeping the input resistance of the order of 10 MΩ or so; this resistance remains constant up to frequencies of 10 MHz and over. The output of the amplifier drives the conventional meter movement. With this system, full scale deflections can be obtained for inputs of just a few microvolts.

For a.c. measurements, a diode circuit is introduced before the attenuator, see *Figure 9.11(c)*. On the application of the alternating input, capacitor C charges up with the polarity indicated to the *peak* value of the input. The diode voltage is then equal to the instantaneous input voltage plus the peak value of the input, that is, the diode output contains a *d.c. component* equal to the peak value of the input and an a.c. component which is filtered out by the combination of R and C_1. The d.c. component is applied to the amplifier by way of the attenuator. Although the input is a peak voltage, the scale of the meter is calibrated in r.m.s. values for sinusoidal inputs.

COMPLEX WAVES

Many alternating quantities encountered in electrical and electronic work are not purely sinusoidal in form, although being repetitive at definite intervals or periods just as pure sinewaves are. By a theorem of higher mathematics known as Fourier's theorem, any such repetitive waveform can be represented by an equation of the form

$$i = I_0 + I_1 \sin(\omega t + \phi_1) + I_2 \sin(2\omega t + \phi_2) + \ldots \ldots$$

or, of course, an equivalent voltage form.

The term I_0 is a d.c. component (which in many cases would not be present) and superimposed on this are sinusoidal variations of different amplitudes, different periods and different phases. Such a wave is known as a *complex* wave.

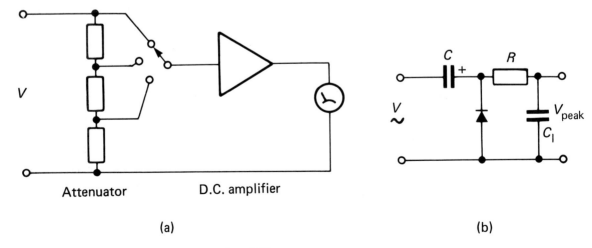

Attenuator D.C. amplifier	
(a)	(b)

Figure 9.11

As we are considering only alternating quantities it is sufficient to take the terms

$$i = I_1 \sin (\omega t + \phi_1) + I_2 \sin (2\omega t + \phi_2) + I_3 \sin (3\omega t + \phi_3) + \ldots$$

each of which has an average value of zero over its particular period, just as a single sine or cosine wave has over its period of $360°$. If we examine each term we see that the *component* frequencies of the complete wave are made up of a frequency $\omega/2\pi$ and multiples of it, twice the frequency, three times the frequency and so on. The frequency represented by the first term, $\omega/2\pi$, is called the *fundamental* or first *harmonic* frequency; the second term $2\omega/2\pi$, is called the second harmonic, the third term $3\omega/2\pi$, the third harmonic and so on. The second, fourth, etc harmonics are known as the even harmonics, while the third, fifth, etc are known as the odd harmonics. So any repetitive alternating quantity can be split up into a fundamental frequency and harmonic frequencies. Sounds produced by the voice or musical instruments always contain a large number of harmonics and it is these which give musical notes their particular quality or 'timbre'.

Similarly for electrical waves, if a complex current or voltage wave is acting in a circuit we can treat it as a series of purely sinusoidal components each acting independently of all the others for purposes of analysis.

The result of combining a fundamental wave and its second harmonic is shown in *Figure 9.12(a)* where the waves are assumed to be in phase at time $t = 0$ and the amplitude of the harmonic is one-third the amplitude of the fundamental. The resultant complex wave is shown in solid line. The equation of this curve will be

$$i = A \sin \omega t + (A/3) \sin 2\omega t.$$

The combination of a fundamental wave and its third harmonic is shown in *Figure 9.12(b)*. Here again we have assumed the waves to be in phase at time $t = 0$ and the amplitude of the harmonic is one-third

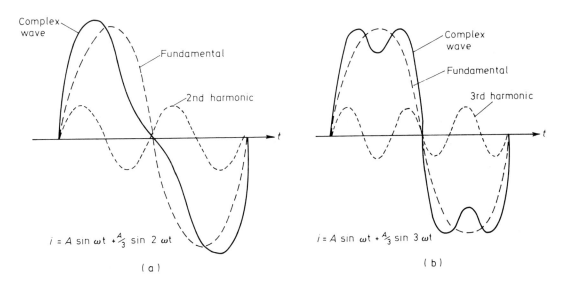

$i = A \sin \omega t + \frac{A}{3} \sin 2\omega t$

(a)

$i = A \sin \omega t + \frac{A}{3} \sin 3\omega t$

(b)

Figure 9.12

the amplitude of the fundamental. This time the equation of the resultant complex wave will be $i = A \sin \omega t + (A/3) \sin 3\omega t$.

The greater the number of harmonics present the more complex does the resultant wave become. This does not mean that its shape becomes very confused, on the contrary, the shape often becomes geometrically neat. A square wave, for example, contains an infinity of odd harmonics, while a saw-tooth wave contains an infinity of all the harmonic sine terms.

(11)   Look at the fundamental and harmonic waves, with their complex resultants, shown in *Figure 9.13*. Identify the harmonics present and estimate the form of the equations representing each of these resultant waves.

If we are going to amplify a complex wave we must make sure that the amplifier we are using is capable of dealing with the whole range of frequencies concealed in the complex wave. This is of paramount importance in amplifiers which are used in test equipment, such as oscilloscopes. There must be no question of the amplifier itself introducing further distortion into the waveform under examination, either by adding additional harmonics of its own or leaving others out. Such amplifiers have to be designed to a rigorous specification if they are to be of any value.

First of all, an ideal amplifier must have a flat gain-frequency response characteristic, that is, it must not amplify some frequencies more than others. If it did so and the output was displayed on an oscilloscope screen, the relative size of the waveform exhibited would change at different frequency settings and accurate measurement would not be possible. Further, if a complex wave was under examination and the amplifier failed to amplify some of its significant harmonics in the right proportions, the output waveform would be quite different from that at the input.

Of equal importance to constancy of gain at all frequencies, the *time taken* for signals to pass through the amplifier must be the same at all frequencies. It might seem at first that the transit-time as it is called would automatically be the same for all frequencies but this is not so. Remember, there are such things as time constants in the coupling components, and the active devices themselves, transistors or values, introduce time delays which are dependent upon frequency.

Suppose the waveform of a fundamental and its second harmonic

(a)

(b)

Figure 9.13

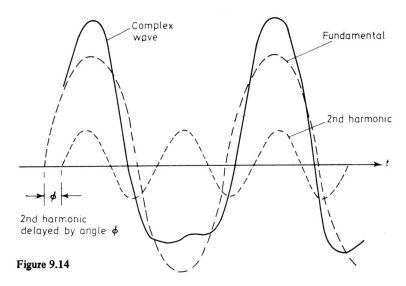

Figure 9.14

shown in *Figure 9.12(a)* is being amplified. If the two components undergo the same amplification but the second harmonic is delayed slightly in transit relative to the fundamental, then the output signal will be of the form shown in *Figure 9.14*. Considerable distortion has occurred and such an amplifier would be of little value in an oscilloscope. The effect would become worse at higher frequency harmonics so that a wave which had a great number of harmonics, such as a rectangular wave, would be seriously distorted.

Modern oscilloscope amplifiers are nearly always designed as d.c. amplifiers so that the coupling capacitors (which contribute to transit-time problems) are not used between stages. The advantages of this are that very low frequencies can be adequately amplified and direct current components are also transmitted.

ATTENUATION

If the voltages to be examined are of large amplitude they cannot be fed directly to an amplifier but must first be reduced or attenuated. The above requirement of faithful transmission by the amplifier must apply equally to the attenuator system. So an attenuator must be independent of frequency and, in most cases, it should have an impedance suited to the kind of circuit to which it is connected.

Most amplifiers are designed to have high impedance inputs so that they do not load the circuits connected to them; if attenuation is to take place at the amplifier input, therefore, a high impedance type of attenuator is called for.

A typical form for such an attenuator is shown in *Figure 9.15*. R_1 and R_2 are the voltage divider resistors (in practice these would be switched in steps of, say, 10 : 1, 100 : 1 and so on), and C_i and R_i represent the input capacitance and resistance respectively of the amplifier following the attenuator. Since R_1 and R_2 will have high values of resistance, the division of voltage across them will only be in the true ratio of the resistance values at low frequencies where the reactance of C_i is extremely high. At high frequencies, C_i progressively shunts R_2 and the attenuation ratio changes accordingly.

Figure 9.15

Figure 9.16

Figure 9.17

To obtain frequency independence, correcting capacitor C_1 is introduced. Then ideally

$$C_1 R_1 = \frac{R_i R_2}{R_2 + R_i} C_i$$

A commonly employed attenuator system is shown in *Figure 9.16*. Here the attenuator is connected into the emitter lead of an emitter-follower which forms the input stage of the amplifier system. The emitter-follower has a very high input impedance but a low output impedance. So the attenuator resistors R_1, R_2, R_3 etc can have low values and the effect of the shunting input capacitance of the following amplifier stage has negligible effect even at high frequencies.

MEASUREMENT OF PHASE

If two sine waves which are of the same frequency are applied simultaneously to the X- and Y-plates of a cathode-ray oscilloscope, then the pattern appearing on the screen will vary between a straight line and a circle depending upon the phase angle between the two waves.

In *Figure 9.17* a resistor R is connected in series with a load impedance Z. The voltage across the resistor is fed to one pair of plates while the voltage across the impedance is fed to the other pair. We then have two sinusoidal voltages of equal frequency but differing in phase applied simultaneously to the deflector plates.

If amplifiers are used, the gains can be adjusted to obtain equal signal amplitudes but the amplifiers must be identical to make the internal phase shift negligible.

The phase angle ϕ can be measured from the shape of the pattern appearing on the screen, and *Figure 9.18* shows in detail how an elliptical pattern is produced. Such a pattern is known as a *Lissajous* figure.

Let the voltage applied to the X-plates be $v_x = V_x \sin \omega t$, and let the voltage applied to the Y-plates be $v_y = V_y \sin (\omega t + \phi)$ where ϕ is the required phase difference.

At the instant $t = 0$, $v_x = 0$ and OA represents the instantaneous value of v_y. Then

$$OA = V_y \sin \phi$$

But V_y is represented by the distance OB, therefore $OA = OB \cdot \sin \phi$.

$$\therefore \quad \sin \phi = \frac{OA}{OB}$$

If the major axis of the ellipse lies in the first and third quadrants, then the phase angle lies between 0 and $90°$. If the major axis lies in the second or fourth quadrants, then the phase angle lies between $90°$ and $180°$. The actual ratio of the horizontal and vertical deflections in the oscilloscope may be quite arbitrary.

This method does not determine which voltage is leading or lagging on the other unless the direction of rotation of the spot is known. It can be determined however, by making a known change in the phase angle (R could be variable) and observing the corresponding change in the position of the ellipse.

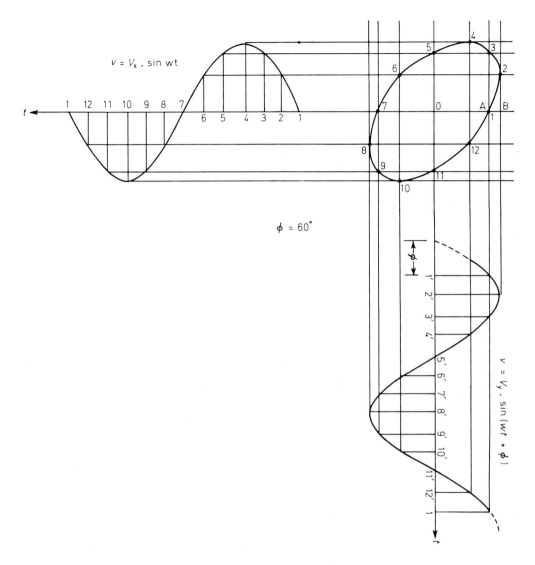

$v = V_x . \sin wt$

$\phi = 60°$

$v = V_y . \sin (wt + \phi)$

Figure 9.18

MEASUREMENT OF FREQUENCY

If sinusoidal voltages of different frequencies are applied respectively to the X- and Y-plates, the pattern observed on the screen can take a great variety of shapes, many of them much too complicated to be of any value. The interpretation of some of the simpler shapes enable the oscilloscope to be used to measure an unknown frequency or to compare two frequencies.

For instance let the unknown frequency f_y be applied, say, to the X-plates while the known frequency f_y is applied to the Y-plates. Then by a process similar to that illustrated for the ellipse in *Figure 9.18*, a Lissajous figure is produced, an example being shown in *Figure 9.19*.

The frequency to be measured is calculated from

$$\frac{f_y}{f_x} = \frac{\text{number of loops along the horizontal direction}}{\text{number of loops along the vertical direction}}$$

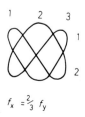

$f_x = \frac{2}{3} f_y$

Figure 9.19

In the case illustrated

$$f_x = \frac{2}{3} f_y$$

When $f_x = f_y$, the pattern produced is a single loop and this is often the best indication to work for there is then no chance of miscounting the side loops. Very wide frequency ratios make the Lissajous figures difficult or impossible to interpret.

The accuracy of the method is dependent upon the accuracy of the comparison (known) frequency f_y. It is not easy to use the method below about 10 Hz or above 1 MHz.

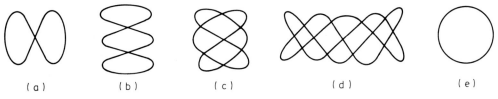

| (a) | (b) | (c) | (d) | (e) |

Figure 9.20

(12)   In *Figure 9.17* a number of Lissajous figures are shown. What is the ratio of the frequencies used in each case. Assume that the unknown frequency f_x is applied to the X-plates.

(13)   Refer back to *Figure 9.14*. Assuming that the X- and Y-plate sensitivities are exactly equal and that resistor $R = 1000\ \Omega$, what would be the value of a capacitor used in position Z so that a circle was obtained on the screen when the input frequency was 50 Hz?

COUNTERS AND FREQUENCY METERS

The measurement of frequency by means of Lissajous' figures on an oscilloscope is essentially a stop-gap method and is rarely used as such outside of demonstration and basic experimental work. Expensive oscilloscopes are available in which a built-in microprocessor provides a direct digital read-out of time periods, frequency and voltage in addition to the normal screen display of the waveform. Marker pips on the screen are set by the operator to indicate horizontal and vertical points on the displayed function and these are interpreted by the microprocessor in terms of frequency, phase or voltage in digital terms. Less sophisticated methods are adequate for general purpose laboratory experiments.

The measurement of frequency over the audio range and up to about 250 kHz can be done quite simply by analogue methods. The general principle in all such designs is to allow a capacitor to charge to a fixed reference level during one half-cycle of the input waveform, and discharge through an analogue instrument during the following half-cycle. The mean discharge current through the meter depends upon the rate at which the capacitor is charged or upon the rate at which the input waveform changes, that is, upon the frequency. The meter is consequently scaled in terms of frequency.

A basic form of circuit is shown in *Figure 9.21*. The input waveform is first converted to a square wave of constant amplitude; it is then used to switch transistor T_1 on and off for each alternate half-cycle. Capacitor C charges during the half-cycle of input when T_1 is off via R and diode D_2 to the potential level set by zener diode Z. On the following half-cycle, T_1 switches on and C discharges through it, diode D_1 and the meter itself. The mean current through the meter is thus proportional to frequency.

The frequency range covered is determined by the value of C; by having a series of capacitors switched into circuit a frequency range of some 15 Hz to 100 kHz — and with care up to about 250 kHz — is easily provided in decade steps. With this method, frequencies below some 15 Hz are seen as slow oscillations of the meter pointer and are not accurately readable; the upper limit is determined by the smallest value of C that can be distinguished from the stray capacitance. Dependence on the whims of circuit strays would not lead to a reliable instrument.

For measurement of frequencies above some 250 kHz, the digital frequency meter is dominant. Even on relatively simple models, frequencies up to 10 MHz can be measured and upper limits of 500 MHz or more are easily obtained by simple pre-division of the input signal.

Digital frequency meters are based on the digital counter which can itself be used for the counting of events such as objects passing on a production line, revolutions of a shaft, human and animal pulse rate and so on, as well as forming the basic 'movement' of the familiar digital clock. Any of these events can be converted into electrical pulses by suitable transducers and these pulses can be counted on a system such as that shown in *Figure 9.22*. This again is in its most primitive form but the principle of all digital counters is based on this. The input, which may be a regular train of pulses or random pulses, is applied to the first of a group of binary converters each of which count from 0 to 9 and provide an output in binary notation, or binary-coded decimal

Figure 9.21

Figure 9.22

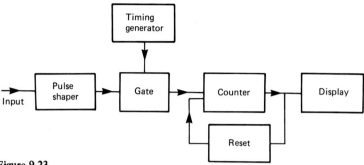

Figure 9.23

(BCD) as it is more usually known. As each converter gets to 9 (or 1001 in binary) it switches back to 0 (0000 in binary) and passes a single pulse on to the next converter in the chain. Hence units, tens, hundreds etc. are counted as the input pulse train continues. To provide an intelligible output, binary decoders are inserted between the converters and the display units. Any calculator will give you an example of such a numerical display. The purpose of the decoders is to change the binary numbers into a form which will illuminate the appropriate sections of the display so that the familiar decimal numbers will appear and indicate the extent of the count.

For the measurement of frequency, the counter is arranged to switch on for a known interval and count the number of input pulses occurring during that period. Such switching cannot be done manually if any sort of precision is looked for, so an all-electronic system is used. This can be switched on and off in precisely controlled periods and at a very high rate; it is usually controlled by a crystal oscillator which can be accurate to better than one cycle in 10 MHz. The crystal output can be divided down to provide, say, 100 kHz, 10 kHz, 1 kHz, 100 Hz, 10 Hz and 1 Hz control pulses, representing time intervals respectively of 10 μs, 1 ms, 10 ms, 0.1 s and 1 s. *Figure 9.23* shows the basic arrangement this time.

The unknown frequency input is first converted into a rectangular pulse train. This then passes to the counter by way of the electronic gate which allows its passage for a fixed interval determined by the output from the crystal controlled timing generator. This output is a single pulse of the required duration, repeated after a time which is long compared with its own duration. Assuming the interval for counting is 100 ms and the counter reads 3287 after receiving an input for that duration, then the frequency would be 32.87 kHz. The gate control pulse must, of course, be suited to the frequency range being measured. It would be of no use to try to measure, say, a frequency of around 100 Hz with a timing pulse of 10 μs. (Why not?)

It is necessary for the counter to be reset before the following count as each subsequent operation of the gate would otherwise cause the counter merely to add to the reading already obtained. All this switching is done electronically within the system and in operation the count is continually updated to take care of any fluctuations in the input frequency when continuous measurement is being made.

(14) The timing generator of a frequency counter operates at a frequency of 10 MHz. If 3600 pulses are counted during the given time interval, what is the frequency of the input?

THE DIGITAL VOLTMETER

The digital voltmeter (DVM) is now an everyday instrument in most laboratories and it offers a number of advantages over analogue instruments: higher accuracy and resolution, no possibility of observational or parallax errors and an extremely high input resistance, constant on all ranges.

The most simple form of DVM is shown in *Figure 9.24*. This method is known as the single-slope technique to distinguish it from the dual-slope which is more commonly used in practice. Both forms are essentially analogue-to-digital converters. Assume that the counter unit is reset to zero and that the output from the integrator is also zero. Then at a time t_1 the integrator produces a ramp–voltage output which increases linearly with time, i.e. the voltage level reached is proportional to time. This ramp level is compared with the analogue input level V_x (the voltage being measured) and when they are equal the output from the comparator changes sign and switches off the gate, which, up until then from time t_1, has been passing a stream of clock pulses through to the counter unit. The count then stops. The time taken for the ramp voltage to rise to the level of the input is proportional to the number reached by the counter; this number is therefore proportional to the input voltage. An additional clock which produces a relatively slow train of pulses is used to reset both the integrator and the counter to zero so that the operation is periodically restarted and the count updated. A 'latching' circuit is also introduced into the counter so that the display is held constant while a following count sequence is taking place.

The single-slope system has disadvantages when it is used in intruments which require resolutions better than 1 part in 10^4 or more. Variations in the integrator due to temperature, time and input sensitivity and in the stability of C and R cause the ramp to be unstable enough to lead to inaccurate and variable readings. The dual-slope system, of which the basic circuit is given in *Figure 9.25(a)*, overcomes most of these problems. As in the single-slope system, the cycle starts with the ramp output set to zero, the counters reset to zero and the voltage to be measured (V_x) switched through to the

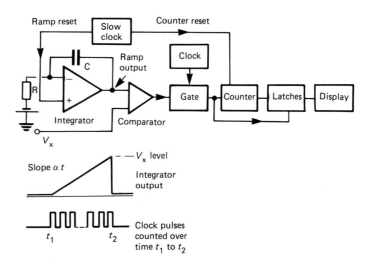

Figure 9.24

input terminal. At a time instant t_1, as before, the integrator produces a ramp output which rises* linearly with time and switches the comparator output when ramp and input voltage levels are equal. This time, however, there is the difference that the ramp is allowed to proceed for a *fixed number* of counts only. So C charges at a rate proportional to V_x for a *fixed* time t_x ($= t_2 - t_1$) and during this period a certain number of clock pulses have been counted. This process is shown for two different input voltages in *Figure 9.25(b)*. At the end of this sequence (at instant t_2) the integrator input is automatically switched to a precise reference voltage, V_{ref}. The sign of this input is such that the integrator ouput is reversed and ramps negatively along a linear path of *fixed* gradient V_{ref}/CR, i.e. the capacitor now discharges at a rate proportional to V_{ref}. The counter resets at instant t_2 and counts until the comparator indicates that the integrator output has returned to zero, time t_3. The control circuits are operated by this transition and set the counter output into the latches where it is displayed as a held count. The counter itself is then reset to zero and the integrator input switches back to V_x. The whole cycle of operation then repeats. *From Figure 9.25(b)*, by proportion

$$V_x t_x = V_{ref} t_{ref}$$

or
$$V_x = V_{ref} \frac{t_{ref}}{t_x}$$

Hence, since t_x and V_{ref} are constants, the count made during the period t_{ref} is proportional to the input voltage and is displayed via the latches as the measured voltage. Notice that the product CR cancels

(a)

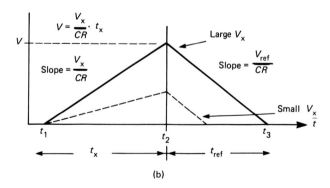

(b)

Figure 9.25

*In practice, the ramp may move negatively but this does not invalidate the argument.

out and does not come into the equation for V_x; this means that the same capacitor and resistor can be used for both the input and the reference integration periods so that variations in C and R have no effect on the accuracy.

The dual-slope technique is slower acting than is the single-slope but this is a minor point for most purposes. Digital meters in general have the disadvantage that they do not give an intelligible display on fluctuating inputs. An analogue meter averages out such fluctuations and provides a mean reading.

Example (15). In the circuit of *Figure 9.25(a)* the clock operates at a frequency of 1 MHz and the reference voltage is 1.35 V. $C = 0.2\ \mu F$ and $R = 10\ k\Omega$. (a) What slope will the charge ramp have for an input of 1.2 V? (b) If time t_x is 1000 counts, what voltage level V will the ramp reach? (c) How long will it take for the integrator to reset to zero?

(a) The slope for an input of 1.2 V will be

$$\frac{V_x}{CR} = \frac{1.2}{0.2 \times 10^{-6} \times 10^4}$$

$$= 600\ V/s$$

(b) Period t_x is 1000 counts of the clock, therefore $t_x = 1$ ms, therefore in 1 ms the ramp would have reached

$$\frac{V_x}{CR} \times t_x = 0.6\ V$$

(c) The slope of the discharge ramp is

$$\frac{V_{ref}}{CR} = \frac{1.35}{0.2 \times 10^{-6} \times 10^4}$$

$$= 675\ V/s$$

therefore time to reach zero from 0.6 V $= \dfrac{0.6}{675} = 8.89 \times 10^{-4}$ s

$$= 0.89\ ms$$

As a check on this last result, we note that during this time the count will be $0.89 \times 1.35 \times 1000$ which, with the appropriate placement of the decimal point, will display as 1.2 V, the input voltage.

Note that in part (c) the slope of the discharge ramp is strictly negative; this omission does not influence the solution for the time of discharge.

THE DIGITAL MULTIMETER

As in the case of analogue instruments, additional circuits must be added to the basic DVM to make it into a multimeter capable of measuring a.c. voltage, d.c. and a.c. current and resistance. Most DVM's have a basic voltage scale with a maximum reading (or 'f.s.d.') of either 200 mV or 2.0 V, strictly 199.9 mV or 1.999 V respectively on the familiar $3\frac{1}{2}$ digit display. This can be extended to read up to

1000 V (which is the maximum for general purpose DVM's) by an attenuator network of precision resistors such as is shown in *Figure 9.26(a)*. Each step down the resistor chain divides the input by 10. So if we had a DVM with a basic full scale reading of 2.0 V and the input was 150 V, we would have to set the switch to position C to accommodate this input within the range of the display. For with 150 V at the input, the B position will have 15 V, the C position 1.5 V and the D position 0.15 V. The correct positioning of the decimal point in each of the ranges is accomplished by another switch, ganged to the attenuator switch. The 470 kΩ resistor in conjunction with the back-to-back zener diodes act as a protection system and limit the input to the DVM to about 3.3 V should an excessive voltage be applied to the input. The 470 kΩ does not degrade the accuracy as the input resistance of the DVM itself is extremely high.

An alternative attenuator arrangement is shown in *Figure 9.26(b)*. This has an advantage in that each range position is independent of the others, unlike that in *(a)* where a failure or change in value of one of the resistors would affect all the ranges except possibly the first. The attenuation ratio this time is clearly $R/(R + 10 \text{ M}\Omega)$ where R is the appropriate switched resistor in each case.

A.C. measurement

The measurement of a.c. voltages requires the input to be first rectified before being passed to the DVM. The same input attenuators may be used for a.c. inputs but the rectifier system has to be something more than a single diode or bridge type circuit. We have already referred to the error arising when low a.c. voltages are being measured due to the non-linearity of the diode below about 1 V, and this would clearly be an unacceptable loss of accuracy in the DVM where the basic measurement might be as low as 200 mV. The problem can be overcome by using what is known as a 'precision rectifier', and a typical circuit is shown in *Figure 9.27*. Two operational amplifiers are used; the first acts as an active rectifier with diode D_1 in the feedback loop. With this arrangement the diode characteristic is linearised down to input voltages of 1 mV or less. The output from this stage of the circuit is a half-wave rectified waveform. This can be filtered and passed to the DVM directly, but by introducing the second operational amplifier the system becomes a full-wave rectifier by combining the input a.c. with the output of the half-wave rectifier. In this way the missing half-cycles

(b)

Figure 9.26

Figure 9.27

are added to the output. This output is then filtered by capacitor C and scaled to the correct r.m.s. value by adjustment of the potentiometer V_R. Diode D_2 might seem redundant, but it is inserted to provide feedback so that the positive half-cycles of input do not overload the first operational amplifier.

> (16) In *Figure 9.26(b)* calculate the values of the unmarked resistors so that for switch positions A, B, C and D the input voltage is divided by 1000, 100, 10 and 1 respectively.

Current measurement

Current input

R_S

R_1

R_2

$R_1 = 99\,R_2$

To DVM

Figure 9.28

The measurement of a.c. and d.c. current can be achieved by measuring the voltage drop across a known resistor. This resistor must be of small value to avoid an excessive voltage drop in the circuit under test, yet at the same time its power rating must be capable of handling the highest current likely to be measured, typically 10 A. A conventional series of shunt resistors can be switched in to suit the current ranges, but an alternative method using an amplifier is a better approach. *Figure 9.28* shows this system; a small value sense resistor is used to drop the voltage and this voltage is then amplified a known number of times, typically 100. Suppose the basic range of the DVM is 2 V; to represent this as a 2 mA scale, say, the amplifier output must be 2 V, hence its input (for a gain of 100) must be 0.02 V. This voltage can be dropped at a current of 2 mA in a 10 Ω sense resistor.

Resistance measurement

D_1

D_2

T_1

T_2

R_1

R_2

R_x

Set resistance range

Figire 9.29

The measurement of resistance using the DVM is accomplished by passing a precisely defined current through the resistance and then measuring the voltage drop across it. The current is obtained from a constant current source and is adjusted in level to suit the range of resistance being measured. For a DVM with a basic 2 V f.s.d., for example, resistances up to 200 Ω could be measured by having a constant current of level 10 mA. The voltage drop for any resistance from 0 to 200 Ω would then be such that it would be interpreted as a resistance value on the display. In the same way, resistances up to 2000 Ω would require a constant current of level 1 mA, and so on.

Constant current generators can be made up from discrete transistors or operational amplifiers may be used. *Figure 9.29* shows a simple circuit using two transistors. Here transistor T_1 which, together with the diodes in its emitter circuit, acts as a voltage reference at the base of T_2, holds T_2 to the constant-current region of its characteristic. The actual level of the current is set by the range switch to provide resistance ranges of (usually) 200 Ω, 2 kΩ, 20 kΩ, and 200 kΩ. A higher range of 20 MΩ is found on most DVM's. The resistors of the input attenuator chain are sometimes used in the dual role of voltage dividers and set-constant-current resistors by way of suitable switching.

A.C. BRIDGES The bridge method for comparing and measuring resistances which has its basic form in the metre slide-wire bridge can be extended from the d.c. mode of operation to the a.c. form; it is then possible to measure

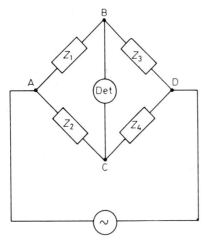

Figure 9.30

inductance, capacitance, frequency, Q-factor, impedance and power factor, among other quantities.

The essential conditions of balance for an a.c. bridge are the same as those for a d.c. bridge; referring to *Figure 9.30*, the bridge will be zero potential across the points BC when $Z_1 Z_4 = Z_2 Z_3$. As the elements in the arms of the bridge may not now be purely resistive, however, the relationship of balance must take into account that there are phase differences in all or some of the bridge arms. Hence the bridge cannot be balanced by adjustment of the magnitude of the arm impedances alone; a further and separate adjustment has to be made with respect to phase angle. So two unknown quantities have to be determined. These are the resistive and reactive components of the unknown arm stated in terms of the constants in the other three arms.

In order to simplify the circuit and keep the number of controls to a minimum, it is customary to make two of the bridge arms purely resistive. Resistance and reactance are then separately balanced out on a third arm against the unknown impedance in the fourth arm.

The technique of balancing an a.c. bridge is rather more complicated than it is for a d.c. bridge. The method is to adjust the resistance-balance control until a minimum indication is obtained on the detector, then to adjust the reactance-balance control until a new and smaller minimum is obtained, then readjust the resistance-balance control, and so on, continually readjusting the two controls in turn until, in theory, a zero or null indication is obtained on the detector.

The detector may be an a.c. voltmeter, or, if the operating frequency is of the order of 1 kHz, a pair of headphones or loudspeaker may be used.

Maxwell's bridge   This bridge is used to measure the self-inductance and effective resistance of a coil in cases where the resistive component is large. There are two basic forms of the bridge, and these are shown in *Figure 9.31(a)* and *(b)*.

In diagram *(a)*, two arms of the bridge, P and Q, situated adjacent to each other, are pure resistances. The adjustable arm Z_1 consists of a calibrated variable inductor L_1 in series with a calibrated variable resistance R_1. The unknown arm Z_2 contains the coil whose inductance L and effective series resistance r are required. It can be proved that the bridge is balanced and the detector reading is a minimum when

$$L = \frac{P}{Q} \circ L_1; \quad r = \frac{P}{Q} \cdot R_1$$

Thus the unknown quantities L and r are obtained in terms of the known quantities L_1, R_1 (read from calibrated scales), and the *ratio* of P to Q. As the results are independent of ω, the exact frequency of operation is unimportant.

P and Q appearing as a ratio in both solutions, can be arranged in values so that a decade multiplying (or dividing) ratio is available as required e.g. if values of 10, 100 and 1000 Ω are used, ratios of 1 : 1, 1 : 10, and 1 : 100 (and the inverse) are immediately to hand. This form of bridge is often known as a *ratio-arm bridge* for this reason.

A disadvantage of this bridge is the presence of an accurately calibrated variable inductor in one of the arms. Such a component is difficult to design, and the modification shown in *Figure 9.31(b)* gets over this difficulty. The resistance arms are now arranged diagonally opposite each other, and the adjustable arm is a variable capacitor C_1 in parallel with a variable resistor R_1. In this circuit the resistive component of the test coil is balanced out by R_1 and the positive reactive component of L is balanced out by the negative reactance of C_1. The variable capacitor is clearly a much better component from the point of view of cost, ease of control and calibration than the variable inductor.

When the bridge is balanced this time:

$$L = PQC_1; \quad r = \frac{PQ}{R_1}$$

Again the results are independent of frequency and give L and r in terms of R_1, C_1 and the *product* of P and Q. For this reason, this bridge is often known as a *product-arm bridge*. If the product PQ is arranged to be 10^6 (e.g. by making $P = 100$, $Q = 10000$) then, when balance is obtained, the reading of C_1 in μF ($= 10^{-6} F$) gives the value of L directly in henries.

The Q-factor of a coil can be estimated from a knowledge of the series resistance r, inductance L and the frequency used on the bridge. As the resistive component r is relatively large in coils measured on this form of bridge, a reasonably good estimation can be obtained.

Hay's bridge This is a modification of Maxwell's inductance bridge and is used to measure inductive impedances having *small* resistive components. In a coil where r is small, Maxwell's bridge requires inconveniently large values of variable resistor R_1; Hay's bridge overcomes this problem by placing R_1 in series with C_1 as shown in *Figure 9.32*. This time the balance condition is:

$$L = PQC_1; \quad r = \frac{PQ}{R_1}$$

where the effective resistance r of the test coil is taken as the equivalent *parallel* component. A simple expression for Q-factor is

$$Q\text{-factor} = \frac{1}{\omega C_1 R_1}$$

hence ω must be known in this case.

The following problems cover instruments in general and not only those items mentioned in the Unit section.

PROBLEMS FOR SECTION 9

(17) An ammeter and a resistor are connected in series across a d.c. supply. The ammeter reads 5 mA. A voltmeter of resistance 25 kΩ connected directly across the resistor reads 25 V. Calculate (a) the approximate value of the resistor, (b) the exact value of the resistor.

(18) *Figure 9.33* shows a circuit used to determine the d.c. resistance of a coil. The ammeter reads 2.5 A, the voltmeter reads 32 V. If the ammeter resistance is 0.1 Ω calculate: (a) the approximate resistance of the coil, (b) the exact resistance of the coil, (c) the p.d. across the coil.

(19) A moving-iron voltmeter has a coil with 100 turns having a resistance of 2500 Ω. The meter gives a f.s.d. with an applied voltage of 100 V. How many turns would be required on the coil if the instrument is converted to read a f.s.d. of 2.0 A?

(a)

(b)

Figure 9.31

Figure 9.32

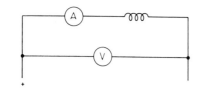

Figure 9.33

(20) A 35 V d.c. supply is connected across a resistance of 600 Ω in series with an unknown resistor X. A voltmeter having a resistance of 1200 Ω is connected across the 600 Ω resistor and shows a reading of 5 V. Calculate the value of resistor X.

(21) A sinusoidal alternating current has a peak value of 5 A. If this current is full-wave rectified what would be the readings on (a) a moving-iron ammeter, (b) a moving-coil ammeter, connected to measure the rectified current?

(22) A voltmeter with a full scale deflection of 25 V has industrial grade limits of calibration of ± 2%. The scale is divided into 100 divisions and the error in observation is $\pm\frac{1}{2}$ division. When used to measure the terminal voltage of a certain power unit, the meter indicates 14.5 V. Between what limits does the voltage probably lie?

(23) Using Maxwell's bridge according to *Figure 9.19(a)* the self-resistance of the coil is given by $r = PR_1/Q$. If the accuracy of each of the bridge resistors P and Q is $\pm\frac{1}{2}\%$ and that of the variable R_1 is 2%, what is the maximum measuring error on the bridge?

(24) A current transformer has a turns ratio of 250 : 1. What current will flow in an ammeter connected to the secondary of the transformer when the primary current is 15 A?

(25) Using the method of construction illustrated in *Figure 9.18*, trace the Lissajous figure resulting from (a) two inputs of equal amplitude and frequency and in phase, (b) two inputs of equal amplitude and frequency, 90° out of phase, (c) two inputs of equal amplitude, but having a frequency ratio of 3 : 2.

(26) In the Hay's Bridge shown in *Figure 9.32*, balance is obtained when $C_1 = 3\ \mu F$, $R_1 = 2500\ \Omega$. If $P = 100\ \Omega$ and $Q = 1000\ \Omega$ and the frequency of the bridge input is 1 kHz, calculate the inductance, self-resistance and Q-factor of the coil under test.

(27) A symmetrical triangular wave is applied to a bridge rectifier type of a.c. ammeter and the reading obtained is 1.5 A. What is the peak current of the triangular wave?

(28) Design a simple ohmmeter using an analogue meter with 100 μA f.s.d. and a 1.5 V cell, so that it will have two ranges, one with a half-scale reading of 500 Ω and the other with 5000 Ω. What would reasonably be the greates value of resistance you might expect to measure with this ohmmeter?

(29) The circuit of *Figure 9.34* is used to measure a resistance connected to points X-Y. What will be the current through the meter when a resistor of 84 Ω is connected across X-Y? If the meter has a f.s.d. of 50 mA, what would be the *lowest* resistance which could be measured by this circuit arrangement?

(30) In the attenuator shown in *Figure 9.26(a)*, the 90 kΩ resistor changes value by +5%. Assuming that all the resistors were originally accurate to 0.1%, what error would there be in measuring 100 V on this meter, taking the basic f.s.d. to be 2.000 V? Is any range likely to be unaffected by this fault?

(31) If you were building the attenuator shown in *Figure 9.26(b)* would you choose a switch which had make-before-break contacts or one with break-before-make contacts? Or doesn't it matter?

$R_M = 64\ \Omega$

12 V

18 Ω

X   Y

Figure 9.34

(32) A digital voltmeter using the dual slope technique has a reference voltage of 2.000 V and a fixed time of 1000 counts. What would be the indicated voltage if the counter read 485 on the down slope?

10 Control principles

Aims: At the end of this Unit section you should be able to:
Distinguish between first and second-order control systems.
Draw a block diagram of a simple control system and describe the function of each part.
Explain the use of proportional control, proportional + integral control, and proportional + integral + derivative control.
Understand the meaning of damping ratio, referring to underdamped, overdamped and critically damped systems.
Differentiate between natural and forced response.

OPEN-LOOP AND CLOSED-LOOP SYSTEMS

The basic elements of automatic control systems have been covered in the second year of the course* and most of the elements used in such control systems should be familiar to you from that previous study. Sensors (or transducers) are used to measure the physical variables such as temperature, pressure, speed, and convert them into electrical signals such as voltage or current. A comparator stage, which may be part of a computer depending upon the complexity of the system, is used to determine the difference (or error) between a reference level (or set point) and a feedback signal derived from part or all of the output of the system. Amplifiers and controllers are then used to amplify the error signal and give it enough mechanical 'muscle' to operate in turn the controlled system, that is, the motor, steam engine, flow valve or whatever is the prime element in the controlled process. To recapitulate briefly, then, and referring to *Figure 10.1*, here we have the basic examples of open-loop and closed-loop systems in diagrams *(a)* and *(b)*. In the open-loop system there is no control in the meaning we generally accept for a controlled process; the principle is that at some point in time the output of a system is set to a desired level as closely as possible and thereafter is left to get on with things without further human or other intervention. This is not to say that such open-loop systems cannot be relied on to give a satisfactory performance provided somebody *does* keep an eye on things and intervenes if the system looks likely to misbehave. Suppose, for example, as *Figure 10.1(a)* shows, a petrol engine is driving a pump. If the throttle setting of the engine is adjusted to suit a particular flow of clear water through the pump and the system is then left unattended, any disturbance, such as the appearance of mud or a similar obstruction to the flow, will cause the engine to labour and possibly stall; alternately, a break in the water flow might cause the engine to speed up to a dangerous level and possibly damage the pump. The open-loop system is untrustworthy because it is *unaware of what is happening at its output* and can take no steps *on its own* to rectify matters if things go wrong.

As soon as there is human intervention (to adjust the throttle setting, for instance) the system is no longer open-loop but closed-loop as shown in *Figure 10.1(b)*. An indication of the variation in the engine

*Electrical and Electronic Principles 2, Unit Section 14. If these notes are available, it would be advisable to read through them again at this stage.

speed would be seen (or heard) by the human operator, suitably interpreted by his brain and his hand would then provide, by way of his
muscle power, the necessary throttle adjustment to put the engine
speed back where it should be. The closed-loop system is differentiated
from the open-loop system in that the closed-loop is *continually aware*
of what is happening at its output; that awareness need not follow from
human intervention, it can be completely automatic.

Figure 10.2 shows the generalised block diagram of a fully automatic closed-loop control system. When a block diagram of this sort is
used to illustrate a particular system, the actual power input to the
controlled system, whether it is electrical, steam or hydraulic power,
is not shown. Only a part, such as a throttle, is strictly a component of
the control chain.

**TRANSIENT AND STEADY
STATE CONDITIONS**

A control system should, in theory, respond immediately to any change
in the physical variable it is supposed to be controlling, and the correction appearing at the output should ideally 'fit' the shape of the
variation occurring at the input. So unless the measured quantity is

(a)

Figure 10.1

(b)

Figure 10.2

perfectly stable (an unlikely state of affairs particularly on mechanical systems) or is changing only very slowly with time, the 'reaction time' of the control system must be considered very carefully to ensure that the output has fully adjusted itself to an input disturbance before a further disturbance occurs.

A measure of the reaction or response time of a system can be found by applying to the input an abrupt change in the condition of the variable; such a rapid change is known as a *step function. Figure 10.3* shows such a variation. There are two fundamental forms of response to a step function.

If the control is a *first-order* system, that is, a system which can be mathematically represented by a first order differential equation, the response is as shown in *Figure 10.4(a)*. The response time, or transient period, is the time taken for the output to get within a specified limit of its final or steady state value. If this curve puts you in mind of the exponential form of an electrical resistor–capacitor charging circuit you are not mistaken. The first-order differential equation

$$\frac{dq}{dt} R + \frac{q}{C} = V$$

derived for the voltage across a capacitor charging through a resistor on page 30 has a solution which involves an exponential equation. Any first-order control system has an output which follows such an equation, and involves systems, electrical or mechanical, which have a *single* energy storage element.

If the control is a second-order system, that is, a system which can be represented by a second-order differential equation, the response can, in very general terms, be anything between the shape shown for the first-order system and that illustrated in *Figure 10.4(b)*. Here an overshoot occurs, the extent of this overshoot being a function of what is known as the damping coefficient which will be explained later. The result of an overshoot is that the response oscillates for a while about its mean final level. The total response time is that period during which the output is settling down to within a specified limit of its final steady state value.

All second-order systems, electrical or mechanical, have *more than one* energy storage element; the resonant electrical circuit, for example, has capacitance and inductance, both capable of storing energy, hence such a circuit is a second-order system.

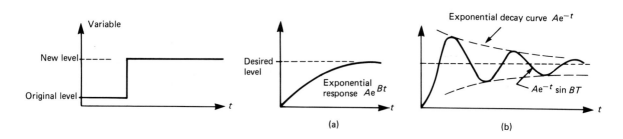

Figure 10.3   **Figure 10.4**

A CONTROL ANALYSIS

Any control system which uses a human operator in the feedback path, as in *Figure 10.1(b)* for example, is *not* a true automatic control. The detection of an error occurring between what the tachometer on the drive shaft reads and what the desired level should ideally be, takes place in the brain of the human controller. His (or her) brain then causes the appropriate muscles to adjust the throttle setting so as to make the *actual* speed equal to the *desired* speed.

Let us examine a similar system but with the human operator replaced by a truly automatic device. Clearly, such a system must be closed-loop, we therefore require the following minimum elements and conditions:

(a) a feedback signal which is derived in some way from the output and which is fed back to be compared with the desired (reference or set-point) signal;

(b) a detector which senses the difference between the feedback signal and the reference signal and which, by way of suitable circuitry, adjusts the output level in such a way that the difference is minimal;

(c) compensation for the correction of the difference mentioned in (b) which must be as quick and accurate as possible in adjusting for any change or disturbance within or external to the system.

Since we have covered the characteristics of electrical generators in an earlier section, and the course in general is concerned with electrical applications, we choose as illustration a wholly electrical system.

Suppose it is necessary to hold the output of a separately excited d.c. generator within tightly specified limits. If a generator is allowed to run without supervision, the output voltage will vary with changes in load current because of the armature resistance voltage drop $I_A R_A$, see *Figure 10.5*. The variation can be corrected or reduced by manipulation of the field current I_F control R; a human operator with his eye on a voltmeter indicating the output terminal p.d. would note the deviation between the reading of the voltmeter and the desired reference voltage (a mental set-point) and adjust the field resistance to bring the error to zero.

We can automate the system up to a point by feeding back the effect of a load change by means of a low resistance winding (R_s) connected in series with the armature, as in *Figure 10.6*. The generator is now effectively a compound machine. Perhaps you might already have appreciated that compounding is a method of automatic control when you worked through d.c. generators earlier on. If so, take a mark. When the load current increases, the armature volts-drop increases but the inclusion of the series winding gives an additional field flux in proportion to the current being drawn; hence the output voltage V does not

Figure 10.5

Figure 10.6

fall as it would without the compounding. For a very precise output voltage, however, even the use of the so-called level compounding is inadequate. The feedback contains the armature resistance R_A which changes with temperature, and hence with I_A (due to heating); also, there is no *amplification* in the loop and the total error is a part of the output.

If we introduce an amplifier into the loop, a more precise control becomes possible.

A system using an amplifier is shown in *Figure 10.7*. Here the output voltage (or a part of it) is compared with a stable reference V_R and the difference is amplified and applied to the field winding. A sudden change in load current reduces the output voltage and greatly increases the error voltage V_e ($= V_R - V$); this error voltage is then amplified and applied to the field winding in such a direction that the field current is increased and the output level restored. The comparator, which senses the error voltage V_e, is an operational amplifier (which you will be covering in your electronics course); this gives an output which can swing either in a positive direction or in a negative direction relative to the mean level of field current, the actual direction depending upon whether the error is positive ($V > V_R$) or negative ($V < V_R$). This output is in turn power amplified and used to increase or decrease the field current accordingly, so restoring the error to zero and the generator output to its desired level.

> (1) Sketch a block diagram of the motor system shown in *Figure 10.6* where the control rheostat R is operated by a human controller.
> (2) Now make a block diagram of the system with the automatic control.

PROPORTIONAL CONTROL

The types of closed-loop control systems we have discussed up to now are known as *proportional* control systems and represent the simplest kind of control. The control signal is derived from the error signal by way of a linear amplifier so that the output is directly proportional to the input. Hence

$$\text{control signal} = k \times \text{error signal}$$

where k is the proportional gain of the amplifier.

However, any amplifier has only finite gain, and although in most control systems the amplifier gain is adjustable, a troublesome effect manifests itself with simple proportional control. *Figure 10.8* illustrates

Figure 10.7

Figure 10.8

this effect; this diagram shows the sort of response we might expect from our circuit system of *Figure 10.7*. Suppose, for example, that the output of the generator is to be held at 100 V. When a sudden load increase occurs, the output drops momentarily to, say, 90 V, but because of the automatic control, recovers in a very short time to what *should* be the 100 V level. However, because of the finite amplifier gain, an offset occurs and the response does not quite rise to the full 100 V level as it should. The effect of proportional control is that the generator field, which in this case needs to be supplied with an increased output from the controller, can only get this increase as the result of an increased deviation (error). Hence the measured value has an offset from its reference value when the system has settled down. To eliminate this offset, the reference level would have to be adjusted.

The effect can be reduced by increasing the amplifier loop gain, but this cannot be carried too far in most cases because high gain can lead to instability. A solution can be found in the employment of what is known as Integral (or Reset) control.

INTEGRAL CONTROL

Integral control is another category of feedback control which is used in conjunction with proportional control. The method is usually known as proportional-integral control (PI), sometimes as reset action, and a block diagram of the arrangement is shown in simplified form in *Figure 10.9*.

It can be demonstrated by more advanced theory that if the error signal is integrated with respect to time, the offset is removed after a sufficient interval of such integration. The term 'integration' is used here in its mathematical sense of a summation; the integral control signal is the sum of *all* the error signals which have occurred since the control process was initially switched on. The overall control signal is then made up of a proportional signal V_P and an integral signal V_I. You might refer back to page 42 at this point and refresh your memory on the operation of the op amp integrating circuit and its effect on a pulse train.

Proportional-integral control eliminates steady state error because the integral action steadily increases the effect of the proportional correction until the offset is negligible. The integral block shown in *Figure 10.9* always causes the overall error to tend towards zero in a time determined by the integral gain control. This control is directly calibrated in units of time, so that if a long period is selected, the reset action becomes slow. Reducing the time of integration speeds it up.

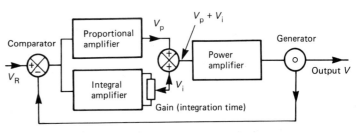

Figure 10.9

A simplified form of practical PI control using analogue circuitry is shown in *Figure 10.10*. Amplifier A compares the reference voltage V_R with the feedback voltage from the generator output, V. If no error exists between the reference and the actual generator output, the output from amplifier A will be zero, and amplifiers P (the proportional amplifier) and I (the integrating amplifier) will have no effect. If an error appears between V_R and V, amplifier A will provide a signal level which is applied to the inputs of amplifiers P and I; amplifier P provides proportional (linear) feedback and amplifier I provides integral feedback. As long as any error is present, the output of the integrator will move up or down to eliminate the error. Amplifier D will be discussed in a moment.

DERIVATIVE CONTROL

The PI system might appear to answer all the difficulties about automatic control but there is still a problem. Suppose that when the system is working normally, a very rapid variation takes place in the generator output, due perhaps to an out of ordinary load current being demanded. The PI control system cannot respond rapidly enough to the new situation because (a) proportional control cannot apply a *large* correction until there is a proportionally large shift from the reference level; (b) integral control is slow to respond because the error signal must be present for some finite time before an output is obtained. Hence the PI control tends, in a rapid change situation, to do too little rather on the late side.

The cure for this problem is to introduce *derivative* control. Here again the word is used in its mathematical sense; derivative feedback produces a signal that is proportional to the time *rate of change* of the error between V_R and V. As soon as an error voltage turns up at its input, the derivative amplifier (amplifier D in *Figure 10.10*) acts as a differentiator and produces a rapid spike of feedback to correct the error as quickly as possible. The effect is very short-lived and is intended to take care of rapid transient variation. *Figure 10.11* shows the general

Figure 10.10

effect of the control of a proportional-integral-derivative (PID) system compared with that of a proportional system alone.

A microcomputer can be made to perform all the functions of the analogue circuit of *Figure 10.10* for a number of PID feedback loops.

NATURAL OSCILLATORY MOTION

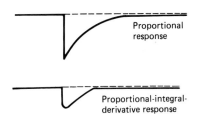

Figure 10.11

Suppose a spring to be attached to the ceiling and at the other end to hold a block which is at rest. There is no motion of any kind and so all the forces acting in the system must sum to zero. The forces acting on the suspended block are (a) the gravitational pull W acting vertically downwards, and (b) the tension in the stretched spring acting vertically upwards on the mass. In the condition of rest the total effective force F acting on the block is

$$F = T + W$$

But F = mass × acceleration, hence since the acceleration is zero, F is zero and

$$T = -W$$

The forces are equal in magnitude and opposite in sense, or in equilibrium.

Suppose now that the block is pulled downwards a short distance and then released. Work has to be done to displace the block and this is stored as strain energy in the spring. When the block is released, this stored (potential) energy becomes converted to kinetic (moving) energy as the block accelerates back to the position of equilibrium. Because of its inertia, the block overshoots the balance point by an amount equal to the original displacement and comes to rest when the same amount of energy is again stored in the spring. Ignoring air resistance, the up and down oscillation of the block will continue indefinitely, maintained by the continual interchange of potential and kinetic energy. We say that the system is *undamped*.

We can sketch a block diagram of this system, and this has been done in *Figure 10.12*. When the block is displaced a distance X_o and released, the output is also X_o. This displacement in the block is fed back by way of the spring and subtracted from the input (which is zero displacement); the error signal is thus effectively $-X_o$. The input to the *spring* is therefore a displacement equal to $-X_o$ and the output is a restoring force; hence the force acting on the block is $-\lambda X_o$ where λ is a constant representing the 'stiffness' of the spring, that is

$$\lambda = \frac{\text{force}}{\text{displacement}} \quad \text{newtons/metre}$$

The stiffer the spring, the greater the value of λ.

Figure 10.12

Feedback from stored energy in spring

(3) Why has the negative sign appeared in the expression for the output force acting on the mass? What is its significance?

(4) Do you think the rate at which the mass moves up and down depends upon the extent of the initial displacement, assuming that the spring is not stretched beyond its elastic limit?

The force acting on the displaced block causes it to accelerate; since acceleration = force/mass, we have

$$\text{Acceleration} = -\left\{\frac{\lambda}{m}\right\} X_o$$

Thus the acceleration is proportional to the displacement and acts in a direction contrary to that in which the mass is moving at any instant, that is, *always towards* the position of equilibrium. When the displacement is zero, the acceleration is zero; when the displacement is at its maximum X_o, the acceleration is a maximum*. This is a condition of simple harmonic motion (S.H.M.) and *Figure 10.13* shows the relationship between the motion and the energy distribution in the system. It is not too difficult to prove that the spring will oscillate at a frequency given by

$$f = \frac{1}{2\pi} \cdot \frac{\lambda}{m}$$

which is the free, undamped *natural* frequency of the system.

DAMPED OSCILLATIONS

If a spring system is set up and put into motion, it does not continue to oscillate indefinitely as our free, undamped example above was assumed to do. Air resistance acts on the block and there are frictional effects brought on by twisting within the spring. The oscillations consequently die away and eventually the system comes to rest. The effect of air and frictional resistance causes the system to be *damped*. Additional damping can be introduced to reduce the overall oscillation time or prevent it altogether; for example, the mass can be immersed in a bucket of water, or, more effectively still, in oil. But do not take the term 'damping' too literally in such cases! Damping not only affects

Figure 10.13

*Do not confuse the acceleration with velocity. The velocity is greatest as the mass passes through the equilibrium position, but the acceleration is then zero. At either end of the oscillation, the velocity is zero but the acceleration is at its maximum.

the amplitudes of successive cycles of the oscillation, it also affects frequency. The frequency of any damped system is always *less* than that of the free natural frequency (the theoretical condition of zero damping).

The last two pages or so might give the feeling that our course has strayed into pure physics, but damping is an essential topic in the study of automatic control systems. We will now get back to our earlier electrical example.

PERFORMANCE CURVES

What we have effectively introduced when we initially displace the block and then suddenly release it is a step function input to the system. The performance of a proportional-integral control system can be evaluated by the same method. *Figure 10.14* shows a series of plots of generator output voltage (for the control system of *Figure 10.9*) varying with time as a heavy additional load is placed on the generator output.

Suppose, as before, that the correct output level is 100 V and under the imposed load this falls momentarily to 90 V. The system cannot adjust itself immediately to restore the output to 100 V and the diagram illustrates four possibilities, all of which depend upon the design of the system. The time taken to make the adjustment is specified by the time constant, a term with which we are already acquainted. It is the time taken for the system to reach 63 per cent of its final level, in this example, the time taken to reach 96.3 V.

Clearly, the time constant is different for each of the curves shown. The differences depend upon the *damping coefficient* or damping ratio ζ. Curve A shows what happens if the system is overdamped; the generator voltage returns to the 100 V level but takes a considerable time to accomplish it. This would not be a very desirable condition. Curve B illustrates the situation if the system is underdamped. The voltage recovers very quickly but overshoots the 100 V level and bounces about for a time around this value before settling down. The frequency of these oscillations conform very nearly to the natural frequency of the system. This situation could lead to problems; the system could interpret each excursion on either side of the correct level as a disturbance and make further, and belated, efforts to correct them. If the correction fed back had a phase lag which gave a total shift of 180° around the loop and the system gain was greater than unity, the oscillation would

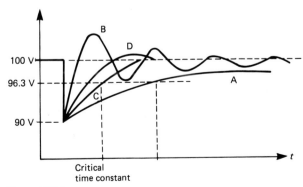

Figure 10.14

either build up at the natural frequency and lead to a completely unstable system or the generator would 'hunt' for a considerable time and fail to settle down.

Turning to curve C, this shows the condition of *critical* damping. In this, the output rises smoothly to the required level with no overshoot and in a relatively short period of time. This seems to be the ideal. If you get hold of an Avometer (or any good quality voltmeter), you can see what is meant by critical damping. Switch to an appropriate voltage range (or you can use the ohms range) and apply a voltage that will bring the pointer close to its full-scale deflection. When you apply the voltage (as a step input), you will notice that the pointer rises very rapidly towards its final position on the scale, slows down quickly and comes to rest at the correct position without overshoot or oscillation about that point. The pointer and its associated system are critically damped.

You may sometimes find a meter that responds as shown in the curve of D; the pointer will overshoot a very small amount (the diagram is exaggerated for clarity), but return at once with no further bounce to the correct scale position and stay there. This is known as the condition of *optimum damping*. You will notice it has a shorter time constant than for critical damping. This is usually the condition the system designer aims for, though it is not always possible to achieve it ideally. Like a lot of other things, automatic control engineering is a subject of compromise from a number of conflicting factors; rapid response, small steady state error and overall stability. Let us look into this last factor in more detail.

(5) Is the mass-spring system described earlier a first-order or a second-order system? If you can, give a reason for your answer.

(6) What would the curve for an unstable system look like on the co-ordinates of *Figure 10.14*?

FREQUENCY RESPONSE AND STABILITY

A short while ago we mentioned damping coefficient ζ. This coefficient (or ratio) is based on the condition of critical damping, and is expressed as a ratio *relative to critical damping*. Hence, for critical damping, $\zeta = 1.0$ and for optimum damping, which is underdamped relative to critical, $\zeta = 0.7$. Overdamped systems have $\zeta > 1$ and underdamped systems have $\zeta < 1$. For the curves drawn in *Figure 10.14* typical damping coefficients would be 0.5 for curve B, 0.7 for curve D, 1.0 for curve C and 1.5 for curve A.

We have so far considered system response to a step input function. Another approach is to consider what happens in the system when changes in the input signal follow a sinusoidal waveform. This might not appear to be as effective in determining response as the step function since the input is unlikely to be a sine wave in practical systems, but it does nevertheless provide a definition of any control system's performance in respect of stability with high accuracy.

The thing that has to be watched in any control system is the overall loop gain and the phase shift encountered around the loop. As we learned in the previous year's work, instability follows from a condition of a 180° phase shift coupled with a closed-loop gain greater than unity.

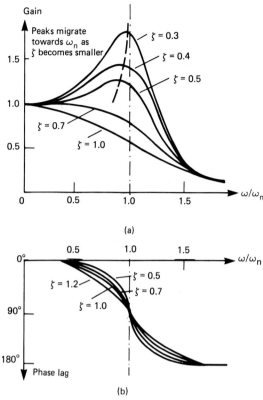

Figure 10.15

Negative feedback then becomes positive feedback and the system supplies its own input independent of any external control signal. The electronic oscillator is an example of an amplifier with a gain exceeding unity and with its output connected back to the input with such a phase that it adds to the existing input. Mechanical systems, too, can have positive feedback problems which usually show themselves in the form of excessive — even destructive — vibration, shuddering and chatter. The loop gain and phase shift of a second-order system are functions of the damping coefficient ζ, so we must examine the relationship between ζ and the gain/phase conditions in the feedback system.

Figure 10.15(a) and *(b)* show respectively typical curves for a given system of the system gain and phase response for different values of ζ. The horizontal axis in both cases expresses the input frequency ω in terms of the natural frequency ω_n.

On the upper diagram, we see that the loop gain of the system is unity irrespective of the value of the damping coefficient for frequencies where the ratio ω/ω_n is smaller than about 0.2, that is, when the input frequency is low. As the input frequency increases beyond this point, however, the system response curve depends upon the value of ζ; for overdamped systems up to the point of optimum damping ($\zeta = 0.7$) the gain falls below unity. This fall relates to the system response illustrated earlier in *Figure 10.14* for the step function input where curve A shows the sluggish recovery of an overdamped control. For underdamped systems, ζ less than critical, the gain increases above unity; this increase also relates to the curves of *Figure 10.14* where curve B shows the effect of overshoot and oscillation around the required control level. Notice that the peak of the gain curves for underdamped systems occurs at a frequency *less* than where $\omega/\omega_n = 1$. It can be proved that the peak amplitude occurs when

$$\text{input frequency } \omega = \omega_n \sqrt{1 - 2\zeta^2}$$

From this we see that the condition $\omega = \omega_n$ occurs when $\zeta = 0$, the theoretical case of zero damping.

(7) At what value of ζ does the term under the square root become negative? What does this imply?

We turn now to the phase curves shown in *Figure 10.15(b)*, which relate the phase difference between input and output signals over the same range of frequencies as for the loop gain response; how many degrees, for example, does the feedback signal (taken from the output) lag behind the input signal? Notice from these curves that as ζ tends to low values, there is an increasing tendency for the phase to change more abruptly from a near zero value to $-180°$ as the frequency ratio ω/ω_n increases through 1. The greater the value of ζ the more gradual the phase change becomes.

(8) Indicate lightly in pencil on the curves of *Figure 10.15(a)* and *(b)* where the gain response and the phase response curves respectively would lie for a case where the damping was zero.

RESONANCE

The curves of *Figure 10.15(a)* probably remind you (for values of ζ below 0.5) of the resonance curves of tuned electrical circuits dealt with in Sections 3 and 4. This is indeed the case, except that here we are dealing with mechanical resonance (some examples of which were mentioned in the earlier sections) rather than electrical, although identical theory can be applied to both. You have probably noticed when riding in a car (unless you are singularly lucky in your choice of car!) that something somewhere will start to chatter as a certain speed is reached. The noise disappears when the speed is either increased or decreased from the point where it is most evident. What we have here is an example of mechanical resonance, very annoying and often difficult to locate. The chatter builds up when the natural frequency of whatever it is causing the vibration coincides with the frequency of vibration of the engine. We have a system in which the input is a periodic wave (from the engine) and the output is a vibration of similar frequency from some other part of the car. Whenever the damping co-efficient of a system is *small* and the system is excited with a sinusoidal form of input at a frequency near to the undamped natural frequency, the output amplitude builds up rapidly to a very high level.

Go back to the spring and block system shown in *Figure 10.12* and assume again as we did there that the damping is negligible. If we make our way around the loop we notice that the output is X_o but the spring input is $-X_o$, so a phase change of 180° has occurred. This, coupled with the fact that under external excitation the amplitude ratio will exceed unity, will turn the negative feedback into positive feedback; in other words, when energy is introduced into the system in such a way that the natural frequency parameter is assisted. Think, for instance, of pushing a child in a swing: how each energising push is given exactly as the swing has reached its limit and begins to go forward, and how the energy of each push is added to that of the moving system so that the amplitude of the swing quickly builds up.

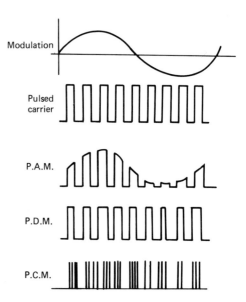

Figure 10.16

When energy is fed in this way into a lightly damped system by applying an input with a frequency which will pass through that of the natural frequency, resonance occurs and the vibrational build-up becomes very intense. This is *forced* response, differentiated from the behaviour due to internal energy storage and release which is the natural response. Forced resonance can be maintained indefinitely as it usually is in electronic oscillators, for example, by the continual input of energy from the associated power supply. In contrast, natural responses die out. In mechanical systems, forced resonance is usually best avoided; this cannot always be engineered with a given design, but various devices which artificially increase the damping can be introduced to overcome or reduce the problem.

So although the natural frequency of a system is not *itself* a response to any external influence, the designer of a control system must arm himself with a knowledge of such natural behaviour so that he can predict, with a good chance of a successful outcome, what might possibly happen when the response of his design is forced by external functions.

PROBLEMS FOR SECTION 10

(9) Define the terms: (a) free natural frequency, (b) damped natural frequency, (c) damping coefficient.

(10) Explain why an undamped spring-mass system will vibrate freely after being initially disturbed.

(11) A mass of 10 kg is suspended on a vertical spring having a 'stiffness' factor of 12000 n/m. What will be the natural frequency of this system when disturbed?

(12) A suspended mass of 5 kg oscillates at a free natural frequency of 3 Hz. What is the spring constant λ for this system?

(13) Define step function. What information about a system's performance does a step function input provide?

(14) A spring–mass suspended system has an undamped period of vibration of 150 ms. It is then damped by a device which introduces a damping coefficient ζ of 0.3. What is the new damped period of vibration?

(15) Make sketch graphs on the same coordinate axes of the response of a spring–mass system to a step function input when the system is (a) underdamped, (b) overdamped, (c) critically damped.

Suggest reasonable values for ζ for each of the graphs.

(16) Is it true that the time constant of a control system is independent of the system's damping coefficient?

(17) Too much proportional gain could possibly cause hunting in a control system. True or false?

(18) An amplifier with feedback will be unstable when the loop gain is greater than unity. True or false?

(19) Explain the use of (a) proportional control, (b) proportional + integral control, (c) proportional + integral + derivative control. What improvement in system performance results from each case?

(20) Complete the following: the behaviour determined by an external energy source is called a . . . . . . response; the behaviour due to internal energy storage is called a . . . . . . response.

(21) Differentiate between first-order and second-order systems. Give *electrical* examples of each.

(22) To what extent is the natural behaviour of a system influenced by the waveform of the forcing function that stores energy in the system?

(23) In a control system for stabilising the speed of a petrol engine, the desired speed is manually set into the comparator. The electrical output of the comparator feeds into an electronic amplifier whose power output operates a magnetic solenoid. This solenoid acts to move the engine throttle which drives (with the output shaft) a tacho-generator. The reading (voltage output) of the tacho is introduced into the comparator.

Draw a block diagram of this system and identify the reference input, the error detector, the controlled output and the feedback element. How might the reference level (representing the desired speed) be derived?

(24) Derive an electronic method of controlling the level of water in a tank. Water flows into the tank from the mains supply and is drawn from the tank through a tap and pipe at the bottom.

11 Principles of modulation

Aims: At the end of this Unit section you should be able to:
Explain the principles of amplitude and frequency modulation.
Know the meaning of side frequencies and sidebands.
Draw phasor representations of amplitude and frequency modulation.
Calculate the power in a modulated wave.
Define the principles of pulse modulation.
Explain the methods of demodulation for amplitude modulated waves.

In any communications system, the information to be transmitted must first of all be converted into an electrical quantity which is time-varying, that is a current or voltage is necessary to represent the signal. In some cases, such as a simple telephone link, the waveform of the signal is transmitted directly to the receiving point as a varying current flowing in wires; in other cases, particularly in radio transmission, the signal is used to 'change' or 'modulate' the output of a high frequency generator. The process of modulation is therefore that of modifying some feature of an otherwise regularly recurring quantity in accordance with the signal. Transmission then takes place by means of the modulated high-frequency wave. The high-frequency unmodulated wave is referred to as the 'carrier' wave; after modulation it is called a 'modulated carrier'.

There are several ways of altering some feature of the unmodulated carrier, though we shall be particularly interested in only two of these. If the carrier frequency is maintained constant and its *amplitude* is varied in accordance with the modulating signal, the carrier is Amplitude Modulated (AM). If, on the other hand, the amplitude of the carrier is kept constant and its *frequency* is varied in accordance with the modulating signal, the carrier is Frequency (or Angle) Modulated (FM).

For either of these systems of modulation (or indeed for any others) the characteristics of the modulated wave are the same, irrespective of the circuits which may have been used to produce the waveform. We shall be interested in this chapter in the general aspects of the modulation process rather than in the circuits necessary to achieve it.

AMPLITUDE MODULATION

In amplitude modulation, as we have just remarked, the amplitude of a high-frequency wave is varied in accordance with the signal to be transmitted. This variation may, in the most simple case (which is, in fact, a quite complicated case), consist of an 'on and off' condition of the carrier, representing the transmission of a code such as Morse.

In general, however, the modulating waveform will be complex, and in the case of speech and music will have a very large number of component frequencies together with their harmonics. If the signal is assumed to consist of a single sine wave whose frequency is low compared with that of the carrier, we may simplify matters somewhat and the modulated carrier will then appear as shown in *Figure 11.1(a)* where the modulated condition to the right may be compared with the unmodulated condition on the left of the figure. We see that the carrier amplitude when modulated varies between the values $(A + B)$ and $(A - B)$. The ratio B/A is known as the modulation depth or modulation factor and is a measure of the depth to which the carrier is modulated. If $B = mA$, then $m \times 100$ is referred to as the percentage modulation and the carrier will be modulated 100% when $m = 1$ or when $B = A$. The amplitude will then vary between twice the unmodulated value and zero as shown in *Figure 11.1(b)*.

We may express modulation depth in terms of the maximum and minimum amplitudes of the carrier as follows:

$$\text{Maximum amplitude} = A + B$$
$$\text{Minimum amplitude} = A - B$$

therefore $2A$ = maximum amplitude + minimum amplitude
$2B$ = maximum amplitude − minimum amplitude

$$\text{Depth of modulation } = \frac{2B}{2A}$$

$$= \frac{\text{maximum amplitude} - \text{minimum amplitude}}{\text{maximum amplitude} + \text{minimum amplitude}}$$

Let the carrier frequency of the wave of *Figure 11.1(a)* be $f_c (= \omega_c/2\pi)$, and the modulating signal frequency be $f_m (= \omega_m/2\pi)$. The expression for the unmodulated carrier is $i = A \cdot \sin \omega_c t$ and for the modulating signal $B \cdot \sin \omega_m t$. After modulation, the *amplitude* can be expressed as $i = (A + B \cdot \sin \omega_m t)$ and the modulated wave is therefore expressed as

(a)

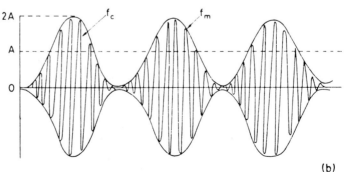

(b)

Figure 11.1

$$i = (A + B \cdot \sin \omega_m t) \cdot \sin \omega_c t$$
$$= A \cdot \sin \omega_c t + B \cdot \sin \omega_c t \cdot \sin \omega_m t$$

which expands into

$$i = A \cdot \sin \omega_c t + \frac{B}{2} \cdot \cos(\omega_c - \omega_m)t - \frac{B}{2} \cdot \cos(\omega_c + \omega_m)t$$

(11.1)

It will be noticed that the amplitude B and the frequency $f_m (= \omega_m/2\pi)$ of the modulating waveform appear only in the second and third terms. Considering these separately, the output current i consists of:

(a) a term $A \cdot \sin \omega_c t$ corresponding to a sine wave at the carrier frequency f_c and of maximum amplitude A;

(b) a term $\frac{B}{2} \cdot \cos(\omega_c - \omega_m)t$ corresponding to a sine wave of frequency $(f_c - f_m)$ and of maximum amplitude $\frac{B}{2}$;

(c) a term $-\frac{B}{2} \cdot \cos(\omega_c + \omega_m)t$ corresponding to a sine wave of frequency $(f_c + f_m)$ and of maximum amplitude $\frac{B}{2}$

Frequency $(f_c - f_m)$ is known as the lower side-frequency, and frequency $(f_c + f_m)$ is known as the upper side-frequency. Such a single frequency amplitude modulated wave is, therefore, equivalent to *three* sine waves: the carrier, the upper side-frequency and lower side-frequency. The amplitude of the carrier frequency component, it should be noted, is independent of the degree of modulation; the other components have amplitudes which vary directly with the degree of modulation and are spaced from the carrier frequency by the original modulating frequency.

If the carrier is modulated by a complex signal wave, *each* frequency component in the signal will produce, in exactly the same way, a *pair* of side frequencies. If a carrier is modulated by N frequencies, therefore, there will be a total of $2N$ side frequencies, and the term 'sidebands' is used to indicate the upper and lower bands of frequencies produced as a result of modulation. The upper sideband therefore extends over the range $f_c + (f_1, f_2 \ldots f_N)$ and the lower sideband over the range $f_c - (f_1, f_2 \ldots f_N)$.

We may now illustrate the process of modulation as a frequency spectrum diagram. Look at *Figure 11.2(a)* where the frequency scale is represented along the horizontal axis and the vertical axis is a purely diagrammatic one representing the presence of a wave. For a single-frequency modulating signal, the sidebands consist simply of the sum and difference frequencies $(f_c + f_m)$ and $(f_c - f_m)$, and there are no frequency components at all in the spaces above and below the carrier. If the carrier is modulated with a complex signal, such as a band of speech frequencies, however, the sum and difference frequencies will themselves be bands of frequencies as we have seen above, occupying the same bandwidth above and below the carrier as the original modulating speech band, *Figure 11.2(b)*. It will be seen that the bandwidth occupied by an amplitude modulated wave is *twice* the bandwidth of the original signal. Thus the modulation of an oscillator of frequency 100 kHz by speech signals in the range 200 Hz to 4000 Hz would produce the additional upper sideband 100.2 to 104 kHz and the additional lower sideband of 99.8 to 96 kHz.

If the carrier frequency is modulated by such a complex band only the highest and lowest frequencies in the band are usually considered, and the sideband limits produced by these are calculated. All the other sideband frequencies lie within these limits. It should be noted that the lower sideband is inverted with respect to the original signal band, that is, the lowest signal frequency is nearest to the carrier f_c in both the upper and lower sidebands.

Power in an amplitude-modulated wave

In any circuit, the mean power dissipated is I^2R watts. The r.m.s. value of a complex wave is obtained from the square root of the sum of the squares of the r.m.s. values of the various components. The r.m.s. value of the modulated current wave of (11.1) above is therefore

$$I = \sqrt{\frac{A^2}{2} + \frac{1}{2}\left(\frac{B}{2}\right)^2 + \frac{1}{2}\left(\frac{B}{2}\right)^2}$$

from which, since $B = mA$:

$$I = \sqrt{\frac{A^2}{2} + \frac{m^2A^2}{8} + \frac{m^2A^2}{8}}$$

$$= \frac{A}{\sqrt{2}} \cdot \sqrt{1 + \frac{m^2}{2}}$$

The total power dissipated by such a current in a resistance R is therefore

$$P_{total} = \frac{A^2}{2}\left[1 + \frac{m^2}{2}\right] R \text{ watts} \qquad (11.2)$$

Now this result is of interest because if we set $m = 0$, the condition for an unmodulated carrier, the power becomes

$$P_{total} = \frac{A^2R}{2}$$

(a)

(b)

Figure 11.2

Hence the additional power when m is finite must come from the source of modulation, and this power resides in the resulting sidebands. The total power in the modulated carrier is then

$$P_{\text{total}} = P_{\text{carrier}} + P_{\text{sidebands}}$$

The ratio of the sideband power to the total power transmitted is obtained from (11.2) above as

$$\frac{P_{\text{sidebands}}}{P_{\text{total}}} = \left[\frac{m^2}{2}\right] \div \left[1 + \frac{m^2}{2}\right] = \frac{m^2}{2 + m^2}$$

When $m = 1$, that is, for 100% modulation (refer back to *Figure 11.1(b)*), the power in the sidebands is seen to be 50% of the unmodulated carrier power. Sideband power does not become an appreciable proportion of the total power until modulation percentages greater than 50% are reached.

Example (1).   Compare the total power and the sideband power radiated when a 10 kW transmitter is modulated to a depth of 30% with that radiated when the modulation depth is 80%, assuming sinusoidal signals.

In general the effective amplitude of a sinusoidally modulated wave is proportional to

$$1 + \frac{m^2}{2}$$

Hence, for 30% modulation:

$$m = 0.3, P_{\text{total}} = 10\left[1 + \frac{0.3^2}{2}\right] = 10.45 \text{ kW.}$$

For 80% modulation:

$$m = 0.8, P_{\text{total}} = 10\left[1 + \frac{0.8^2}{2}\right] = 13.2 \text{ kW.}$$

The sideband power has therefore increased from 0.45 kW to 3.2 kW as the modulation increased from 30% to 80%.

PHASOR REPRESENTATION

Phasor representation would be extremely complicated for complex modulation, but if we consider a carrier wave modulated by a single frequency sinusoid of constant amplitude, the phasor representation of an amplitude-modulated wave can be illustrated in a fairly straight-forward and simple manner. The phasor representing equation (11.1) is then a phasor rotating f_c times per second, at the same time varying in amplitude f_m times per second between the limits of $(A + mA)$ and $(A - mA)$; see *Figure 11.3(a)*. This effect may be treated as if the carrier wave was of fixed amplitude with two side frequency phasors rotating in opposite directions from one of its ends. The lower side frequency rotates in a clockwise direction at f_m Hz. The upper side frequency rotates in an anticlockwise direction at the same frequency. From *Figure 11.3(b)* it is seen that the side frequency phasors always make equal angles with the carrier component phasor, and so the resultant of the three phasors is always in line with the carrier phasor. The resultant thus has a constant frequency and variable amplitude.

Figure 11.3

Example (2). An amplitude-modulated voltage is represented by the expression $e = 5 (1 + 0.5 \cos [3140t]) \sin (2\pi\, 10^5\, t)$ volts. Find: (a) the modulation depth, (b) the modulating frequency, (c) the carrier frequency, (d) the peak instantaneous value of the modulated wave. If this modulated wave is applied across a resistance of 80 Ω, what power will be dissipated in the resistance?

This is a typical kind of question relating to expressions of modulated waveforms and should be followed carefully.

Now $e = 5 (1 + 0.5 \cos [3140t]) \sin (2\pi\, 10^5\, t)$ volts

(a) Comparing this with our 'standard' equation

$$(A + B \sin \omega_m t) \sin \omega_c t = A (1 + m \,.\, \sin \omega_m t) \sin \omega_c t$$

the modulation depth is seen to be 50%, i.e. $m = 0.5$

(b) The modulation frequency is $\dfrac{3140}{2\pi} = 500$ Hz

(c) The carrier frequency $f_c = \omega_c/2\pi = 10^5 = 100$ kHz

(d) The peak instantaneous value of the modulated wave is

$$5 (1 + 0.5) = 7.5 \text{ V.}$$

The power dissipated in a resistance R by a voltage E (r.m.s.) is $E^2 R$.

The power in the carrier is therefore $\dfrac{5}{\sqrt{2}} \times \dfrac{1}{80}$ W

The peak sideband voltage is $\dfrac{mA}{2}$ i.e. $\dfrac{5 \times 0.5}{2} = 1.25$ V, and so the r.m.s. voltage is $1.25/\sqrt{2}$ V.

Hence the total power dissipated

$$= P_{\text{carrier}} + P_{\text{sidebands}}$$

$$\dfrac{\left[\dfrac{5}{\sqrt{2}}\right]^2 + \left[\dfrac{1.25}{\sqrt{2}}\right]^2 + \left[\dfrac{1.25}{\sqrt{2}}\right]^2}{80} \text{ W}$$

$$= \dfrac{12.5 + 1.5625}{80} = 0.174 \text{ W}$$

FREQUENCY MODULATION

We have just seen how information can be transmitted by varying the amplitude of a fixed frequency carrier wave. Such information can also be transmitted by effectively reversing these functions, that is, the amplitude of the carrier may remain fixed and the modulation take place by means of changes in its frequency. Such modulation is known as Frequency Modulation (FM) or angle modulation.

In frequency modulation the amplitude of the modulating signal is used to change the frequency of the carrier from its unmodulated value f_c so that the frequency *deviation* from this unmodulated value is, at any instant, proportional to the *amplitude* of the signal. Suppose, by way of a numerical example, that a carrier wave of frequency 1000 Hz is frequency-modulated by a square wave signal with a period of 40 ms (f_m = 25 Hz) and of such amplitude that the maximum frequency deviations are ± 200 Hz. The wave-form of the modulating signal, the unmodulated carrier and the modulated carrier are shown respectively in *Figures 11.4(a) (b)* and *(c)*. In a 20 ms half-period of the modulation there are 16 cycles at the lower frequency of 800 Hz, and in the next 20 ms half-period of the modulation there are 24 cycles at the upper frequency of 1200 Hz; and so on. The figure is not to scale.

There is thus a cyclic variation in frequency, the *rate* at which this cyclic variation occurs corresponding to the signal *frequency* of the modulation. For a sinusoidal modulating signal, this variation will have its peak value when sin $\omega_m t$ = ± 1. The instantaneous carrier frequency will then be

$$\omega = \omega_c + D_1 \cos \omega_m t$$

where D_1 is proportional to the *amplitude* of the modulation. D_1 is the *frequency deviation* and is expressed strictly in rad/sec, although it is often stated in kHz. It might appear that the frequency limits would be $\omega_c \pm D_1$ and hence the bandwidth required would be $2D_1$ kHz. This is not so; typically the maximum value of D_1 is 75 kHz.

Let a carrier be represented as $A \cdot \cos \omega_c t$. Although the frequency at any instant is $\omega_c + D_1 \cos \omega_m t$, this cannot be substituted directly for ω_c in the carrier expression. Here ωt is the total electrical angle

Figure 11.4

turned through by the signal up to a time t. It is directly proportional to ω since ω is constant, but in f.m. transmission, ω is not constant, and the total angle covered up to time t is

$$\theta = \int (\omega_c + D_1 \cos \omega_m t) \, dt$$

$$= \omega_c t + \frac{D_1}{\omega_m} \sin \omega_m t$$

whence the expression for the carrier becomes

$$A \cdot \cos \left[\omega_c t + \frac{D_1}{\omega_m} \sin \omega_m t \right] \tag{11.3}$$

By analogy with the case of amplitude-modulation it might be expected that 100% modulation would occur when the maximum value of the frequency swing equalled the unmodulated carrier frequency, so that the carrier would be swept between the limits 0 and $2\omega_c$. Such a system is completely impracticable. As mentioned above, an arbitrary upper limit (usually 75 kHz for high quality transmission) is set for the frequency swing and this is the *frequency deviation D*, where $D = D_1$ max. This upper limit may then be considered the equivalent of 100% modulation.

The choice of this limit is decided by two primary factors: signal-to-noise ratio, and the bandwidth required for transmission. As will be noted later, the limit should be as high as possible to secure a good signal-to-noise ratio, but low to reduce the necessary bandwidth.

Since the frequency deviation D corresponds to the maximum amplitude of the modulating signal, it is possible to introduce a modulation factor defined by

$$m = \frac{D_1}{D} = \frac{\text{frequency swing}}{\text{frequency deviation}} = \frac{\text{modulation amplitude}}{\text{peak modulation amplitude}}$$

whence

$$\frac{D_1}{\omega_m} = m \cdot \frac{D}{\omega_m} = m_f \text{ the modulation index}$$

Hence, modulation index $m_f = \dfrac{\text{actual frequency deviation}}{\text{modulating frequency}}$

and the expression for the modulated carrier may be written

$$A \cdot \cos \left[\omega_c t + m_f \cdot \sin \omega_m t \right] \tag{11.4}$$

Figure 11.5 illustrates the effect of different modulation percentages on the carrier frequency.

Figure 11.5

The particular value of the modulation index for $m = 1$ is called the *deviation ratio* δ, hence

$$\delta = \frac{D}{\omega_m} = \frac{\text{the rated system deviation}}{\text{modulating frequency}}$$

δ is selected in the course of the design of an f.m. system, it being a determining factor in the transmission of significant sidebands, those of amplitude greater than 1% of the carrier amplitude.

For high-quality v.h.f. broadcasting the maximum deviation is 75 kHz so that for an upper limit of 15 kHz for the modulation, the deviation ratio is 5. For v.h.f. mobile communications, the deviation is usually limited to about 15 kHz with an upper modulating frequency of 3 kHz, so that the deviation ratio remains the same. The minimum bandwidth occupied by broadcast transmitters is therefore about 150 kHz which depends upon the amplitude of the modulating signal, not its frequency. A practical bandwidth is given approximately by the expression $2 (f_d + f_a)$ where f_d is the maximum deviation and f_a is the maximum modulating frequency, and this allows for higher modulation products than the simple $2f_d$ bandwidth suggested above.

PULSE MODULATION

Modulation

Pulsed carrier

P.A.M.

P.D.M.

P.C.M.

Figure 11.6

Clipping levels

Figure 11.7

In both amplitude and frequency modulation, the carrier wave is continuously present. There are methods of modulation where the carrier wave is made discontinuous in the form of a train of rectangular pulses. The modulation process is then to vary some characteristic of the pulses in accordance with the modulating signal. Three possibilities are of interest:

(a) the amplitude of the pulses may be varied; this is known as pulse amplitude modulation, PAM;

(b) the duration of the pulses may be varied; this is known as pulse duration (or pulse width) modulation, PDM;

(c) the pulses may be arranged in a binary coded sequence to provide what is known as pulse code modulation, PCM.

Figure 11.6 illustrates all three methods of pulse modulation, assuming a single frequency sinewave modulating signal.

Like its A.M. counterpart, pulse amplitude modulation suffers from distortion arising from amplitude variations due to noise getting on to the signal over the transmission patl.. By using pulse duration modulation this problem can be overcome to a great extent by symmetrical 'clipping' of the signal so that the noise is removed without affecting the required modulating content; see *Figure 11.7*. Distortion can still be present, however, caused by the irregular edges on the clipped pulses which go to vary the actual pulse width.

Pulse code modulation has advantages over both PAM and PDM; if the modulating signal is first converted to a digital code, it is only necessary at the receiver to determine the presence or absence of a signal. Communication is possible by this method over very noisy systems.

DEMODULATION

Demodulation, or detection, is the process of recovering from the modulated wave the information which it has carried. The carrier wave

Figure 11.8

has done its job in acting as the bearer of the modulation; at the receiver, therefore, the two components must be separated again, the carrier wave being jettisoned as it were.

The detection of amplitude modulated waves is much simpler to execute (and rather easier to understand!) than is the detection of frequency modulated waves. We need here only the elementary principles of amplitude demodulation, a process which goes under the name of 'envelope' detection and which is simply a diode half-wave rectifier D with a reservoir capacitor C across a load resistor R, see *Figure 11.8*. To begin with, imagine that the load resistance R is removed. If now a high frequency carrier wave of constant amplitude is applied at the point shown, the current which will flow through the diode during the positive half-cycles will charge the capacitor C, causing the cathode terminal to become positive with respect to the anode. The charge will continue and after a short while the voltage across C will attain the peak value of the applied signal, when the diode will cease to conduct. The capacitor will then maintain this value of direct voltage, as no discharge path is available.

Now let the resistance R be considered to be in position across C and refer to *Figure 11.9(a)* and *(b)*. During the first positive half-cycle of the signal input, diode current will flow and C will receive a charge, the cathode going slightly positive with respect to anode. During the following negative half-cycle of input, the anode will be below the potential of the cathode so that no diode current flows, and the capacitor will partially discharge through R. This process continues, and finally a position of stability is obtained when the positive peaks of the input cycles just draw sufficient current to keep the mean voltage across C at a steady value which this time will be somewhat less than peak V_1.

Suppose now the signal amplitude to change to a new level V_2. The additional amplitude will cause the diode to 'over-conduct' from the position of equilibrium it was in, and the mean voltage across C will rise until a second stage of stability is reached, with the voltage rather less than peak V_2.

When the amplitude of the input decreases to a level V_3, however, the diode will for a few cycles remain non-conducting and C will discharge through R until the peaks of the input cycles once more cause diode current to flow.

We thus see that provided the transitional periods can be made to occupy a few cycles only, the voltage across C will follow the variations of the modulation envelope, and a varying d.c. signal output representing the original modulation obtained; *Figure 11.9(c)*. The 'ripples' in this output are due to the small amount of discharge of C between succeeding positive half-cycles of the input signal and are eliminated in a suitable filter circuit.

The choice of the values of C and R is a compromise. R must be large or a considerable portion of the capacitor charge will leak away when the diode is not conducting. Hence during the stable periods, V_c will be considerably less than the peak values V_1, V_2 and V_3 for example. On the other hand R must be small so that falling transitions as from V_2 to V_3 occupy a very short time and the new lower amplitude level is quickly assumed. But a small value of R does not permit a rising transition as from V_1 to V_2 to take place quickly and many cycles are lost before the new higher amplitude can be attained. Further, the diode when conducting has a comparatively low resistance and the average

value of this resistance over a complete input cycle must not be too
small or the input source will be too heavily damped. To obtain a large
average value of resistance, the diode must conduct only over a very
small fraction of the complete input cycle; this calls for a large value of
R. A compromise value of R for input frequencies between 50 kHz and
10 mHz is 0.25 to 0.5 MΩ.

For the choice of capacitor value, C must be small for two reasons: a
small value will produce a large terminal voltage for a small accumulation
of charge, and transitional periods such as V_1 to V_2 will be made as
short as possible. Similarly, for a given value of R, a small capacity will
discharge quickly on such transitions as from V_2 to V_3. C, however,
must be many times the capacity of the diode itself, so that at the signal
frequency its reactance is sufficiently low compared with that of the
diode capacity that substantially the whole of the input signal is applied
to the diode.

If the input is sinusoidally modulated, the voltage appearing across C
and R will contain the low-frequency modulating voltage and the network will offer an impedance Z, where

Figure 11.9

Figure 11.10

$$\frac{1}{Z} = \sqrt{\frac{1}{R^2} + \frac{1}{X^2}}$$

so that $$Z = \sqrt{\frac{(RX)^2}{(R^2 + X^2)}}$$

The low frequency output is then

$$IZ = IR \cdot \frac{X}{\sqrt{(R^2 + X^2)}}$$

where I is the mean diode current. Thus, as the frequency increases, the response falls from a maximum value of IR to some fraction of IR. Suppose a falling off in response of 10% is acceptable at the high frequency limit of the modulating signal. Then the voltage across CR will be $0.9IR$, i.e.

$$\frac{X}{\sqrt{(R^2 + X^2)}} = 0.9$$

and $$1 + \frac{R^2}{X^2} = \frac{1}{0.9^2} = \frac{1}{0.81} = 1.235$$

therefore $$\frac{R^2}{X^2} = 0.235$$

and $$\frac{R}{X} = 0.485 \approx 0.5$$

Thus X must not be less than $2R$.

For an upper frequency of 5 kHz, and a value of R of 100 kΩ, C then evaluates to 160 pF. In practice, a value of about $50 - 100$ pF is usual for modulating signals up to some upper frequency of $12 - 15$ kHz.

In the practical detector of amplitude modulated signals, a more complex circuit than that of the simple diode-CR combination is required. This is because the diode output will consist of three components: (a) the required low-frequency modulation, (b) a d.c. component, (c) an r.f. ripple component. The modulation is required free from both the d.c. and the r.f. components, and this is usually done by dividing R into two parts R_1 and R_2, where R_1 is approximately one-tenth of R_2, and then placing an additional capacitor C_1 across R_2 of such a value that the impedance of R_2C_1 to the r.f. component is much less than the resistance R_1 alone. At the same time, C_1R_2 must present an impedance to the modulation which is much greater than R_1. If R_2 is about 100 kΩ, R_1 is usually 10 kΩ and C_1 is 100 pf. The modulation developed across R_2 (which is often used as a gain or 'volume' control) is applied to a following amplifier stage by way of a large value coupling capacitor which blocks off the d.c. component of the diode signal. A signal can also be obtained from the same output as a.g.c. voltage, though a separate a.g.c. diode is usual. A complete circuit is shown in *Figure 11.10.*

PROBLEMS FOR SECTION 11

(3) Why is a high-frequency carrier needed for radio transmission?

(4) How many types of modulation are possible with a direct current carrier?

(5) What kind of modulation is used in a simple telephone system?

(6) An amplitude modulated wave has a maximum value of 4.5 V and a minimum value of 2.3 V. What is the depth of modulation?

(7) A carrier wave of frequency 1 MHz is amplitude modulated with audio signals within the range 200–3000 Hz. What side frequency bands are generated?

(8) A 500 kHz carrier wave is amplitude modulated by a signal of frequency 2 kHz having a strong third harmonic content. What side frequencies will be present in the transmission?

(9) The power in an unmodulated carrier is 100 W. When amplitude modulated by a single frequency, the power rises to 104.5 W. What is the depth of modulation?

(10) How would the power in an unmodulated carrier compare with the power in the same carrier when frequency modulated?

(11) If an F.M. transmitter uses modulating frequencies up to 15 kHz and the maximum deviation is 75 kHz, what is the approximate bandwidth required for the transmission?

(12) What is meant by 'side frequencies' and 'sidebands'? Differentiate between these terms.

A sinusoidal carrier is amplitude modulated by a sinusoidal signal. The total power in the modulated wave is 540 W and the depth of modulation is 40%. Calculate (a) the carrier power, (b) the power in each sideband.

(13) A carrier wave $A . \sin \omega t$ is amplitude modulated to a depth of 50% by a signal of
(a) sinusoidal form at 1 kHz,
(b) a square waveform of period 1 ms.
Sketch the modulated waveform after the manner of *Figure 11.1(a)*, showing for each waveform the period of the carrier and the signal.

(14) An A.M. voltage is represented by

$$v = 5 \left[1 + 0.6 \cos (6280t)\right] \sin (2\pi 10^4 t) \text{ volts}$$

Find:
(a) the modulation depth
(b) the modulation frequency
(c) the period of the carrier
(d) the peak value of the modulated wave
(15) What function does a demodulator serve?
(16) Describe a simple way of demodulating an amplitude modulated wave.

Solutions to problems

Most solutions are not given to any better accuracy than two decimal places and in many cases are rounded off to exact figures.

UNIT SECTION 1

(5) $E_{oc} = 12$ V, $R_G = 18.57$ Ω, $I = 0.22$ A
(6) $E_{oc} = 3.8$ V, $R_G = 2.4$ Ω; $R_L = 5.2$ Ω
(15) (a) -23 dB; 80 dB
(16) (a) 10^9; (b) 2.5
(17) The power loss is about 386 dB which is a ratio of 4×10^{38}.

Hence the input would have to be 4×10^{36} W! In real life amplifiers would be used.

(18) 2.095 V
(19) 10.5 V, 0.15 Ω
(20) 6.203 V, 0.034 Ω
(21) 1.0 Ω, 36 W
(22) (a) $E_{oc} = 10$ V, $R_G = 9$ Ω; (b) $E_{oc} = 4$ V, $R_G = 0.8$ Ω; (c) $E_{oc} = 4.5$ V, $R_G = 5.25$ Ω; (d) $E_{oc} = 1.6$ V, $R_G = 2.4$ Ω.
(23) 59 mA
(24) 26.8 Ω
(25) 1.6 V, 25.6 mW
(26) (a) $I_{sc} = 1.11$ A, $R_G = 9$ Ω; (b) $I_{sc} = 5$ A, $R_G = 0.8$ Ω; (c) $I_{sc} = 0.86$ A, $R_G = 5.25$ Ω; (d) $I_{sc} = 0.67$ A, $R_G = 2.4$ Ω.
(27) $E_{oc} = 11.2$ V, $R = 1.52$; $I_{sc} = 7.35$ A, $R = 1.52$.
(28) 67.1 mA
(29) 53 mA
(30) 102 mV; 52.3 Ω; 1.95 mA; 50 mW.
(31) 3.2 Ω
(33) 2.3 Ω
(34) (a) 316 mW; (b) 50 μW; 560 μW
(35) 13.7 dB, 31 dB; 17.26 dB
(36) 0.62 V
(37) 9.54 dB

UNIT SECTION 2

(2) 500 Ω; 60 mA
(3) (a) 100 V, (b) 40 V, (c) 0
(4) $C = Q/V = It/V$; $R = V/I$. Then $CR = t$ (time)
(7) 80 kΩ. (a) 1.25 mA, (b) 1.75 V/s
(8) You should read off V_c as about 63 V, approximately 2/3 of V.
(12) See *Figure A.1*. Final voltage V is the same in each case but the time constant CR is different for each case.
(13) See *Figure A.2*. Final charge is different for each value of C.
(14) $E = LI/t$ so $L = Et/I$; $1/R = I/E$. Then $L/R = t$ (time)
(15) 0.1 s
(20) 40 mA; 100 V.
(21) 250 Ω; 40 mA.
(22) (a) 1 s, (b) 300 kΩ, (c) 33.3 kΩ.
(23) 10 V/s; 8 V/s; 6 V/s; 4 V/s; 2 V/s.

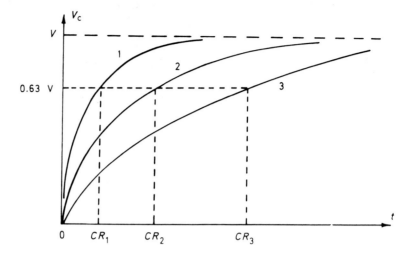

1. Small value of R
2. Medium value of R
3. Large value of R

Figure A.1

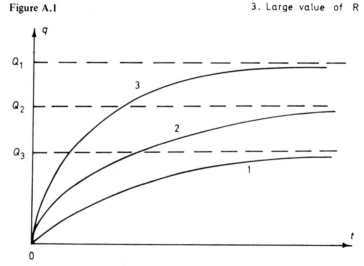

1. Small value of C
2. Medium value of C
3. Large value of C

Figure A.2

(24) 62.5 kΩ, 3.125 MΩ.
(25) (a) $v = 150\,(1 - e^{-t/2})$ volts; (b) $i = 1.5e^{-t/2}$ mA
(26) 80 A/s; 1.0 A
(27) $R = 8\ \Omega$, $L = 5.33$ H
(28) (a) 50 mA, (b) 0.1 s, (c) 33 V.
(29) 1 kΩ; 60 mA
(30) (a) 100 V, (b) 60.7 V, (c) 4 mA
(31) (a) 0 V, (b) 100 V, (c) 13.5 V
(32) (a) 0 V, (b) 0 V, (c) 86.5 V
(33) (a) 5000 μC, (b) 1840 μC, (c) 0.184 mA
(34) (a) 1.0 A, (b) 0.02 s, (c) 0.632 A

(35) 6.67 A in resistor, 20 A in coil; 2.71 A
(36) 1.84 A; 0.139 s
(37) 129 Ω.
(38) (a) 28.6 V, (b) 71.4 V, (c) 714 μC, (d) 25.5 mJ,
(e) 71.4 μA. 19.66 s
(39) 20 μF.
(42) (i) 52.3 ms; (ii) 23.2 ms

UNIT SECTION 3

(1) 314.2 Ω
(2) 2500 Hz
(3) 6 mA
(4) 69.2 μF
(7) $R = 38.8$ Ω, $L = 154$ mH; 953 Hz
(10) 306 Hz
(11) Put $V = IZ$, $I = V/Z$ into the true power expression VI
$\cos \phi$.
(14) 5100 W
(15) (a) 17.3 Ω, (b) 11.55 A, (c) 1600 W, (d) 0.694 lagging
(16) Use the circuit of *Figure A.3*. No power is consumed by
the capacitor, power delivered by the supply is i^2R or $i V_2$. Then
p.f. = true power/apparent power = $iV_2/iV_1 = V_2/V_1$

Figure A.3

(19) $Q = \omega L/R$. Put $\omega = 1/\sqrt{(LC)}$ then $Q = \dfrac{1}{\sqrt{(LC)}} \cdot \dfrac{L}{R} =$

$\dfrac{1}{R} \sqrt{\dfrac{L}{C}}$. To have a high Q-factor, R must be small and the ratio
L/C must be large.
(21) (a) ωL; (b) impedance; (c) $1/\omega C$; (d) leads, $90°$;
(e) proportional.
(22) 2 A, 0.318 A; 0.894 A
(23) 11.5 V
(24) (a) 18.6 Ω, (b) 10.75 A, (c) 57.3°, (d) 1156 W
(25) (a) 17.8 Ω, (b) 5.62 A, (c) 63.5°
(26) 200 Ω
(27) 0.47 lagging
(28) (a) 96 Ω, 184 mH, (b) 106 μF, (d) 0.96 lagging
(29) 31.5°, 0.82
(30) 178 Hz
(31) Frequency, 0.28 A, 69.3°; 400 Ω, 1.6°
(32) (a) unity, (b) capacitive, (c) zero, (d) watts
(33) (a) 5.06 μF, (b) 157.4 V, (c) 5 W
(35) 33.3 μH
(36) 9.95 kHz, 1.26 kHz
(37) Circuit A is inductance with resistance; circuit B is
capacitance with resistance. Circuit A: 0.055 H and 20 Ω;
circuit B: 46 μF and 20 Ω.
(38) $R = 4.4$ Ω, $X_L = 33$ Ω. X_L αf therefore if frequency is
doubled X_L is doubled. Since $X_L \gg R$ doubling X_L doubles Z,
hence if the voltage is doubled, the current remains about the
same.
(39) 1.94 kW; 2.48 kVA; 1.54 kVA
(40) 0.083 Ω
(41) 50
(42) 1.32 kW; 0.65 kW

UNIT SECTION 4

(2) (a) 12.5 A, (b) 36.9° lagging

(3) (a) 0.15 A, (b) 667 Ω, (c) 212 mH

(5) 0.03 A; 24.8°

(6) 1.415 A; 2.06 A

(7) 2250 Hz; (a) 6960 Ω, (b) 8766 Ω

(9) 795 kHz; 33.3 kΩ

(14) (a) I_R = 2 A, I_c = 3.78 A; (b) 4.28 A, (c) 46.73

(15) (a) 9.17 A, (b) 10.9 Ω, (c) 35 mH

(16) 59.5 μF

(17) 15.9 μF; 0.57 A

(18) 2 A; 0.314 A; 2.025 A

(19) (a) 40 V, (b) 126 mA, (c) 74 mA.

(20) 15.9 mH; 45°

(22) 1.88 to 0.91 MHz. No, for negligible R the resonance formulae are identical for series and parallel circuits.

(23) 31.6

(24) 39.3 μF

(25) (a) unity, (b) capacity, (c) unity

(26) 19.2°

(27) 0.45, 62.3°

(28) 0.47

(29) (a) 173.2 Ω, (b) 93.3 W

(30) (a) 5 V, (b) 32 mW, (c) 0.895, (d) 0.064 μF in parallel with AB.

(31) 1275 W

(32) I_L = 0.71 A, I_c = 1.0 A, I = 1.137 A

(34) 1.32 kW; 0.65 kW

(35) (a) 77.6; (b) 8.84 kHz

UNIT SECTION 5

(2) (a) 1125 turns, (b) 2.25 A, 3 A, (c) 225 W

(8) 80 turns

(9) 578 turns

(10) 1.133 A

(11) (a) 48 V, (b) 0.32 A, (c) 0.064 A, (d) 15.36 W

(12) (a) 200 lamps, (b) 0.417 A

(13) (a) 5.33 to 1, (b) 0.169 A, 0.9 A, (c) 40.5 W

(14) 28.125 kΩ

(15) 3.53 to 1

(16) (a) 3.375 Ω, (b) 0.135 Ω

(17) 28 mW; 4.47 to 1; 156 mW

(18) (a) 300 V, (b) 271 V

(19) N = 3.16

(20) 0.4 H; 56.7 Ω

(21) 3.33 μF; the impedance is increased at the primary, hence the effective capacitance is *reduced*.

(22) 102 W

UNIT SECTION 6

(4) 433 V, 250 V; unbalanced 250 V, 250 V, 433 V.

(7) Apparent power = $\sqrt{3}I_L V_L$ volt-amps; reactive power = $\sqrt{3}\,I_L V_L$ sin ϕ volt-amps reactive

(8) 0.094 V

(9) 1 m

(10) 0.143 V

(12) 208 V

(13) $V_p = 289$ V, $I_p = I_L = 2.89$ A; $V_p = 500$ V, $I_p = 5$ A, $I_L = 8.67$ A

(14) Star 2.5 kW; delta 7.5 kW

(15) 17.32 kVA; 0.866

(16) 41 A

(17) 415 V

(18) Star: $I_L = 4.62$ A, $P_r = 2.56$ kW; delta: $I_L = 13.85$ A, $P_r = 7.68$ kW

(19) 27.2 A

(21) 17.35 A in both cases.

UNIT SECTION 7

(3) As B increases the relative permeability of the iron falls, hence the reluctance of the iron increases and the e.m.f. ceases to rise linearly.

(7) 220 V; 250 V

(8) The machine would not excite.

(9) 203.4 V

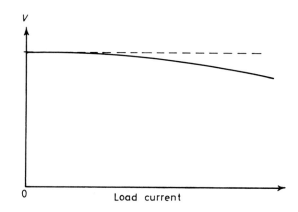

Figure A.4

(10) See *Figure A.4*. The field flux is maintained constant by the external supply, so the e.m.f. generated is also constant. The slight fall in the output voltage is due to the armature resistance reducing the output at high values of load current.

(11) $E = V_B + R_A (I_L + I_F)$ where $V_B = V + R_F (I_L + I_F)$ this time.

(12) 114 rad/s

(14) Unless you have had experience of machines before, this might have been difficult. The field is weakened slightly by magnetic distortion produced by the rotating armature. This is known as armature reaction.

(18) (a) electrical, mechanical, (b) $\dfrac{\text{output power}}{\text{input power}}$ (c) poles,

(d) two, (e) Φ

(19) 17.86 mWb

(20) 300 conductors

(21) 385 V

(22) 280 V

(23) -215 V

(24) 178 rad/s

(25) About 40%

(26) 164 kW

(27) (a) Φ, (b) Φ, (c) opposes, (d) gross

(28) 272 Ω; 230 V

(29) 62.5 N-m

(30) 491 r.p.m. Inefficient because of the heavy power loss in the series resistor.

(31) 52.2 rad/s

(32) 62.5%

(33) One-sixth; 14.3 A, 5.714 kW

UNIT SECTION 8

(1) Transformers require less iron and copper at higher frequencies.

(2) (a) 3000 rev/min, 314 rad/s; (b) 1500 rev/min, 157 rad/s; (c) 1000 rev/min, 105 rad/s.

(3) $N = 60f$

(4) 100%. Standstill here means that the rotor is held stationary though power is supplied to the stator.

(5) s times f

(6) 5%; 1425 rev/min

(7) 1.67 Hz; 3.3%

(8) 3%

(9) (a) 750 rev/min (b) 731 rev/min (c) 1.25 Hz

(12) 4%

(13) Yes, but a rotating field cannot be produced from a single-phase supply. The single phase motor is not self-starting.

(14) 16 poles

(15) 49.8 Hz, 1572 rev/min

(16) 1 : 24.25

UNIT SECTION 9

(1) No. At balance the meter reads zero so its calibration error is immaterial.

(3) No. This is a deliberate example of what *not* to do. The error in the instruments is $\pm 2\%$ and the limits of the readings obtained can only be given to this accuracy. Hence it is not correct to state that the resistance value lies between 30.147 and 26.837 because this implies an error no worse than 1 part in 10^4 or 0.01%!

(4) No. The systematic error has already been allowed for in the evaluation of R.

(7) When I_2 measures 9 A $\pm$ 0.135 A, I_1 remaining at 10 A $\pm$ 0.2 A, the value of I_3 becomes 1 A $\pm$ 0.335 A, a possible error of 33.5%! This shows that the determination of I_3 by the method described becomes more inaccurate the closer the values of I_1 and I_2 are to each other.

(8) $\pm 4\%$

(9) Better to use a single meter. The *ratio* of two quantities is then unaffected by the error of the meter.

(11) (a) $A \sin \omega t + \frac{1}{2}A \sin 2\omega t$; (b) $A \sin \omega t + \frac{1}{2}A \cos \omega t$.

(12) For the ratio $f_x : f_y$ you should get (a) 2 : 1, (b) 1 : 3, (c) 2 : 3, (d) 5 : 2, (e) 1 : 1

(13) 3.18 µF
(14) 2778 Hz
(16) 10010 Ω
     101010 Ω
     1111111 Ω
     ∞

In this last case the resistor would be omitted.
(17) (a) 5 kΩ; (b) 6.25 kΩ
(18) (a) 12.8 Ω; (b) 12.7 Ω; (c) 31.75 V
(19) 20 turns
(20) 2.4 kΩ
(21) (a) 3.54 A; (b) 3.18 A
(22) 14.1 to 14.9 V
(23) ± 4%
(24) 60 mA
(25) (a) A 45° line; (b) a circle; (c) see *Figure 9.16*
(26) 0.3 H, 40 Ω, $Q = 47$
(27) 2.96 A
(29) 27 mA; 38.6 Ω
(30) Meter would read 104.4 V
(31) Preferably MBM
(32) 0.485 V

UNIT SECTION 10

(1) See *Figure A.5*.
(2) See *Figure A.6*.
(3) The block swings to the other side of the equilibrium level. Energy is interchanged between the block and spring.
(4) The up and down movement (the frequency) is not affected by the initial displacement.
(5) Second-order; it has *two* energy storing elements.
(6) An oscillation about the 100 V level which *increases* in amplitude.
(7) When $\zeta < 0.707$. For $\zeta > 0.707$ the term becomes 'imaginary' and there is no longer a peak at ω relative to ω_n.
(8) See *Figure A.7*.
(11) 5.22 Hz.
(12) 1776 N/m.
(14) 157.2 ms.
(16) No.
(17) True.
(18) False; instability also depends on phase shift.
(20) Forced; natural.

Figure A.5

Figure A.6

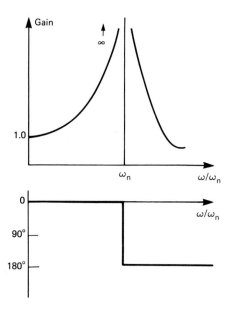

Figure A.7

UNIT SECTION 11

(3) High frequencies are radiated more efficiently than low frequencies.

(4) One only. The amplitude is the only thing that can be varied in a direct current. Amplitude here = magnitude.

(5) Amplitude modulation.

(6) 32.4%.

(7) 999.8 – 997 kHz, lower side band; 1000.2 – 1003 kHz, upper side band.

(8) 494 kHz, 498 kHz, 500 kHz, 502 kHz, 506 kHz.

(9) 30%.

(10) Unchanged. Frequency modulation has no effect on the peak (and hence r.m.s.) value of the carrier.

(11) 180 kHz. Use the approximate formula in the text.

(12) (a) 500 W; (b) 20 W.

(14) (a) 60%; (b) 1 kHz; (c) 100 μs; (d) 8 V.

Index